RIVER

RESCUE

3d Edition

Also Available from AMC Books

Paddling Guides
Classic Northeastern Whitewater Guide
Quiet Water Canoe Guide: New Hampshire/Vermont
Quiet Water Canoe Guide: Maine
Quiet Water Canoe Guide: Massachusetts/Connecticut/
    Rhode Island
Quiet Water Canoe Guide: New York
Quiet Water Canoe Guide: Pennsylvania
River Guide: New Hampshire/Vermont
River Guide: Maine
River Guide: Massachusetts/Connecticut/Rhode Island
Sea Kayaking along the Mid-Atlantic Coast
Sea Kayaking along the New England Coast
Whitewater Handbook

Hiking Guides
White Mountain Guide
Maine Mountain Guide
Mount Desert Island and Acadia National Park
Massachusetts and Rhode Island Trail Guide
North Carolina Hiking Trails
West Virginia Hiking Trails

Nature Walks
Nature Hikes in the White Mountains
Nature Walks in and around New York City
Nature Walks in Eastern Massachusetts
Nature Walks in Central Massachusetts
Nature Walks in Southern New Hampshire
Nature Walks in Southern Maine
Nature Walks in Southern Vermont
Nature Walks in the Berkshire Hills
Nature Walks in the New Hampshire Lakes Region
Nature Walks in Northern Vermont
Nature Walks near Philadelphia

RIVER RESCUE

3d Edition

A MANUAL FOR
WHITEWATER SAFETY

Les Bechdel & Slim Ray

APPALACHIAN MOUNTAIN CLUB BOOKS
BOSTON, MASSACHUSETTS

Cover photographs: Philip DeRiemer; front cover insets, Slim Ray; back cover, Glenn Oakley
All photographs by Slim Ray unless otherwise noted.
Illustrations: Jan AtLee
Cover Design: John Sizing
Book Design: Carol Bast Tyler

Library of Congress Cataloging-in-Publication Data
Bechdel, Les.
  River rescue : a manual for whitewater safety / Les Bechdel & Slim Ray.
  —3rd ed.
        p.   cm.
    Includes bibliographical references (p.) and index.
    ISBN 1-878239-55-4 (alk. paper)
      1. White-water canoeing—Safety measures. 2. Rafting (Sports)—
  Safety measures. 3. Rescue work. I. Ray, Slim. II. Title.
    GV788.B435   1997
    797.1'22'0289—dc21   96-53448
                                                                      CIP

The paper used in this publication meets the minimum requirements of the American National Standard for Information Sciences—Permanence of Paper for Printed Library Materials, ANSI Z39.48–1984.

**Due to changes in conditions,
use of the information in this book
is at the sole risk of the user.**

Printed on recycled paper using soy-based inks.
Printed in the United States of America.

10 9 8 7 6 5 4 3 2   98 99 00 01 02 03

Contents

*This book is dedicated to the memory of
Rick Bernard and John Dolbeare,
friends lost on the river.*

Foreword

Time and the river roll onward, and paddle sports keep developing at a pace and into new areas of skill that make those of us who have been involved for a long time just shake our heads.

Runs formerly considered extreme, such as the Narrows of North Carolina's Green, now see heavy weekend use, often by boaters in their first or second year of paddling who enjoy squeezing in two or three runs a day. Young men and women are spending literally hundreds of hours in play holes around the country perfecting routines of linked maneuvers—cartwheels, McTwists, wingovers—of astounding complexity that once only existed in the cartoons of William Nealey. And, on a broader and more pervasive note, more people than ever are getting out on whitewater rivers—almost 300,000 people on the Nantahala alone in 1996 *so far*, with the season not yet over. Sometimes amidst all this enthusiasm and newly developing skill, things go wrong—sometimes terribly wrong—and, for the most part, paddlers of all skill levels are still underprepared with plans and techniques for the quick resolution of rescue situations. This summer, there were two foot-entrapment deaths on the Nantahala. One of them was at almost exactly the spot where I had helped extricate a person from a foot entrapment several years ago. This time, there weren't enough people who knew what to do close at hand.

Just this past summer, I was leading a group of young boaters down their first encounter with fairly steep water—a small Class III–IV stream near my home in Asheville. I was accompanied by instructors from the camps where I work. The instructors are young but highly skilled boaters: they are capable of moves in boats that I cannot even approach. Below one of the first drops, where we were setting up safety for the kids about to come through, I asked one of the instructors sitting in a rescue boat what he would do if a kid got vertically pinned in the first drop. He looked alarmed at the thought, and I could see that the scenario had not crossed his mind. I watched the emotions of doubt and anxiety play across his face, then the intense look of concentration as he began to work out a plan, rejected it, worked out several more possibilities, and then settled on an idea of tag lines and shore-based rescue. We talked over his plan. I suggested several options or revisions of his idea. We had a good plan in place before we signaled the boats to come through. Later that day on the river, he told me that it had never crossed his mind what he would do had a pin occurred; he was just sitting below the drop, ready to pick up swimmers.

Now, if I had really thought a vertical pin was a possibility, I would never have allowed the campers to run the drop in the first place. The point is that the instructor and I ran through a plan of what to do if such an unlikely and frightening event took place. That plan would have saved us several minutes of possibly precious time if anything had gone wrong. It was simple, it could be applied quickly, and it posed the minimum of risk to rescuers. The need for having such plans in place is always with all boaters, on all classes of water, at every bend and horizon line in the river. It is now a need for more people than ever before.

Because of that need, I welcome this new edition of *River Rescue* by Les and Slim. I value that they are still out on the rivers and in the field, working with professional guides and emergency services personnel in applying and evaluating plans that work and plans that don't. Unless you are on the rivers full time these days, it is impossible to keep up with these developments. A book such as this, updated with the wealth of experience possessed by Les and Slim and the people with whom they have worked, can go a long way toward giving you the preparation to make plans of your own. I know I will be reading it again as a much-needed refresher course, and will pay particular attention to the new chapter "Rescue on the Run," which deals with boat-based rescues in big water—an area that really has needed more attention.

We can't entirely eliminate risk from the sport of running whitewater rivers and streams. But we can intelligently manage the risks we take, and the focus of that risk management means a sharpening of perceptions that brings greater awareness, pleasure, and—yes—safety to our experiences out there. I am grateful that Les and Slim have had, and continue to have, leadership roles in the sharpening of those perceptions, and I hope that boaters of all skill levels will read this edition and use it to enhance their own river experiences everywhere.

Gordon Grant
Instruction Coordinator, Camps Mondamin and Green Cove
Former Head of Instruction, Nantahala Outdoor Center
September 1996

Prologue: Two Rescues

A Drowning on the Chattooga

It was a trip like any other. After a high-water year the Chattooga had finally settled down to a medium level (about 1.8 feet), and we had started to relax a little. There were six rafts and a safety kayak on the trip. Rick Bernard, an expert paddler, had traded a raft guide slot on another trip to be safety boater. It was a fine November day and we did not expect trouble. There were no problems moving through the Five Falls area, and when we reached Jawbone, the next-to-last rapid of the series, we waited for Rick to run through first. He decided to catch the eddy above Decapitation Rock, a huge undercut boulder about halfway through the rapid. This was common practice for safety boats, and Rick had done it before. The danger of the move is that this steep, small eddy flows out directly into the undercut end of the rock.

Rick caught the other eddies in the rapid nicely but hit the eddy above "Decap" low and began to slip back. We had seen this, too; the boater must flip here deliberately to avoid hitting the rock with his head. As Rick slid under the rock, we watched the downstream side to see him roll. Nothing happened.

The next thing we saw was his hand reaching up from beneath the rock to try to find a hold. An alert guide threw a rope, but Rick was unable to hang on to it. After a few more seconds the hand disappeared. Shortly after that his life jacket washed out.

Rick's boat was pinned about a foot from the stern and folded underneath the rock. It was made mostly of nylon and other synthetic fibers that would not tear (a breakaway cockpit would have been of no use in this situation anyway), and the problem was compounded by the lack of footbraces. Since the boat was now facing downstream, the force of the current was pushing Rick against the front of the cockpit rim.

There were people on the other side of the river, including one of our rafts, but communication was difficult because of the noise of the water. It took several long minutes for them to understand exactly what the situation was. Even then, the rescue attempt was hampered by inadequate equipment. Rick's boat was barely visible from the top of the rock, and the whole force of the current slammed into the upstream side of the rock. We had ropes but nothing else, not even a carabiner, to hook onto the boat. The boat's grab loops were out of reach, and although I was able to reach and release his sprayskirt in the hope that the boat would fill up and wash off, I couldn't get a rope around the boat. We tried every method we could think of for more than an hour, as hope for Rick's life faded.

Dave Perrin, the trip leader, had to think about the rest of the people on the trip. It was getting late and we were overdue. The guides ran the rafts through Jawbone and met the customers below. Dave appointed a substitute leader, and the trip set off for the take-out. At the same time he sent a runner out to notify our company of the situation. Since we expected help, Dave and I stayed there.

Just before dark Payson Kennedy (director of the Nantahala Outdoor Center), Andrew Stultz, Bruce Hare, and a member of the local search-and-rescue outfit showed up. With fresh people and ideas we renewed our efforts. We didn't want to leave our friend under that rock! Finally Andrew formed a coil of rope and dropped it in above the rock right where Rick's boat had gone in. The water sucked the rope in just as it had the boat. In the gathering darkness we secured the rope to the boat and passed it over to the other shore. Pulling directly against the current, it was all the six of us could do to pull it out. It had taken us five hours to find the right combination for the recovery.

Slim Ray

Rescue on the Bío-Bío

In January 1981 three commercial rafting outfitters were making their way through the infamous Nirreco Canyon of the Bío-Bío River in Chile. Our group was scouting a quarter-mile-long Class V rapid called Lava South and had pretty much concluded it was too big for our paddle rafts. After constant rain the river was running more than 20,000 muddy cubic feet per second, and things looked ominous.

With another outfitter, who was camped below the rapids, we watched the third outfitter's rafts crash their way through Lava South. The size of the rapid made control marginal, and the rafts were barely making it into the eddy above the next rapid, Cyclops (another Class V).

As we watched I saw an emergency signal from one of our guides at the top of the rapid. A raft was coming through upside down and one of the passengers was backstroking weakly for the left shore. We lost sight of him for what seemed an eternity in the big waves. When he flushed out in the tail waves, he was floating face down.

Three of us—all employees of the Nantahala Outdoor Center: Dick Eustis, Drew Hammond, and I—were on a fifteen-foot cliff overlooking the fast current that led into Cyclops rapid. We all saw what had happened, and each of us reacted differently: Dick dove into the water immediately. I followed, and Drew, who was farther downstream, began getting a throw rope ready. A boatman from the other company was already on his way to his oar rig to back up the rescue. Each of us acted on instinct, based on his position relative to the victim. There was no time for discussion, only action.

Dick swam to the victim and tried to give mouth-to-mouth resuscitation while they were both still in the water, but he wasn't successful in the big waves. I reached the victim, and we started swimming him in, using a sidestroke, with each of us holding a lapel of his life jacket to keep him on his back.

Drew made a remarkable rope throw, but it was a long one, and only Dick was able to grab the end. The force of the current on the three of us was too strong, so I let go and swam for it. Drew did a dynamic pendulum belay, running downstream as Dick and the victim swung across the eddy line.

John, a boatman from another company, was there in his oar rig, and he pulled the victim out of the water onto a large dry box. A quick check confirmed that the victim was not breathing. Dick started mouth-to-mouth resuscitation, and Drew began the chest compressions. In their haste they were initially out of sync, but John started counting and got things together for effective resuscitation.

His friends across the river couldn't help us but shouted that his name was Billy. Within a few minutes Billy started to vomit, and we had to roll him on his side. I checked his pulse at the carotid artery on his neck to measure the effectiveness of the compressions and then arranged for a backup CPR team.

After a few minutes of this Billy blinked his eyes and moved. We stopped CPR, he moaned, and by God he was breathing on his own! He started shivering violently but was still unconscious. We cautioned each other that we might have to restart CPR. We moved him from the raft to a tent with a caterpillar pass and began warming him under sleeping bags with our bodies. He regained consciousness that night and was able to walk the next morning.

In retrospect, it was fortunate that we were in the right place at the right time. But without preparation, skill, and organization, that luck wouldn't have mattered.

Les Bechdel

Two stories. A drowning in one and a successful rescue in another. How and why did these events happen? These narratives give a first-hand account of what happens in a whitewater emergency. You may not understand now exactly what went on or why, but the purpose of the rest of the book is to answer those questions.

Whitewater is a challenging sport and the rewards are great, but the inherent risk of injury or death must be recognized. Too much that has been written about whitewater either ignores this danger entirely or overdramatizes it to impress the reader. We've tried not to do either. The safety of any adventure sport is directly related to the knowledge of and preparation for its hazards. You will better enjoy your sport if you are better prepared to deal with its dangers.

Introduction

Many things have changed on the river since we completed the first edition of *River Rescue* in 1985. River-rescue techniques continue to change and develop, and it is more important than ever to share experiences and techniques with others. Paddle sports are booming. In 1996 the American Canoe Association, using data from the National Survey on Recreation and the Environment (NSRE), put the number of people who paddle in the United States at 24.2 million. Of this number, there were 13.2 million canoeists, 1.4 million kayakers, and 15.2 million rafters. The downside of this popularity is that river overcrowding is becoming a serious problem in many areas of the country, and the overall number of accidents has increased. In 1995, ACA Safety Chairman Charlie Walbridge tallied forty-one whitewater river fatalities: four canoeists, eight kayakers, and twenty-nine rafters. While many of the rafters were novices clearly in over their heads, one of the more disturbing trends continues—the increase in accidents and drownings among expert paddlers. People are running harder water at higher levels than ever before, and safety margins have shrunk accordingly. Sadly, some of those lost have been our friends.

On the bright side, however, safety awareness is higher than ever, especially among recreational paddlers, and rescue gear like carabiners, knives, and Prusik loops are now commonplace. Outfitters now routinely include river-rescue techniques as part of staff training, and some require rescue training for prospective guides. The American Canoe Association recently introduced a rescue course and requires it for instructors who teach on Class III water. Kayaks now have larger cockpits, factory-installed broach loops, and improved wall-locking systems. Rescue life jackets finally have been approved by the Coast Guard and are starting to appear in sizable numbers on the river, as are customized, close-fitting recreational life jackets.

A persistent problem that remains when analyzing river safety is the lack of a national clearinghouse for collecting statistics, accounts of drownings and near misses, and descriptions of new safety and rescue techniques. All readers are encouraged to send accident reports, photos, or clippings of rescue- and safety-related material to the Safety Committee of the American Canoe Association (7432 Alban Station Blvd., Suite B-226, Springfield, VA 22150-2311). This information is gathered into an annual report available to paddlers nationwide.

Rescue systems and concepts of safety differ from one area of the country to another, so we've tried to incorporate systems and techniques we have used and found to be effective. This doesn't mean that if a technique isn't in this book it doesn't work or shouldn't be used, just that we've used the ones we've described and know that they do work. Readers familiar with previous editions will find that we have reorganized the chapters, expanded information in several areas, and added techniques like dynamic safety on big rivers or "rescue on the run," including righting rafts in midcurrent.

This book is not a "how to paddle" or a first-aid book. We assume the reader has a basic knowledge of whitewater paddling and knows some of the rudiments of first aid. We strongly recommend that all paddlers take a first-aid course, preferably one that emphasizes wilderness protocols; it is essential for anyone who works or plays on a river. We also urge all paddlers to take a practical, hands-on river-rescue course such as the ones given by the American Canoe Association or Rescue 3. You can't learn river rescue from a book or video, no matter how good.

Another positive trend is the sharing of knowledge among different areas of the country and the world, as well as within the larger search-and-rescue community. International conferences on safety and rescue have allowed us all to benefit from each other's knowledge and experiences. There is still insularity and provincialism in the paddling world (usually expressed as "my way is the only safe way"), however, and we hope this book will add to a greater understanding of the different situations and problems in each.

Les Bechdel, McCall, Idaho
Slim Ray, Asheville, North Carolina

*The face of the river, in time, became a wonderful book...which
told its mind to me without reserve, delivering its most
cherished secrets as clearly as if it had uttered them with
a voice. And it was not a book to be read once and
thrown aside, for it had a new story to tell every day.*

Mark Twain, *Life on the Mississippi*

1

River Sense

When something goes wrong on the river there seem to be two types of people: those who have foreseen the trouble and are already taking corrective steps—and the rest of us, who are standing there with mouths agape trying to figure out what's going on. The first type of person always seems to be just where he's needed at the critical time. Such people have "river sense."

People are not born with river sense; it's something they develop over time. It involves perfecting skills, understanding equipment, and appreciating the forces and hazards of whitewater. It involves an ability to evaluate other people's paddling skill, a sense of group dynamics, and effective communication with other people. It involves being alert at all times on the river.

River sense means accident prevention. Most river accidents and drownings are a result of a combination of poor planning, improper equipment, and plain ignorance. In the spring of 1984, for example, five rafters drowned after attempting to run a low-head dam on the Potomac River. Evidently they had no idea of the power of the deadly hydraulic at the base of the dam. Accidents of this nature can be prevented, and they are doubly tragic because they lead to unnecessary regulation by well-meaning public officials who often don't understand that there are better, less restrictive ways to save lives.

Characteristics of Whitewater Rivers

Four factors should be considered in assessing the difficulty of a whitewater river: elevation loss, volume of flow, geomorphic make-up of the riverbed, and hazards. Other factors, like weather and accessibility, also must be considered, but they do not, strictly speaking, define the difficulty of the river.

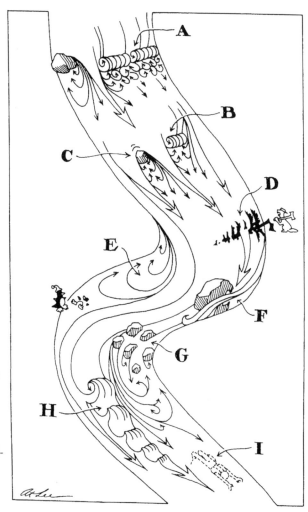

1.1 River features and hazards: (A) ledge hydraulic, (B) hole, (C) rock with eddy below and pillow upstream, (D) strainer, (E) bank or shore eddy, (F) undercut rock, (G) boulder sieve, (H) standing waves, (I) submerged undercut rocks.

Elevation loss in the United States is normally expressed in vertical feet per mile, usually as an average figure over the section normally run: the net vertical drop between two points one mile apart. Outside the U.S. this average is normally expressed as a percentage; e.g., 5 percent, equal to about 250 feet per mile. Averages can be deceptive, however, since some rivers concentrate their elevation loss in one steep section, thus hiding a difficult section with easy water before and after. For example, Section IV of the Chattooga has an average drop of about 50 feet per mile, but in the quarter-mile of the Five Falls it averages well over 200 feet per mile. Rivers like this are called pool-and-drop rivers. Other rivers, like the Arkansas River in Colorado, have a more consistent elevation loss. These rivers are often more dangerous, since they may have no calm pools in which to recover after a difficult section. Furthermore, there may be the risk of a long swim in cold water if things go wrong. Thus continuous Class III water may be more dangerous than pool-and-drop Class IV water.

Volume of flow must be considered along with elevation loss in determining the difficulty of a river. Flow in the United States is measured in cubic feet per second (cfs) and elsewhere in cubic meters per second (cms or cumecs; 100 cms is about 3,500 cfs): it is the volume of water that passes a given point on the riverbank in one second. Elevation loss and volume of flow are often inversely proportional: a big river like the Colorado typically flows 8,000–15,000 cfs (226–425 cms) (it ran more than 100,000 cfs [2,832 cms] in the spring of 1983) through the Grand Canyon, yet the average drop is just over 8 feet per mile. Some of the scarier creek runs can drop more than 400 feet per mile (10 percent) but typically carry a scant 200–300 cfs (6–8 cms). In general, the higher the numbers, the hairier the paddling. Right now the outer limits of navigability are represented by rivers that combine big continuous water with lots of elevation loss.

The riverbed itself partly determines the difficulty of the run. Narrow riverbeds may have tight turns and constrictions, and are more likely to be blocked by fallen trees, rock slides, or an intrusion of boulders from a side canyon. The geomorphic makeup of the riverbed will largely determine the presence or absence of undercut rocks, boulder sieves, potholes, and ledges. All create unseen hazards. Two examples of rivers with extreme geomorphic hazards are the Chattooga in South Carolina/Georgia and the Gauley in West Virginia (see figures 1.2 and 1.7).

1.2 *A geomorphic hazard: the Chattooga's infamous Bull Sluice pothole at very low water. Hazards like this are hard to see at higher water. A paddler drowned here in 1982.*

The nature of the gorge through which the river flows also dictates the commitment a paddler must make. Paddling a river in a steep-walled canyon is a much more serious undertaking than paddling one that has a road alongside.

Hazards

A whitewater hazard is any obstacle or condition that is capable of harming a boater. It may be a hard object like an undercut rock or a fluid one like a hydraulic. Most whitewater paddling can be looked at as the avoidance of hazards. To avoid them you should understand what they are and how they work.

Holes. The novice is often surprised to learn that not all surface water in a river flows downstream. Powerful upstream currents and waves in the form of eddies, hydraulics, and "holes" can be serious hazards under certain conditions (see figure 1.3).

ANY FLOATING OBJECT MAY BE HELD BY BACKWASH

1.3 A typical hole caused by water flowing over a rock.

An eddy is an upstream current that forms behind a surface object in the river or behind a riverbank. As the water flows around the object it piles up on the upstream side and then flows in behind the object, creating a reverse current. The line between the upstream and downstream currents is the eddy line. Larger and faster flows produce a marked difference in height between the upstream and downstream currents. Eddies and eddy lines in large, swift rivers can themselves be a hazard as serious as any you may find on the river: the eddies have a strong reverse current and the eddy lines can be studded with crosscurrents and whirlpools.

Water also forms a reverse current when it flows over a submerged object such as a ledge or boulder, creating one of the most enjoyable but dangerous features of the river, the hole. There are many words for it (*pourover, hydraulic, stopper, reversal, sousehole*), but in this book we'll use hole to mean the general phenomenon of a reverse current that tends to trap and hold a buoyant object.

Small holes are great fun to play in—when you want to. Boaters love to see who can go in the biggest one, stay the longest, and do the most stunts. But there are a few things to remember: don't stay in until you're exhausted, because getting out is harder than getting in. And look downstream before you go in: what's down there if you have to come out of your boat?

Large holes can be deadly and are capable of holding boats and boaters for extended periods of time. Smooth ledges with no breaks in them and low-head dams form the worst holes (see figure 1.13). This type of hole is often called a hydraulic. A hydraulic is frequently hard to see from upstream, and the regular nature of the backwash makes it nearly impossible to get out of without help.

On bigger rivers, breaking waves also can form holes as the tops of the waves fall back upstream. Large ones are quite capable of flipping rafts and giving boats a thrashing, but they are generally less dangerous than hydraulics, since an upside-down raft, a swamped boat, or a person will usually flush through. However, mishaps like this often set the stage for worse things on a large, cold, continuous river.

1.4 Some holes are fun to play in...

1.5 ...*and some aren't.*
(Roger Phillips)

Undercuts and Potholes. It's sometimes sobering to see a river at low water and realize what you have been paddling over when the water was high. The geological reasons for undercuts (large rocks that are narrower at the bottom than at the top) and potholes (smooth, eroded depressions in rocks; sometimes the rock will be worn right through to form a tunnel) are not important to the paddler, but their existence and location are. At higher water undercuts often can be recognized by the absence of an upstream pillow of water, and frequently they will have water boiling up behind them. The danger of an undercut is that a boat or a person can be pushed under it and trapped by the force of the water, pinning the boat or entrapping an extremi-

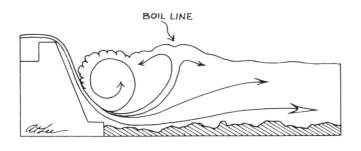

BOIL LINE

1.6 *A hydraulic caused by a low-head dam.*

1.7 Another common hazard on some rivers is the undercut rock. An undercut is a likely pinning spot and should be avoided. (Robert Harrison/Whetstone Photography)

The Force of the Current

The force of water against an obstacle does not, as you might expect, increase in linear proportion to the velocity of the current. If a current of 3 feet per second exerts a force of 17 foot-pounds on your legs, you might reasonably think that a 6-feet-per-second current would exert a force of 34 foot-pounds. *This is not so.* The force of water increases in proportion to the *square* of the velocity of the current. Thus, if the current velocity doubles, the force of the water increases fourfold.

Current Velocity	Average Total Force of Water lbf/kgf		
mph/kph	*(on legs)*	*(on body)*	*(on swamped boat)*
3/2	16.8/7.6	33.6/15.3	168.0/76.2
6/3.7	67.2/30.5	134.0/60.8	672.0/305.0
9/5.6	151.0/69.0	302.0/137.0	1512.0/686.0
12/7.5	269.0/122.0	538.0/244.0	2688.0/1219.0

ty. Undercuts also collect logs and other river debris, which form strainers and increase the risk of entrapment. The most dangerous undercuts are the ones on or near your line through a rapid, the ones the current pushes you directly into.

Waterfalls. When you look downriver and see the river disappear over a definite line across the river, it indicates a significant gradient loss. Sometimes these horizon lines identify rapids while others conceal a true waterfall (see figure 1.16). Waterfalls are best scouted before running, since you can never tell what debris has become lodged in the deposition zone at the bottom.

Entrapment. One of the biggest dangers of an unplanned swim in a shallow, rocky river is entrapment, a general term for getting any body extremity, usually a foot or a leg, caught against the bottom by the force of the current. Often a person unfamiliar with whitewater will attempt to stand on the river bottom and walk to shore. This is

1.8 Running big waterfalls such as The Gorilla on North Carolina's Green River has become more popular in recent years.

an invitation to get a foot caught in a tapered crack between two rocks or in an undercut ledge. Once the limb is caught it is held there by the force of the current. Escape is difficult, and it is likely that the person will drown. If the river is fairly deep (more than about four feet) the chance of foot entrapment is smaller, unless the drops are very steep—in vertical or near vertical drops the swimmer

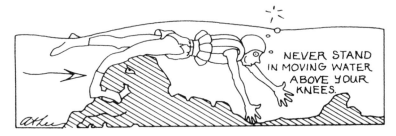

1.9 *Foot entrapment.*

is forced from a horizontal position to a more or less vertical one, which increases the risk of entrapment in a boulder sieve or rock crevice at the bottom of the drop.

Left Crack of Crack-in-the-Rock Rapid on the Chattooga is a good example of a place where body entrapment is a danger. The opening is very narrow and tapers down to less than the width of a person's body at the bottom. At higher water the crack fills in and

1.10 *Left Crack of Crack-in-the-Rock Rapid is just wide enough to wedge a paddler's body in and hold it with the force of the water. The danger level is somewhat higher than the level in this photo.*

the water will carry a swimmer over the deadly tapered section; at very low levels there is not enough water to carry a swimmer into it. At medium levels, however, it is a killer: the water carries the victim directly into the taper and wedges him there with the full force of the current.

Strainers. Fallen trees and accumulations of debris can form strainers: water flows through, but a solid object like a boat or a person won't. A strainer can completely block a narrow river. Strainers are particularly dangerous because they look so innocent. Frequently they are also hard to see, especially when a fallen tree trunk is stripped of branches and is partly submerged. In the summer of 1987 five people drowned when their raft struck a massive strainer on Canada's Ellaho River. Trees are not the only danger, though: smooth, water-worn boulders pushed down from a side creek can form boulder sieves at low water and trap boats and people or, at high water, form a series of hydraulics.

1.11 Kayakers crossing a half-submerged log on Colorado's Piedra River. Unlike fixed hazards, such as low-head dams and undercuts, strainers can be a surprise, since they can be created or can move overnight.

Debris. In addition to all the hazards nature has put in our way, there are man-made ones to contend with. Especially in the eastern United States, many rivers have all sorts of debris left over from the days of mills, dams, and logging that can pin or spear a boater. Bridge pilings are particularly likely to pin rafts or boats since they have little if any upstream water cushion. One kayaker was entrapped and drowned by an industrial conveyor belt someone had thrown into the river!

Low-Head Dams. Low-head dams and weirs deserve special mention, since they continue to cause drownings. They are common in many areas of the country and appear as a uniform feature all the way across the river. They form the perfect hydraulic: they are regular, difficult to see from upstream, and almost impossible to get out of without help.

An important feature by which to recognize a hydraulic at the base of a low-head dam is the boil line. This marks the boundary between the water flowing back upstream and the downstream flow. The water in the backwash is white, frothy, and aerated, while the water flowing downstream is darker and smooth. At the line where the two meet, the water appears to be boiling up. *Anything that gets farther upstream than the boil line will be pulled into the hydraulic by the backwash.* Rescuers must keep this in mind. Several firemen and

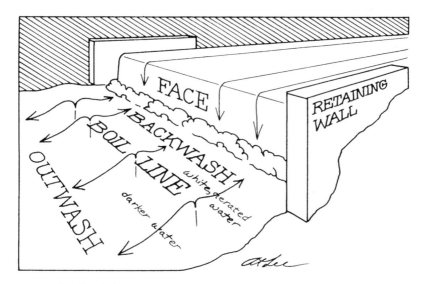

1.12 *A low-head dam.*

1.13 *Low-head dams can be deadly. A kayaker and his would-be rescuer drowned in this one near Rockford, TN. The kayaker was caught in the back-wash and was unable to escape. The rescuer tied himself to a rope and attempt-ed to swim above the dam. He drowned when the rope snagged on an obstacle and he was held underwater. A second rescuer also tied himself to a rope and narrowly escaped a similar fate. (Michael Patrick/ Knoxville News-Sentinel)*

search-and-rescue personnel who were not aware of these hazards have drowned while attempting to rescue people from hydraulics below low-head dams. One woman rescued from the backwash of a low-head dam commented that she had been through much worse-*looking* rapids. With good reason low-head dams are called "drown-ing machines."

This all points to the need for good educational preparation. Know what you're looking for and looking at.

Big/Cold Water. Even without the dangers of hydraulics and holes, big and continuous whitewater is itself a hazard for a person out of a boat or raft. Breathing, not to mention rescue, is difficult no mat-ter how good your life jacket, and must be carefully timed. Swimming in this kind of water can lead to "flush drowning" if the swimmer aspirates enough water. Long, cold swims quickly bring on hypothermia, a lowering of the body's core temperature, which robs the swimmer of his strength, judgment, and, if prolonged, his consciousness and eventually his life. (For details see the chart on page 256 in chapter 12.)

A combination of the two can be even more deadly, since an unprotected person falling into cold water (below 25°C/77°F) often experiences a gasping reflex, causing him to aspirate water rapidly and drown. Glacier-fed rivers often peak during warm weather, producing a combination of warm air, which often inhibits the wearing of proper protective clothing, and big, cold water.

Rating the Rapids

Interpreting the classifications of river rapids causes a lot of confusion. The American Whitewater Affiliation (AWA) International Scale of River Difficulty grades rapids in Classes I to VI, from "easy" to "extreme risk of life."

The "Grand Canyon" or "Deseret" scale, sometimes used in the West, rates rapids on a scale from 1 to 10. The problem with both of these scales, though, is that they attempt to define a fluid phenomenon with an arbitrary number. One person's Class III is another's Class IV. Paddlers are getting better, and by today's standards older guidebooks often overrate rapids. Nantahala Falls, for example, which was at one time rated a Class V at high water, is now considered by many to be an easy Class III. Some western boaters have taken to downgrading rapids as a matter of course. A Class VI that has been run successfully becomes a Class V, and, after a few more runs, a Class IV.

The result of all this is a "system in chaos," which in some ways is worse than no system at all. Several changes, such as an open-ended decimal scale similar to that used by rock climbers or a separate letter added to the numerical classification for the danger exposure factor, have been proposed but not adopted. Right now the only way to be sure how difficult a river is, is to compare notes with other paddlers. Compare the new river to one you've already paddled: maybe it's harder than Noname Creek but easier than the Bottomdrop River. Get specifics like the gradient and volume; don't settle for vague descriptions like, "It's only Class IV," or, "It's easy." And no scale should be a substitute for your own judgment.

International Scale of River Difficulty

This is the American version of a rating system used to compare river difficulty throughout the world. The system is not exact; rivers do not always fit easily into one category, and regional or individual interpretations may cause misunderstanding. It is no substitute for a guidebook or accurate firsthand descriptions of a run.

Paddlers attempting difficult runs in an unfamiliar area should act cautiously until they get a feel for the way the scale is interpreted locally. River difficulty may change each year due to fluctuations in water level, downed trees, geological disturbances, or bad weather. Stay alert for unexpected problems!

As river difficulty increases, the danger to swimming paddlers becomes more and more severe. As rapids become longer and more continuous, the challenge increases. There is a difference between running an occasional Class IV rapid and dealing with an entire river of this category. Allow an extra margin of safety between skills and river ratings when the water is cold if the river itself is remote and inaccessible.

The Six Difficulty Classes

Class I: Easy. Fast-moving water with riffles and small waves. Few obstructions, all obvious and easily missed with little training. Risk to swimmers is slight; self-rescue is easy.

Class II: Novice. Straightforward rapids with wide, clear channels that are evident without scouting. Occasional maneuvering may be required; but rocks and medium-sized waves are easily missed by trained paddlers. Swimmers are seldom injured and group assistance, while helpful, is seldom needed.

Class III: Intermediate. Rapids with moderate, irregular waves that may be difficult to avoid and can swamp an open canoe. Complex maneuvers in fast current and good boat control are often required; large waves or strainers may be present but are easily avoided. Strong eddies and powerful current effects can be found, particularly on large-volume rivers. Scouting is advisable for inexperienced parties. Injuries while swimming are rare; self-rescue is usually easy, but group assistance may be required to avoid long swims.

Class IV: Advanced. Intense, powerful but predictable rapids requiring precise boat handling in turbulent water. Depending on the character of the river, it may feature large, unavoidable waves and holes or constricted passages demanding fast maneuvers under pressure. A fast, reliable eddy turn may be needed to initiate maneuvers, scout rapids, or rest. Rapids may require "must" moves above dangerous hazards. Scouting is necessary the first time down. Risk of injury to swimmers is moderate to high, and water conditions may make self-rescue difficult. Group assistance for rescue is often essential but requires practiced skills. A strong Eskimo roll is highly recommended.

Class V: Expert. Extremely long, obstructed, or very violent rapids which expose a paddler to above average endangerment. Drops may contain large, unavoidable waves and holes or steep, congested chutes with complex, demanding routes. Rapids may continue for long distances between pools, demanding a high level of fitness. What eddies exist may be small, turbulent, or difficult to reach. At the high end of the scale, several of these factors may be combined. Scouting is mandatory but often difficult even for experts. A very reliable Eskimo roll, proper equipment, extensive experience, and practiced rescue skills are essential for survival.

Class VI: Extreme. These runs often exemplify the extremes of difficulty, unpredictability, and danger. The consequences of errors are very severe, and rescue may be impossible. For teams of experts only, at favorable water levels, after close personal inspection and taking all precautions. This class does not represent drops thought to be unrunnable, but may include rapids that are only occasionally run.

Preparation

General. Adequate, functioning equipment is critical for safety. Equipment preparation includes jobs like patching boats and repairing life jackets and helmets, tedious work best done in the off-season rather than the night before the first spring trip. It also means having the right equipment and having it *with* you.

Some paddlers go to great lengths and cost to prepare their equipment but do very little to prepare themselves either physically or mentally. Knowing your own physical abilities and limitations is important. Equally important is knowing that they change with the seasons. Boating is a seasonal sport, and after a winter's layover few of us are at the same peak of paddling ability as we were last fall. It's better to warm up on a few easy rivers than to begin pushing the limit the first day out. Your chances of injury (not to mention muscle soreness) are much less if you've maintained a regular fitness and stretching routine over the winter.

Time spent off the river can be used to expand your abilities and horizons—the middle of a rapid is not the best place to practice your strokes. If your roll is weak, get in a pool or on a lake and sharpen it up. Many clubs sponsor weekly pool rolling sessions during the winter months. Education in general is an important part of paddling. Practice and expand your paddling skills in the controlled environment of a clinic. Take a class in rescue techniques, first aid, or cardiopulmonary resuscitation (CPR) so you don't have to guess what to do in an emergency. Learn from books, magazine articles, club slide shows, outfitter's presentations, and paddling guides.

Pretrip Considerations. Before you get on the water, gather information about where you're going. A thorough knowledge of the river is essential, and a remote creek requires more research than a popular river run.

Consider the river. Where will you put in and take out? Are there any alternatives? How long is the run, and can it be completed in the

1.14 What class is it? Present classification systems are vague and should be applied with caution.

1.15 Education is an important part of paddling. Here students in the Rio Grande River near Taos, NM, practice a strainer drill, in which a student must go from a feetfirst swimming position into a headfirst one to cross the strainer.

time available? Add some extra time for lost shuttles, playing, and emergencies, and remember that the days are shorter in the spring and fall. What is the level of difficulty of the river? How much will it change if the water goes up? Where are the river gauges (and what are the safe levels?), the major rapids and hazards, and emergency evacuation access points and trails? What about the location and phone numbers of the nearest rescue squads and hospitals? Are there landowner problems? Save yourself the pleasure of looking up the wrong end of an irate farmer's shotgun and find out before you leave. Are guidebooks or USGS topographical maps available for the river and the surrounding area?

Screen participants for paddling ability. It is much easier for a trip organizer to say no to an unqualified friend over the phone than at the water's edge, but judging paddlers you've never met or seen paddle is difficult. Ask some discreet questions (Do you understand the risks? Do you know what to do in an emergency? Can you roll?). Inquire about rivers they have paddled or the names of others they have paddled with to get an idea.

Arrange for shuttles. There is no better way to get any trip off to a bad start than by a poorly organized shuttle. A botched shuttle can compromise the safety of the trip if it puts you on the river much later than expected and forces the group to bend safety rules to hurry. Some forethought about meeting locations, finding drivers, hiding keys, avoiding trespass on private property, and learning about road conditions will contribute to a timely start. A good map is a big help, and the mechanical condition of the shuttle vehicles must be considered. Almost everyone has a story about the shuttle that got lost, got stuck, or broke down.

Have a contingency plan. What happens if the water is too high or too low? Or if the river is dam controlled and there is no release? Can other sections of the river be run? Are there other rivers in the area of the same level of difficulty? Finding out river levels and local weather conditions is an art. Driving all night to get to a river only to find it in flood invites rash acts.

On the Water. Once at the river, get together and discuss the trip so that everyone knows what the plan is. Talk about the length of the trip and the nature of the river, and compare notes about the weather and water temperature to help determine what to wear.

Choose a leader. Paddlers tend to be independent and informal and sometimes resist this, but in the organizing stage of the trip and especially in an emergency there are good reasons for having a leader. A leaderless group may be disorganized in an emergency, and that is the very time instant action and coordination are needed. Small paddling groups (three to five people) of nearly equal ability seldom formally choose a trip leader, but in that case each individual must accept responsibility for his own actions and be prepared to assist other group members in any rescue function. In informal, "common adventurer" groups like this, individual initiative must substitute for leadership.

Designate a lead and sweep boat, so that experienced paddlers will be first and last on the river. In larger groups (ten or more boats), two or three boats can stay together as "buddy boats" the whole day. This spreads the impact of a large group over more of the river. Major rapids and a description of the takeout should be noted before starting. Times should be agreed on, so as to keep the group moving during the day and to avoid getting caught out after dark.

Someone should carry a first-aid kit, a spare paddle, and a repair kit, and everyone should know which boats these are in. In general, the first-aid kit should be carried by the most medically competent person in the group, and it should stay near the sweep boat. Groups of more than ten boaters should consider having more than one first-aid kit and spare paddle.

Scouting

Scouting is looking before you paddle. It is the last step in preparation before actually going into a rapid. This is normally done in unfamiliar or difficult rapids, but it's always a good idea, even if you've run the rapid before. If the water has been up, for example, there might be a strainer down across the river.

When do you scout? A ledge or big drop will appear first as a horizon line across the river. The noise of the water may be louder and mist and spray apparent. Difficult rapids often appear in areas of geologic change, which you can spot by watching the shoreline. Do the contours of the land drop suddenly? Is there a staircase appearance to the boulders on shore or in the treetops? Is the river narrowing down and the banks rising? All these are invitations to scout.

Some people are able to scout almost everything in their boat, eddy by eddy. But most paddlers can't, and the best way is to walk.

1.16 Sometimes horizon lines aren't easy to see from a boat. This one conceals a 12-foot drop on the Nantahala. Scout what you can't see.

If possible, scout from both shores. You'll be amazed how the perspective changes. Scout from river level if possible: if you look down on the river from above, things flatten out and don't look as big as they really are. Obvious routes seen from on high have a way of getting lost in a confusion of waves and holes once you are on the water. Pick markers to designate your line; a particular boulder, a wave, or a landmark on shore will help define your route.

An experienced paddler will study the rapids carefully and plan the run almost stroke by stroke. However, an all too common attitude among decked-boat paddlers is, "If I miss my line and flip, I'll just roll up at the bottom." Such nonchalance has gotten some people into trouble. Consider the consequences if things go wrong and have a contingency plan ready. Where are the eddies? If you end up swimming, which way will you go? How close is the next rapid?

Group scouting is usually best, because it allows for an exchange of opinions and gives the trip leader a chance to suggest tactfully that some paddlers should walk. Peer-group pressure can be a source of trouble. There is nothing wrong with running something a little over your head as long as adequate safety precautions are taken, but there are those who will encourage you to run something just to see you get hammered. If you don't feel up to it, portaging is always an honorable option.

1.17 *Scout as a group. If you're not confident of your ability, portaging is an honorable option.*

Leadership

Paddling is an individualist's sport, and often leadership and team-work are purposely avoided. Yet organization, whether for a trip or for a rescue, is vital and requires leadership. This doesn't mean giving orders, except in an emergency, but designating a member of the group to give directions may make the difference between a well-organized trip or rescue and a disaster.

A good trip leader is a person with experience and river sense. He should have good judgment and adequate interpersonal skills to get along with the rest of the group, and he should be a skilled paddler. "Getting along" might be the ability to organize things without appearing to give orders and to say no politely to an unqualified paddler wanting to join the trip. Good leadership may mean walking around a rapid you'd like to run yourself in order to encourage a weaker paddler not to run it, or it may mean keeping your eye on someone who has taken repeated swims and might be becoming hypothermic. It means acting as a clearinghouse of information for the other trip members and always checking everything. The trip leader is not always the strongest paddler in the group, but he should be someone with a cool head and the ability to organize and make decisions.

When getting organized for a river trip you need to take a good look at the people you are going with. At one extreme are those people who invite novices along just to see them get munched; at the other extreme are those who refuse to let anyone but the best come because they don't want to take time out from boating for teaching or assistance. Experts sometimes seem either to lose perspective about the skill needed to paddle difficult water, or to play it down deliberately in order to make themselves look better. This makes it hard for others to gauge such rapids objectively. Add this to the vagueness of the present rapids classification system and you have a situation in which it's easy to get in over your head. If measuring your own skills against an uncertain standard seems hard, it is even harder to measure someone else's. Ultimately the individual must determine his own qualifications, but the trip leader and the other paddlers should express candid opinions on the matter. Rather than asking whether a prospective group member can paddle Class IV water, the leader should ask what rivers he has run and at what water levels. At the put-in, some practice rolls or braces will tell the good leader more about the person's ability than will any amount of verbal description.

The "What If" Factor

Good river sense demands a special type of awareness. As you paddle you are tuned in, often on a subconscious level, to your own performance and to that of other members of the group. You are aware of the hazards of a particular rapid and are always ready to begin a rescue if necessary. Thinking like this works well when scouting rapids. As you scout, pick out the hazards and potential trouble spots. Are there ways of avoiding or minimizing the hazards? If there is a flip or a swim, what will happen? What rescues could be used? In the back of your mind you are always asking yourself, "What if something goes wrong—where is it going to happen, and how can it can be prevented?"

At first you will have to think consciously about the "what if" factor, but after some practice it will become automatic. Your mind will be continually assessing potential problems, discarding some alternatives, and working out the details of others. Some may criticize this as pessimistic paddling, but by avoiding accidents and being ready for trouble we are able to be more positive about paddling in general. The test comes when something goes wrong. Time for rescue is measured in minutes and sometimes seconds. The "what if" factor may mean the difference between success and failure.

We close this section with an account by Charlie Walbridge of a drowning on the South Fork of the Clearwater River in Idaho. (Full details may be found in the *Best of the River Safety Task Force Newsletter 1976–1982*, published by the American Canoe Association in 1983.)

The kayaker in question was clearly in over his head, having lost a boat on another, easier river just two days before. He flipped, swam, and drowned in the first rapid of the run. Walbridge notes that the victim "had a tendency to 'follow' people, feeling that, in or out of his boat, he'd probably make it."

Trusting in probability is a poor substitute for good judgment and a realistic assessment of one's abilities in any case, but what about the other group members? "Many in the group felt," says Walbridge, "that someone should have said something to Chuck." There does not seem to have been a designated trip leader, but on the other hand "no one expected him to attempt the river that day; he jumped in the water at the last minute." Chuck's miscalculations were his own, but other people in the group were aware of them and did not make their reservations known.

*Show me an adventure and I'll show
you a lack of preparation.*
Roald Amundsen, Arctic explorer

2

Equipment

On the river, proper equipment is often as important as good judgment. We have seen too many trips ruined by improper or missing equipment, and inadequate equipment has been linked to a number of accidents. Unfortunately, equipment problems can affect everyone on a trip, not just the individual paddler.

The general heading "equipment" includes personal gear the paddler wears; safety equipment like ropes and throw bags, which are usually carried separately; and the watercraft being paddled, whether a raft, a canoe, or a kayak. The choice of equipment is determined by the difficulty of the water, the time of year, and the location of the river. Obviously, a first descent in the Andes and an afternoon float on the Buffalo River will require different equipment. But the minimum, always, is a life jacket for everyone and a helmet for decked boaters.

For some people, the preparation is almost as much fun as the paddling. We see them outfitting boats and patching gear on long winter evenings. Some are equipment freaks, who have dozens of gadgets they'll never use; there are others whose idea of getting ready for the season is to buy a new roll of duct tape (these are usually the ones who have forgotten something important, need a shuttle, and just remembered that they cracked their paddle last fall). On the river you should be able to concentrate on paddling and not have to worry about equipment failure. You must choose your own equipment, but there are some specific criteria, discussed in this chapter, that everyone should consider.

We must stress, however, that no piece of equipment, however effective, can substitute for experience, skill, and judgment. Rescue equipment can create more problems than it solves if improperly used. It is the responsibility of each individual paddler to become proficient with any equipment he or she chooses to carry.

Safety Equipment

Life Jackets. The primary purpose of the life jacket is quite simple: to help keep your head above water so you can breathe. (We say "help" because in turbulent water no life jacket will keep your head above water all the time.) Some compromises must always be made, balancing flotation, comfort, fit, and mobility, but in general the fit and function of a life jacket are more important than an arbitrary amount of flotation. Newer life jackets function more as active swimming aids than as passive floating assists.

The Coast Guard calls life jackets *personal flotation devices* (PFDs) and with typical organizational mania has classified them into Types I through V. We need to consider only Types III and V, since the others are useless for whitewater. Coast Guard–approved life jackets are required by many river-management agencies, but approval is no indication of the riverworthiness of a particular life jacket, since Coast Guard testing primarily reflects offshore ocean-rescue criteria. The approval process is lengthy and expensive, and has actually inhibited life jacket design.

Type III PFDs are meant for paddlers: they are cut for comfort and mobility and have a minimum of 15.5 lbs (7 kg) of flotation. The best ones are cut in vest fashion and use closed-cell foam for flotation. The amount of flotation varies with the manufacturer, and some "shorties" are cut very short to provide improved mobility for kayakers with a minimum of flotation. In general, the bigger the water, the more flotation you will need. (The Type IV PFD is made to be thrown, not worn, so it does not fit in here.) Some PFDs are rated in categories III *and* V, hence the designation III/V.

Type V is a catchall category for those PFDs that do not fit into Types I–IV. This includes PFDs designed with commercial whitewater rafting in mind. These have more flotation and a buoyant collar

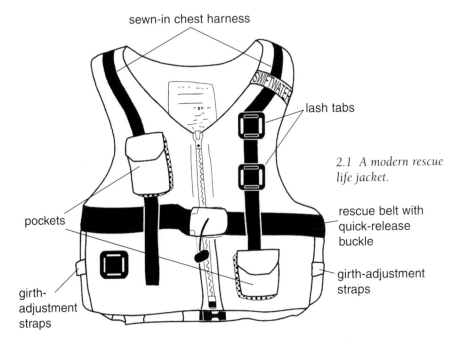

sewn-in chest harness

lash tabs

2.1 *A modern rescue life jacket.*

rescue belt with quick-release buckle

pockets

girth-adjustment straps

girth-adjustment straps

intended to help turn the unconscious wearer face up (fine for a lake but of little use in whitewater). Many Type Vs are bulky and uncomfortable for paddlers to wear.

Life jackets have other benefits besides flotation. The foam will protect you if you fall while scouting, or cushion your back if you're swept into a rock either in or out of your boat. A snug, well-fitting life jacket is also warm: it provides more than an inch of insulation for the critical trunk area of the body.

None of this is going to matter if you don't have your life jacket on, whether because you didn't wear it or because it came off when you most needed it. The tattered, faded life jacket with shrunken foam is still considered by some to be the emblem of the true river veteran. Forget that image. A good test to see if the time has come to retire "ol' faithful" is to jump in the water holding onto your life jacket so that it stays in place. If you end up floating with your nose underwater, it's time. Then try jumping in without holding onto it. If the life jacket comes up over your head, fix the waist tie or consider buying a new one.

In part because of excessive regulation, U.S. life jacket design has been relatively static, with the most innovative designs coming from Europe. Many U.S.-made life jackets are really suitable only for swimming Class III water. Many still fit too loosely and have inadequate waist ties made of nylon tape tied with a bow knot. Newer, tight-fitting designs have been appearing, however, and some more progressive manufacturers now offer things like add-on crotch straps and multiple, heavy-duty locking straps. There is considerable room for improvement here, and some distributors have begun offering nonapproved (but better) life jackets and letting the paddler decide what is best.

One of the most useful features pioneered by the Europeans has been the addition of an integral rescue harness to the jacket (see figure 2.1). This makes strong-swimmer rescues quick and easy and, since the harness or belt is easily released, safer.

This system also can be used to tie into a shore belay, incorporated with a sit harness for rappelling or vertical lowers, or can be the critical point of attachment for rescuing an entrapment victim. In the better jackets this system has been skillfully integrated into the design so that it is totally unobtrusive until needed (see figure 2.2).

Here are some features to look for when picking a life jacket:

- The jacket should fit as close to the body as possible. This helps prevent it from coming off, increases insulating ability, and allows maximum freedom of movement. It should have a positive locking waist-tie system and a girth-adjustment system that prevents the jacket from riding up in turbulent water.

- The jacket should allow maximum freedom of movement, especially around the arms and shoulders.

- The jacket should allow the attachment of add-on crotch straps.

- There should be outside pockets for essential items such as Prusiks and carabiners.

- The jacket should have a quick-release system for attaching a rope to the life jacket for strong-swimmer rescues.

- The jacket also should have an optional "cow's tail" for towing swamped boats.

There are some modifications you might want to make to your life jacket. One is to attach a whistle; another is to add a knife. Many newer designs have "lash tabs" which allow a knife to be quickly and

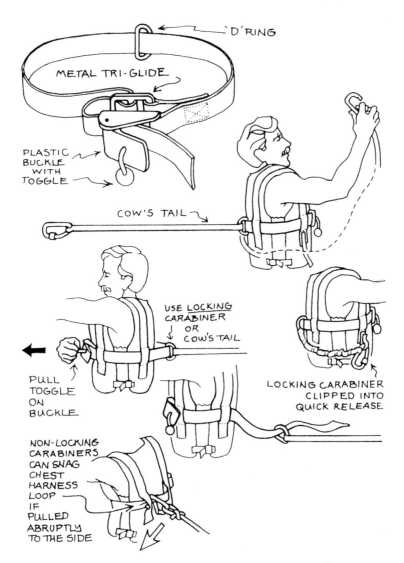

2.2 *A quick-release harness or belt built into a life jacket allows a res-cuer to get free of a tethering line in an emergency. A cow's tail makes clipping into a line easier.*

easily attached. Paddlers should also be aware of the snag potential of anything they choose to hang on their life jackets. Carabiners, Prusik loops, and the like may snag or clip into ropes, branches, or other obstructions in the river, causing a potentially life-threatening situation. The preferred solution is to carry equipment in pockets designed for the purpose. If this isn't possible, tie things like Prusik loops in tightly so that they don't hang down, and turn the gates of carabiners in against your body.

Rescue Harnesses. This is a separate chest harness that fits over the life jacket, where it may be used for a strong swimmer rescue or to tied into a shore belay. Some European paddlers also use the harness as an attachment point *for the paddler* if he is vertically pinned. They carry a small throw bag attached to the harness which, if the boat is pinned, the paddler throws out to potential rescuers. Considering that attaching a line to a vertically pinned kayak can be quite difficult, this is a sensible option. Using a rescue harness over a life jacket is one way to add rescue capability while keeping an approved life jacket.

Tow Belts. This tow system works exactly like the tow systems described later in this chapter, except that it is attached directly to the life jacket or worn as a belt around the waist. It has a quick-release device (Velcro™ or a buckle) and is not attached to the boat. The tow is done with a short (8–10 ft[2.4–3 m]) line with a carabiner on the end which fits into a small bag on the back. Some tow belts have a throw rope stuffed in one end and do double duty as a throw bag as well. This is a handy system for busy instructors who switch boats often.

Helmets. These are a must for decked boaters. We recommend them on difficult rivers for rafters and canoeists, too. If you use a helmet, get one worth having (see figure 2.3). Some sold today give little more than a false sense of security. Ideally, a helmet should protect not only the top of your head but also your temples and the back of your head. As more broken noses and lost teeth are reported, we are seeing more and more paddlers adding face guards to their helmets.

Carabiners. The carabiner is a true multipurpose river tool: it can secure gear in boats, substitute for a pulley in many situations, attach haul lines to pinned boats, and do a multitude of other things. It is a good idea for everyone to carry at least one and preferably two; complicated rescues sometimes need a lot of carabiners.

There are many different kinds of carabiners. For river use, get an aluminum alloy one—it is lighter and won't rust. Some carabiners have a locking device on the gate, which keeps the gate from

2.3 Helmets come in all shapes and sizes. This one features a removable face guard.

opening at inopportune times. This is an excellent safety feature, although there is the possibility of the gate clogging with sand. Newer designs use coarser threads that reduce the chance this will happen. If the lock jams on a carabiner you can often release it by using a Prusik loop as a strap wrench (see figure 2.5). If you don't have a locking carabiner, use two non-locking carabiners clipped in so that they open in opposite directions.

D-shaped carabiners are usually stronger than the oval ones, but probably the best all-around design for paddlers is a large oval-shaped locking carabiner. The large size and gentle radius of this design also make it an excellent choice for a Münter hitch belay (see figure 9.20), and some have an opening large enough to allow passing a knotted half-inch rope.

Many paddlers like to wear their carabiners on their life jackets, attached at the shoulder or the waist. However, you can injure your shoulder or collarbone if you flip over in a decked boat and the carabiner gets between you and a rock. There have also been several cases of carabiners on life jackets inadvertently clipping into lines at the wrong moment. If possible, carry them in a pocket, tucked safely out of the way.

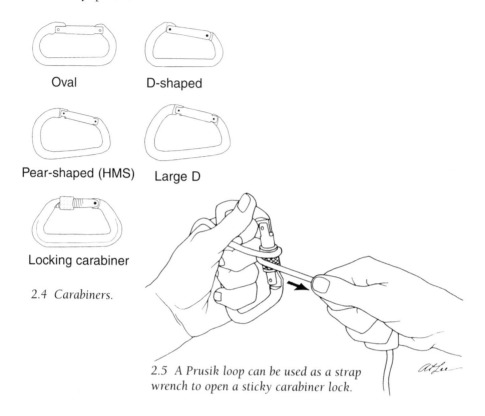

Oval

D-shaped

Pear-shaped (HMS)

Large D

Locking carabiner

2.4 Carabiners.

2.5 *A Prusik loop can be used as a strap wrench to open a sticky carabiner lock.*

Pulleys. Although carabiners can be used as substitutes on the river, pulleys *do* reduce friction and give greater pulling power to **Z**-drags and similar mechanical haul systems. While there are some excellent small pulleys available, some are designed only for light use. Look for models with sealed bearings and robust construction.

The size of the pulley and the number you carry depend on your boat, the amount of cargo you can carry, and the diameter of the rope with which you plan to use it. As a rule of thumb, choose a pulley whose diameter is at least four times that of the rope. Kayakers using 3/8"(9.5 mm) throw bag rope can get by with 1–2"(2.5–5 cm) micro pulleys, while a rafter on an extended trip who plans to use a 1/2"(13 mm) static rescue rope for unpinning rafts might want to carry 2–4"(5–10 cm) rescue pulleys.

Two recent innovations are worth mentioning. One is the "Prusik-minding pulley," whose squared-off sides catch the Prusik knot and keep it from jamming when working a **Z**-drag. Rock Exotica now makes a 2"(5 cm) model small enough for kayakers to

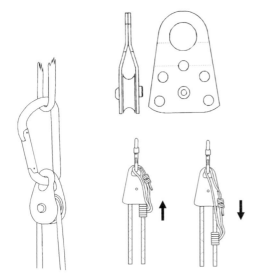

2.6 *A strong, lightweight pulley greatly reduces friction in rope work. The squared-off sides of the Prusik-minding pulley keep the knot from feeding into the pulley's throat.*

carry. The other is a nylon roller, marketed by Petzl, that can be clipped on to any carabiner to make it into a makeshift pulley.

Pulley Bags. A neat solution for the problem of carrying pulleys and keeping all your rescue gear together, the pulley bag attaches to the rescuer's end of a throw bag rope and holds pulleys, carabiners, Prusiks, and the like. When not in use the bag fits inside the throw bag, and comes out first in an emergency.

The Prusik. The Prusik is a mountaineering hitch designed to cinch on a haul line when placed under tension. When the tension is relaxed, however, it will slide freely. Boaters often call this pre-tied loop of cord, as well as the knot, a Prusik. It's an invaluable piece of

2.7 *The pulley bag attaches to the end of the throw bag rope and holds a number of accessories—for example, pulleys, paddle hooks, and carabiners. The pulley bag is stuffed into the mouth of the throw bag for storage, then held when the bag is thrown.*

equipment for quick tie-offs, anchor ties, hitching systems, and **Z**-drags. Prusik cord, usually 5–6'(1.5–3 m) of soft-lay, 1/4–5/16"(6–8 mm) kernmantle nylon rope, is smaller in diameter than the haul line, and it is usually tied into a loop with a double fisherman's knot. The following diameters are suggested starting points, although we recommend that you test any combination before using it, since some combinations of ropes and cord work better together than others. Prusik cord has to be sized according to size of rope.

Rope size		Prusik size
3/8"(9.5 mm) throw bag rope	=	6 mm
7/16"(11 mm)	=	7 mm
1/2"(13 mm)	=	8 mm

Outfitters catering to rock climbers stock this kind of line. Many rescue teams have begun to use Prusiks in pairs, i.e., two unequal-length Prusiks. This increases their holding power and provides a backup if one fails.

Webbing and Slings. Webbing is generally stronger than the cord used for Prusiks and makes excellent material for anchors and sit harnesses. A soft flat or tubular nylon webbing can be substituted for Prusik loops. Made into slings, good-quality 1"(25 mm) climbing webbing can be used in much the same way as the Prusik loops described above. Use a Kleimheist knot (see figure 9.21.2, page 190) to cinch it on a rope for hauling.

Paddle Hooks. This is another piece of gear originally designed for the steep rivers of the Alps. Paddle hooks come in several designs and sizes, but the most common is a small one that clamps to the edge of the paddle (see figure 2.8). The hook is clipped to a haul line; the paddle serves as an extension to place the hook on a convenient attachment point on the boat (such as the grab loop or the cockpit rim). One manufacturer makes a clamping system whereby two paddles can be joined blade-to-blade for an even longer reach. Paddle hooks also can be used with oars, either attached to the blade or to the oar clip on a pins-and-clips rig.

Knives. These are recommended for recreational paddlers and are essential for the river professional. The right knife can cut a boat or an entangled rope, or cut through the floor of a broached raft to free

2.8 The paddle hook clamps to the blade of a kayak paddle and extends the paddlers reach during rescues.

someone. Some of the haul-line systems we will describe in later chapters can develop tremendous loads when pulling on a pinned boat. If someone's arm or leg gets snarled in the line, a sharp knife will get him free. Les used his knife this way one day on the Nantahala when he came upon a raft towing a boy on an inner tube. When the raft hit a rock the boy was dumped into the water. When he came up, his head was caught in a noose of parachute cord. A submerged tree limb speared the inner tube and pulled the cord tight around his neck. "I leapt out of my canoe," Les remembers, "brandishing my knife like Errol Flynn. I cut the cord and swam the kid to shore. The rafters never noticed he was missing. I decided right there that my silly-looking knife was worth every penny."

Get a sturdy knife with a nonrusting blade, a nonslip grip, and a positive locking sheath that can be operated with one hand. Many paddlers use folding knives, but these can be hard to open with one hand. If you choose a folder get one with a locking blade. Keep your knife handy; strap or sew it to the chest, shoulder, or waist of your life jacket.

Knives can cut through the polyethylene plastic used in white-water boats. We found that a very thin, sharp blade works best; thicker blades tend to jam in the cut. It is essential to pull the blade

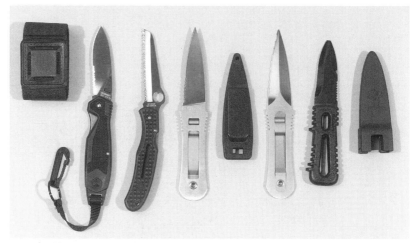

2.9 River knives come in a variety of shapes and sizes. (NOC Photo)

at a 45° angle to the cut. To cut the triple layer of the cockpit rim you must have a blade with a serrated edge. Most of the "river knives" sold today are less than ideal for cutting boats. Their blades are too thick, and it is next to impossible to get a decent grip on their metal skeleton handles.

We await the ideal river knife.

Saws. A lightweight folding saw will cut through a boat or a strainer with little hesitation and is handy to have in camp. Several lightweight saws are now available (see figure 2.10.1). An alternative is to purchase a 10"(25 cm) reciprocating saw blade, tape one end as a handle, paint it, tie a small lanyard on it, and shove it into your front foam wall. Then forget it until the day you need it.

Whistles. Every paddler needs a loud, reliable whistle that can be heard over the roar of the water. It is also handy if someone gets lost walking. Choose one without a cork ball (this will swell and render the whistle unusable) and attach it to your life jacket so it will be there when you need it.

First-Aid Kit. The contents of your first-aid kit will vary greatly according to the location, season, duration, and anticipated difficulty of any trip. For popular rivers near well-traveled roads you may need no more than a simple "ouch pouch." Extended day trips in remote locations with a group require a more comprehensive kit, one able to deal with serious lacerations, broken limbs, illnesses,

2.10.1 Designed by one of the authors, the kayak rescue kit includes a throw bag, two pulleys, a paddle hook, a large oval carabiner, and a small saw; it fits (except for the saw) into the throw bag and weighs only 2 pounds, 8 ounces.

and insect-sting reactions (anaphylactic shock). Wilderness expeditions require things like hypothermia thermometers and tooth-fracture treatments, as well as an array of prescription drugs available only through a doctor. (The contents of first-aid kits are discussed in more detail in appendix C.)

Emergency Kit. Often carried with the first-aid kit, this is intended to cope with emergencies other than physical injuries. A butane lighter or fire-starting kit is a good idea if there is a chance you might be caught out overnight or a need to warm a hypothermia victim. You might carry an extra set of contact lenses or glasses, if they are essential, or a small space blanket. Some paddlers keep items like this in a waterproof container sewn into their life jackets.

Improvised Gear. Some items must be improvised on the spot. For example, several persons have been rescued from low-head dams by fishermen who have used jumper cables from their cars.

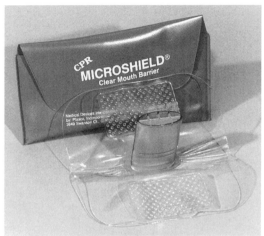

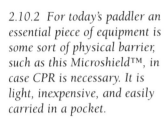

2.10.2 For today's paddler an essential piece of equipment is some sort of physical barrier, such as this Microshield™, in case CPR is necessary. It is light, inexpensive, and easily carried in a pocket.

Ropes. River ropes can be divided into two main categories according their intended use: throwing or hauling. Ropes are made either by the traditional method of twisting or braiding fiber strands together, or by the newer technique of kernmantle construction, in which the strands are laid parallel in a core and covered with an abrasion-resistant woven sheath. Most climbing and rescue ropes are kernmantle ropes. For a simple throwing rescue, the construction (and the strength) of the rope is relatively unimportant. What is important for a river throw rope is that it should float, not absorb water, and be easily handled.

A certain amount of dynamic stretch is beneficial, since it will reduce the shock loading when stopping a swimmer. For most purposes a simple 3/8"(9.5 mm) braided polypropylene rope will suffice. However, when used for haul lines, and especially for lifelines (that is, where a person is suspended by it), rope quality and strength become critical. For a haul or anchor line we want a rope that has a high breaking strength and will not stretch under load. This means having a static or low-stretch (as opposed to a dynamic, or climbing) kernmantle nylon rope of 7/16–1/2"(11–13 mm) in diameter.

So far, in spite of a number of attempts, no one has come up with a single rope entirely suitable for both purposes: polypropylene throw bag rope is too weak and stretchy for serious mechanical rescues and is unsuitable for lifelines; nylon rope absorbs water and doesn't throw well. Spectra™ ropes that have a low-stretch synthetic core with a polypropylene kernmantle sheath are becoming pop-

2.11 *Four types of river ropes. Top to bottom: 3/8"(9.5 mm) polypropylene kernmantel (tensile strength aprox. 2600 lbf[1200 kgf]), with a 6 mm nylon Prusik loop attached; 3/8"(9.5 mm) braided polypropylene (1,800 lbf[816 kgf]); 1/2" twisted polypropylene (1800 lbf[861 kgf]); and 7 mm(1/4") Spectra® (4500 lbf[2041 kgf]).*

ular. These 3/8"(9.5 mm) ropes have a tensile strength of 4,500 lbs (2,041 kgf) and a good "hand." They are expensive, however, and do not float as well as all-polypropylene ropes.

Throw Bags. The vast majority of throwing rescues are made with throw bags: a simple nylon sack stuffed (rather than coiled) with a rope and a disk of foam to float the bag. It is the primary tool of rescue for the river runner, and every paddler should consider carrying one.

Throw bags typically contain 50–70'(15–21 m) of 3/8"(9.5 mm) braided polypropylene rope, with tensile strength in the 1,700–2,000 lb(771–907 kgf) range. Throw bags are easily stowed in the boat and can be quickly deployed, at least for the first throw. It does take time to restuff the bag after a throw, and second throws with loose rope are more difficult. There is also a risk that the bag may become snagged, and there is no way to control the amount of rope thrown.

Throw bags come in a wide variety of styles and lengths. Some "boutique bags" have 1/4"(6 mm) ropes that are only 40–50'(12–15 m) in length. These are very popular with kayakers because they make for a very compact bag and are easier to throw. However, we have

2.12 *Throw bags come in many shapes and sizes. The bag at the left rear is made of a nylon mesh to reduce "bucketing" and to allow easy drying.*

found that rope smaller than 3/8"(9.5 mm) in diameter is often weak and very hard on the hands. One popular variation is a small bag that can be worn on a paddler's waist, ready for instant deployment. Some designs combine this with a tow system.

Throw bag ropes are usually marginal for mechanical rescues, although the introduction of Spectra™ has certainly helped. Neither we nor their manufacturers recommend that you use them for Tyroleans or similar lifelines except in an emergency.

Pin Kits. Outfitters and wilderness rafters on difficult rivers should consider carrying a "pin kit" to help free pinned boats. This would consist ideally of a 150–300'(46–91 m) of 7/16"–1/2"(11–13 mm) low-stretch nylon kernmantle rope, six large locking carabiners, four 2–4"(5–10 cm) rescue pulleys, several 8 mm Prusiks, and six 10'(3 m) anchor slings made of 1"(25 mm) tubular nylon webbing. With this kind of pin kit you would be equipped to set up Telfer lowers, Tyroleans, and other technical rescues.

Clothing

Proper clothing is as important as any other piece of equipment. Synthetic piles and drysuits have virtually replaced the traditional wool and neoprene. Whatever you wear, the object is the same: to maintain the body's core temperature. In order to do this, certain critical areas, the trunk and head especially, must be protected against heat loss.

On the river the problem is that the paddler is constantly wet and may at any time be immersed in cold, moving water. The water acts in two ways: the body is made wet by waves or spray, the water evaporates in the wind, and the body is rapidly chilled (windchill hypothermia); or, when the body is immersed in cold water, rapid and severe heat loss by convection takes place, which quickly leads to acute immersion hypothermia.

Paddlers usually dress with the assumption that they are going to stay in their boat. This can lead to problems if the assumption proves wrong, either because of a swim or because they have to get in the water to do a rescue. The best rule is to overdress.

Outer Layer. The first defense is an outer layer that will protect the body from the chilling effect of the wind. Usually this consists of a paddling jacket and pants made of some kind of coated fabric to keep spray and waves off the bare skin. Both jacket and pants should be cut loose enough to fit over the insulating layers underneath.

Insulating Layer. Wool, nylon, and polypropylene pile or knits all make excellent insulators under a paddling jacket and pants. In milder conditions they can be worn alone. The same layering principle applies here as in mountaineering: two or three thin layers are better than one thick one. Avoid cotton clothing altogether—it will not keep you warm when wet.

The new synthetics are so good that they have led some paddlers to advocate eliminating wetsuits and drysuits altogether. This can be a serious mistake, however, particularly for novices, because neither synthetic materials nor wool will protect you in the water. Water will flow right through any woven fabric and directly over the skin, causing an abrupt and massive heat loss to the body. This may be an acceptable risk for experts (although the drowning of at least one expert paddler has been traced to this), but if you're still learning and expect to swim a lot, keep reading through the wetsuit and drysuit sections.

Wetsuits. Capable of replacing both the insulating layer and the outer layer, the wetsuit was developed for skin divers. Made of neo-

2.13 Dressing for the river. (Rex Rystedt/Canoe & Kayak)

EXTREME COLD CONDITIONS

Pogies: Paddlers who opt for direct contact with the paddle prefer these coverings instead of gloves.

Skull Cap: Extra head coverage provides warmth and helps to prevent "ice cream" headaches.

Helmet: Full, shorty (shown), or either with a face protecting mask or bar.

Personal Flotation Device: Various styles for comfort, mobility and warmth.

Drysuit: Full-body garment that blocks water from your torso and keeps warmth in; does not protect hands, head, or feet.

Underneath: Drysuit liner "bunnysuit," plus additional layers—such as polypropylene top and bottom—to suit your comfort and warmth needs.

Booties: Protect the feet from cold and terrain.

COLD CONDITIONS

Gloves: Various styles—usually in neoprene—fit for comfort and warmth.

Helmet: Always wear a helmet!

Personal Flotation Device: Always wear a PFD!

Paddle Jacket or Dry Top: Repels water and cold from upper torso while retaining warmth.

Wetsuit: Neoprene Farmer Johns and Janes, or pants, are ideal in this ensemble.

Underneath: Extra layering provides extra warmth.

Booties: A good choice for wear in all conditions.

WARM CONDITIONS

Helmet: Use your noggin, don't bash it.

Personal Flotation Device: Keep on keepin' it on.

Short-sleeve Dry Top: Optional upper torso protection without long sleeves.

Underneath: Try a birthday suit.

Shorts: Many styles for fit, function, and fashion.

Sandals: Choose a watersport style that will stay on during a capsize or swim.

prene in a variety of thicknesses and coverages, it works by letting a small amount of water in between the skin and the neoprene. The body warms this thin layer of water, which then acts just like any other insulating layer. If the wetsuit is fitted properly (that is, tightly) this warm water will be held against the skin even when the wearer is in the water. The neoprene also acts as a shield against waves and spray.

Against these advantages, however, it must be said that wetsuits are stiff, constricting to the active paddler, and somewhat uncomfortable. "Plumbing" arrangements are tedious for men and next to impossible for women. Wetsuits do not lend themselves well to layering, although the newer generation of thinner, more flexible wetsuits developed for surfing is much better on this count.

Drysuits. Since its introduction to paddling in the mid-1980s, the drysuit has revolutionized cold-weather paddling. Worn over normal insulating clothing, the full drysuit has openings at the wrist, ankle, and neck closed with tight-fitting latex rubber seals. With water mostly sealed out and the body kept dry, heat loss is minimal; in fact, heat buildup is sometimes a problem. Many river runners opt for the dry top that can be used alone or in conjunction with a farmer john–style wetsuit. Drysuits are expensive and require a fairly high level of maintenance: the latex seals wear out, and the expensive waterproof zippers sometimes jam.

Boats and Rafts

Whitewater river craft can be divided into three broad categories: rafts, open canoes, and decked boats. All have benefited over the years from improved designs and technology, and these improvements now allow us to extend the limits of the sport to ever higher levels. In extreme whitewater, however, the consequences of mistakes or equipment failure are often severe. To reduce the risks of accidents, it is important to maximize the safety features of each type of craft.

Rafts. When selecting a raft, look for multiple air chambers (four or more) and construction from high-quality materials such as neoprene, PVC, or hypalon. There should be an adequate number of D-rings attached to the sides for your purposes, and these should be large and securely attached. The hand lines along the sides should

2.14 Oar rafts are popular for extended trips.

2.15 A paddle raft.

fit snugly to prevent accidental entanglement of arms or legs. Paddle rafts should be fitted with foot cups to help people brace in.

The two most important factors in determining what class of water the raft can handle are the size of the raft and the load it is carrying. Size means not only the length and width of the raft, but also the diameter of the tubes and the upturn of the ends, all of which affect the amount of water taken on. Bigger is not always better—maneuverability must be taken into account on many rivers. Do not base your calculations on the manufacturer's figures from the raft's data plate. These are for calm water only. A reasonable guideline for whitewater load rating is to figure one-half the length of the raft plus the guide (for example, a 14' boat can carry eight people—one-half of 14=7; plus guide= 8).

Self-bailing rafts have inflatable floors laced or glued into the tubes, allowing the water to run out without having to bail it out with a bucket. They are also easier to unwrap when pinned because the floor does not catch the current as much as in conventional rafts. Without a doubt, self-bailing rafts have made river running safer and much less work.

2.16 *Catarafts, such as the one in the foreground, have become much more popular in recent years. They combine stability and automatic self-bailing. (Kris Walker)*

Catarafts also have become popular. These craft have a frame suspended between two pontoonlike tubes. Since there is no floor or open compartment to fill up, these boats have no swamping worries and will punch through bigger holes than a conventional raft. They do mean a very wet ride and do not have the carrying capacity of a traditional raft.

Any raft must always be prepared for a flip. All too often, gear is left strewn about the raft floor. Everything should be tied or clipped securely into the raft before you start, and should be kept that way. Any lines and throw bags must be secured so that they do not entangle swimmers. It is possible to right a flipped raft, even in the midst of a rapid. "Flip lines," pioneered by western rafters, are pre-rigged lines attached at one end to **D**-rings on the side of the raft or to a rowing frame. With the raft upside down, a boatman can grab the flip line, stand on the opposite tube, and flip the raft over in mid-current.

In an oar boat, beware of shoehorning yourself into the rowing compartment, because you will need some space if the downstream oar hits a rock. In one incident on the Bío-Bío River in Chile, an oar was driven completely through a boatman's thigh because of a crowded rowing compartment. Make sure that all of your cargo is

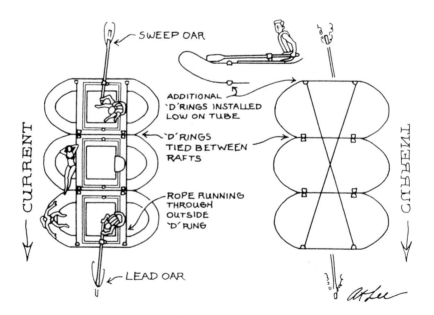

2.17 *A triple-rigged raft. Left: view from above. Right: view from below.*

properly tied in and that your passengers can't get hurt or entrapped by a shifting load.

On big rivers, consider outfitting rafts for double or triple rigging. When two or three rafts are tied together, the combined mass is less likely to be flipped or stopped by a hole. To prepare for this, install additional **D**-rings low on the tubes so that the rafts can be tied together top and bottom, which will prevent them from flipping over onto each other.

Decked Boats. Proper outfitting of a decked boat is important for safe paddling. *Outfitting* means finishing a boat and fitting it to yourself, after you buy it but before you paddle it. Almost any boat needs a certain amount of modification so that the paddler can fit snugly in the boat, although this is not nearly as much of a hassle as it once was. The key here is to be tight enough to "wear" the boat yet not be wedged in so tightly that a quick exit is difficult.

Most whitewater kayaks today are made of rotomolded plastic. This material is extremely tough but not very rigid. It requires internal bracing to keep the decks from collapsing, usually with 3–4" minicell foam walls mounted vertically under the bow and stern, parallel to the length of the boat. The harder the water and the more playing you do, the bigger and stronger the walls must be. Better boat designs lock the walls, seat, and thigh braces together into a single rigid unit. The paddler braces his feet on adjustable footbraces, although some manufacturers now offer a bulkhead-type footbrace that fits alongside the standard walls.

Some European boats, however, are designed differently, since many boat builders there believe that the danger of a vertical wall's collapse outweighs its benefits. Instead they use an adjustable transverse bulkhead under the deck that also acts as a footbrace (the Prijon is a good example; see figure 2.18). This allows more room for the paddler's legs and ensures that he will not go forward if the boat hits an obstruction.

Many U.S. boat builders, however, have realized the safety value of larger cockpits, something else that has been a feature of European boats for some time. A large cockpit allows easy exit in an emergency. Another solution is the "keyhole" cockpit: a long, narrow, cockpit in which the paddler can raise his knees (see figure 2.19).

While on the subject of design, a word about squirt boats is appropriate. These small stunt kayaks have attracted a growing following, especially in the eastern U.S. squirt boats require constant

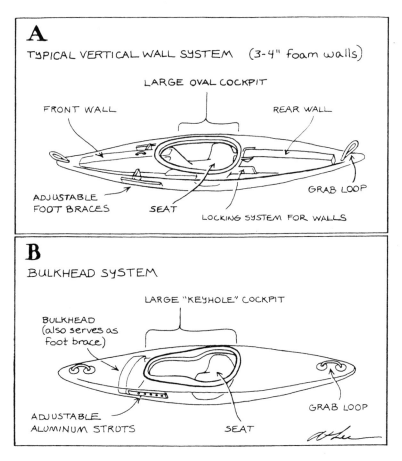

A

TYPICAL VERTICAL WALL SYSTEM   (3-4" foam walls)

LARGE OVAL COCKPIT

FRONT WALL

REAR WALL

ADJUSTABLE
FOOT BRACES

SEAT

GRAB LOOP

LOCKING SYSTEM FOR WALLS

B

BULKHEAD SYSTEM

LARGE "KEYHOLE" COCKPIT

BULKHEAD
(also serves as
foot brace)

ADJUSTABLE
ALUMINUM STRUTS

SEAT

GRAB LOOP

*2.18 A safely outfitted boat should have sturdy, braced walls or bulkheads
to keep the deck from collapsing, strong grab loops, airbags, footbraces,
and thigh braces. Most U.S. boats use the system shown in A, with vertical
sidewalls running the length of the boat, while many European boats use
the system shown in B, with a keyhole cockpit and a transverse bulkhead
which also serves as a footbrace.*

expert attention and are tiring to paddle, especially in cold water,
since the paddler is usually in it up to his armpits. These boats dive
like submarines and some of the accepted maneuvers, like mystery
moves and splats, invite pinning or broaching. They have been
involved in a number of accidents. We do not pass judgment on any
paddler's choice of boats, but the dangers of these little craft are not
to be taken lightly.

2.19 *Most modern kayaks have adopted larger, longer cockpits that allow a paddler to escape more easily in an emergency.*

Other important safety features are the grab loops on the bow and stern. These should be securely attached at bow and stern and be sturdy enough to haul a pinned boat out. If your boat is ever pinned (with or without you in it), the grab loops are almost always the primary point of attachment for the haul line. Another critical item is the "broach loop" (see figure 2.20), which is a steel cable or nylon loop mounted in front of the cockpit. This offers another point of attachment for a pinned boat, and in the best of circum-

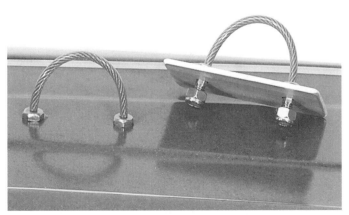

2.20 *Broach loops, such as this Perception "security loop" have become standard equipment on most kayaks. In addition to adding an attachment point for rescue, it can be used to lock the kayak to a rack.* (NOC Photo)

stances may allow a haul line to pull the front deck up enough to free an entrapped paddler's legs.

Another useful feature to consider is a towing system for getting swamped boats back to the shore. Most paddlers rely on the "bull-dozer" method: putting their bow in the cockpit of the swamped boat and pushing it to shore. A more efficient way is to use a towing system that puts you in the normal ferry position upstream of the swamped craft. The center-mounted system (just aft of the cockpit) allows the tow boat to swivel and therefore control the ferry angle

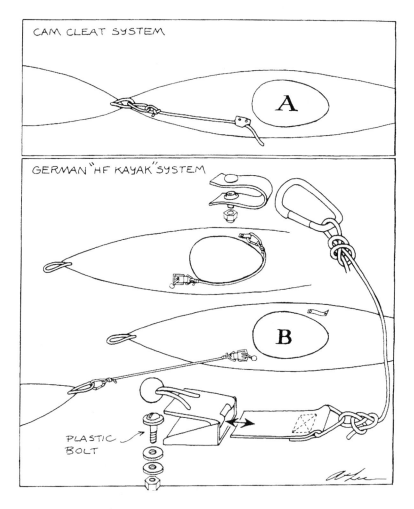

2.21 Two types of tow systems.

more precisely. Any tow system should have a foolproof release system, unless you like the idea of having a thousand-pound anchor permanently attached to your boat. One German tow system attaches to the hull with a plastic through-bolt that will break under pressure, even if the paddler is unable to release it. Be sure to test the release on any tow system before you use it. Any of the several tow systems shown here (see figure 2.21) will work well. Most are inexpensive and easy to install. They use the jam cleat, a standard sailing item available through most marine hardware stores, to make a quick-release system. You can now buy preassembled towing kits, from simple ones that use the jam cleat to the more expensive imported items.

Sit-on-Tops and Inflatable Kayaks. The sit-on-top kayak does away with the deck (and the feeling of claustrophobia that goes with it). The paddler sits on top and holds himself in with thigh straps. This obviously reduces the chances of entrapment, although it does expose the paddler more. An inflatable kayak (see figure 2.23) has similar outfitting, but has inflated tubes like a raft. Recent models have rigidity approaching that of a plastic kayak, with corresponding performance. Most high-performance designs are self-bailing and have a foam floor insert for added rigidity.

2.22 *The "Sit-On-Top" kayak allows for easy entry and exit. (Carlos Steward)*

2.23 Inflatable kayaks combine stability with ease of entry and exit. Although popular with novices, there are high-performance models available as well. (Carlos Steward)

Open Canoes. The new generation of open canoe designs has allowed open canoes to run water once reserved for decked boats. The Grand Canyon is now routinely run in canoes, and even the Niagara Gorge has been done.

Some people choose the open canoe because of the reduced risk of entrapment. Walls are not necessary, as they are in decked boats, but a fixed foam block, or "horse," placed under the thwarts will go far toward eliminating the danger of a canoe pin or paddler entrapment. Commercially available molded plastic "saddles" serve much the same purpose. Air bags displace water and make the boat take on less water (and easier to swim to shore), but they do not add any structural strength to the canoe in the event of a pin. It is critical that the air bags are securely affixed to the canoe. Another system of flotation, popular in New England, involves attaching a 4" layer of ethafoam to both sides of the outer hull of the canoe, which gives more room to carry duffel on wilderness trips.

Canoeists often install thigh straps or braces to improve their control over the boat. Straps should have a quick-release feature and be made of a wide, stiff material that won't snag the paddler in a wet exit. Position them so that they don't come up around your groin but fit lower down, toward your knees. Velcro™ makes an

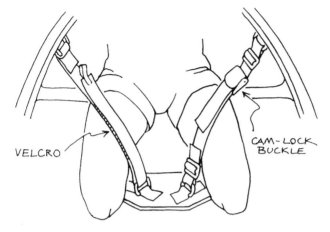

VELCRO

CAM-LOCK
BUCKLE

2.24 Thigh straps are an integral part of the outfitting of whitewater canoes. They should allow the paddler to exit without entanglement. In order to avoid the type of entanglement described in chapter 10, both straps should have a positive release such as Velcro™ or a quick-release buckle.

excellent strap fastener, since, unlike a buckle, it will release under strong pressure.

Unless you line your canoe a lot, there is little reason to use end lines ("painters") more than 8'(2.5 m) long. The loose painter becomes a hazard in an upset and may snarl the paddler. Store it under shock cord when it is not in use. If you have aluminum gunnels, go over them periodically with a file and remove any sharp edges. We don't recommend wooden gunnels or thwarts for serious whitewater. They can be a hazard if they break into spearlike splinters when the boat pins. A spare paddle is a good idea, but make sure the hold-down system works: you should be able to get the paddle easily, but have it secure if the boat overturns.

When we first wrote *River Rescue,* the minimalist look was "in." Carrying a knife, carabiner, or Prusik was considered the mark of a sissy or a terminal tech-weenie. Now fashions have changed, and we see guides with half a dozen carabiners and yards of sun-baked, deteriorated, Prusik cord dangling loosely from the backs of their life jackets. Sometimes too much equipment can get you into trouble. One Utah boatman flipped out of his oar boat one day in the middle of a rapid, and made a lunge for the chicken line on the way out. He missed, but the carabiner on the shoulder of his life jacket didn't. Thus attached, he went down through the rapid's tail waves, his face smacking into the metal oar frame every time the raft crested a wave. After that he carried his carabiners in a pouch.

3

Self-Rescue

Rivers keep flowing, regardless of our personal misfortunes. An important lesson for all paddlers to learn from this is that you have to take care of yourself on the river. In chapter 1 we saw the importance of preparation, both mental and physical, and of good judgment. We also discussed some of the leader's responsibilities for the safety of the group and the individual. In this chapter we'll concentrate on the individual paddler and on how he can deal on his own behalf with some of the hazards we've defined.

We recommend that you don't paddle alone, but even in a group the responsibility for your own safety rests in large part with you. You are the one who wants to paddle, and you are the one ultimately who must take the blame for your miscalculations. It follows that you should be able to rescue yourself.

The Eskimo Roll

For those in decked boats, the quickest and most obvious means of self-rescue is the Eskimo roll. It is the best insurance policy you can invest in, and like any other aspect of the sport it requires practice. A good roll is a real boost to your self-confidence, which in turn reduces the likelihood of more serious mistakes. Nevertheless, there is also a time to swim. Overconfidence and misplaced pride ("I never

3.1 Mishaps are part of the fun on the river, but be ready for self-rescue when they happen. (Glenn Oakley)

come out of my boat") are as bad as too little confidence. In open water it is all right to keep trying to roll, and if you scouted thoroughly you should know when you turn over whether a hazard is coming up. Often it's a matter of experience: novices tend to bail out too soon and experts to stay in too long. Experience will give you almost a sixth sense for where you are in a rapid when you find yourself upside down.

Swimming with Boats

Although the number of open canoeists who know how to roll is increasing, most must still rely on the swimming technique of self-rescue. When that last low brace falls and you capsize, get to the upstream side of the boat when you come up. If things look bad, abandon the boat and swim for shore. If it seems safe to do so, work your way to the upstream end of the boat, grab the painter (but don't wrap it around your arm), and swim the boat to shore. Sometimes it is possible to right a swamped boat and paddle it to shore.

Rafters can also use self-rescue after a flip. While a raft cannot be rolled, it can be righted in midriver (the next chapter, "Rescue on the Run," describes in detail how to do this). If the flip happens close to shore, the best bet is usually to get the boat into shore rather than to right it in deep water. One way to do this is for the rafters to climb on top of the capsized raft and paddle it to shore, after first checking to see what is downstream. Another method is to unleash the bow line or clip a throw bag rigged so that a crew member can grab it, swim to shore, and pendulum the raft in (figures 3.3 and 3.4). In other situations, a throw bag can be thrown from shore with a carabiner preattached. If this is not possible, the crew can try to swim the raft to shore by holding on to the **D**-rings or painters.

Swimming with a boat or raft can be more dangerous than swimming without one, especially on rocky rivers, where there is a chance of getting squashed between the boat and a rock. In big water the extra buoyancy of your boat is an asset, but stay on the upstream side. Wide, cold rivers, such as those in Canada and Alaska, present another problem. Although the whitewater may not be difficult, a swimmer may become hypothermic before reaching shore. With a swamped decked boat a paddler can sometimes reduce his exposure

3.2 One method of self-rescue for the rafter is to get on the upside-down raft and paddle it to shore. Obviously this only works in fairly calm water.

3.3 Another method of rafting self-rescue: a throw bag is tied and clipped to the bow D-ring of the raft...

by crawling on top of the boat and paddling it like a surfboard. If the situation permits, companion boats may stabilize the swimmer's boat enough to permit a deep-water reentry.

It's always a good idea, if you can, to hang on to your equipment if you have to swim. However, bear in mind that equipment is cheap and lives are not. This may sound obvious, but at least one paddler drowned on the Chattooga because she chose to hang on to her boat

3.4 ...and the rafter unclips the bag after the flip, swims to an eddy, and pendulums the raft in.

rather than to throw a rope and was entrapped in the Chattooga's infamous Left Crack.

Swimming in Whitewater

We recommend that every paddler swim a "safe" rapid at least once a season to renew his respect for the force of the water and to keep in practice if his roll fails. Novices and experts alike should do this. Especially in cold or difficult water, head for shore as fast as possible. Swim aggressively: boating techniques like ferries and eddy turns can be used out of the boat as well as in it to help you move toward the shore (see figure 3.5). Rescue yourself: *never assume someone else will do it.* Charlie Walbridge notes in the *Best of the River Safety Task Force Newsletter* that "many experts make lousy victims." Often the transition from hero paddler to helpless victim is a hard one, and one reason for this is that paddlers seldom practice swimming.

Defensive Swimming. On shallow, rocky rivers the standard position for swimming in a rapid is lying on your back with your feet downstream (see figure 3.7). This reduces the danger of foot entrapment. Try to maintain a horizontal position as near to the surface as possible, always looking downstream and preparing to fend yourself off rocks with your feet. Don't float passively from one rapid to the next: angle your head toward shore, kick with your legs and backstroke with your arms. A sidestroke works well in deeper water or when extra power is needed, such as when crossing an eddy line.

Aggressive Swimming. In deeper water, where the danger of foot entrapment is minimal, or when there is a critical eddy to catch, roll on your stomach and do a crawl stroke. Keep your head out of the water as much as possible in order to keep your bearings. In big waves you must time your breathing for the troughs of the waves (see figure 3.8). If the situation dictates, eddy out behind rocks in midriver to rest, catch your breath and plan your next move, or perhaps sit tight and wait for a rescue boat. If you enter the water from a rock, or from shore, *never dive headfirst.* This is an invitation to a cervical spine injury. In deep water, you can do a modified shallow-water dive with your chest hitting the water first. The initial distance and momentum gained by diving can make a big difference when entering the current.

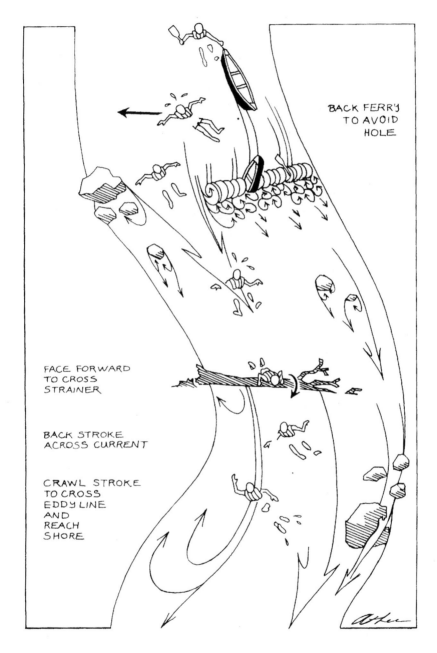

BACK FERRY
TO AVOID
HOLE

FACE FORWARD
TO CROSS
STRAINER

BACK STROKE
ACROSS CURRENT

CRAWL STROKE
TO CROSS
EDDY LINE
AND
REACH
SHORE

3.5 *Swim aggressively, using techniques like ferries and eddy turns to move across the river to safety. Here a swimmer ferries across the main current toward the eddy line, crosses a strainer, then breaks through the eddy fence with a crawl stroke.*

3.6 *Two canoeists swimming in whitewater. They are upstream of the boat, facing downstream, with their feet up and in front of them.*

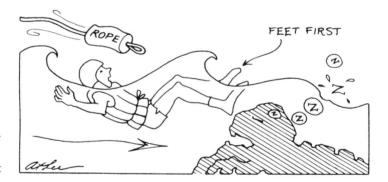

3.7 *Defensive swimming in shallow water.*

Strainers

If you find yourself swept unavoidably toward a tree-choked strainer you should change your position from feet-first to headfirst (see figure 3.9). A feet-first position will tend to make you wash under the trunk or limbs, which is the last thing you want. Try to swim faster than the current, using a crawl stroke, and look at the tree. Is

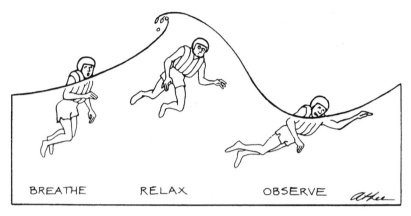

3.8 Swimming in big, deep, water requires timing your breathing for the troughs of the waves. Since the danger of foot entrapment is minimal, a crawl stroke may be the best option for getting ashore quickly.

the trunk slippery? Are there limbs you can grab? You must try to get up on the tree and out of the current. As you hit the tree, let the force of the current assist you in keeping your momentum up as you crawl onto it. If your boat is floating with you, don't let it block your movements or pin you against the tree. In river rescue classes we routinely set up a smooth "strainer" held in the current with ropes and let students practice swimming up and over it. This an excellent demonstration of the power of moving water.

If you can't get up on the tree, whether because the current is too fast or the trunk too large, a last resort is to dive underneath it, head first. Time your breathing and plan on pulling yourself through the branches. Don't let your body get parallel to the main trunk, or you will be pressed against it.

3.9 Strainers. If a strainer is unavoidable, swim toward it headfirst and pull yourself up and over it.

Entrapment

The best way to deal with entrapment is to avoid it. This means not trying to walk in water deeper than your knees and swimming with your feet up and in front of you when in shallow water. Once an entrapment occurs, it is difficult, if not impossible, for the victim to escape unaided. It is hard to stand if your foot gets caught, and if your whole body is immersed, the force of the water will be more than twice as great as on the entrapped limb. If you are entrapped, though, you may be able to gain valuable rescue time if you can push yourself off the bottom and dog paddle with your hands. If the water is not too swift, you may be able to get an occasional breath and survive until someone can reach you. In one such situation a man survived for more than two hours until he was rescued.

Broaches, pins, and boat entrapments will be covered in more detail in chapter 8, but here we'll consider some things a paddler can do to help himself in these situations. A boat is broached when it is pushed sideways onto a solid object by the current and held there. The danger of broaching is that the boat may collapse and entrap the paddler. In a broach, the severity of the situation depends on the position of the boat and the amount of water pushing on it. Only experience can give you a real appreciation of this, but if the water pressure is great enough to blow your sprayskirt off the cockpit rim, you are in dire danger of wrapping the boat, and it's time to get out in a hurry. You may have a chance to lean into the rock and push yourself off it with your hands.

Sometimes you can push off with your paddle or shift your weight so that the boat moves, but remember that the boat may wrap at any time: you must be prepared to get out as quickly as possible. The more doubtful you feel about the situation, the less time you should spend trying to get the boat off. A quick exit is usually the best choice; remember, though, that the same rocks that pinned the boat may entrap you also.

Holes

Paddlers in decked boats surf holes to practice balancing in the hole and then paddling out. They enjoy doing this, but they also know that sometime in the future they will find themselves in a hole by accident and may need those escape skills. Before surfing an unknown hole, look at it carefully. Is water flowing out of the sides? Is there a weak spot in the backwash to escape through? Consider

3.10.1 Escaping direct-ly downstream from a hole can be difficult.

3.10.2 Instead, move to the ends of the hole...

3.10.3 ...and try to catch the water flow-ing downstream.

also what is downstream if you have to swim out. Some paddlers experiment by sending in a friend first ("Sure, it's okay. Surfed it last week. Go ahead while I take your picture."). While this method has its adherents, it doesn't win friends.

The best system of self-rescue in a hole is to paddle out. Try different directions: some sections of the backwash may be weaker than others. In most cases it is easier to escape out of the side of a hole (see figures 3.10.1-3). Paddle forward and backward, stroking on both sides in a kayak, not just on the downstream bracing blade. Rock the boat backward and forward to build momentum, putting in a maximum-effort stroke at the end of the hole and attempting to catch the downstream-flowing water with your paddle. For most paddlers, a reverse stroke powered by the large muscles of the torso is more powerful than a forward stroke. Canoeists should be able to switch and brace on either side. If paddling fails, turning over in the hole and extending the paddle will sometimes allow the downstream current beneath the backwash to catch your body and the paddle and pull you out.

As a last resort, pop the sprayskirt, allowing water in, and hope the less buoyant boat will wash out with you still in it. Keep trying to get out, but don't make the mistake of letting yourself become exhausted. In a violent hole it takes a lot of effort to stay in control: if you can't get out, swim for it early. The best escape is to flip upside down and dive down under the backwash.

An open canoe caught in a hydraulic will almost always swamp quickly, which may cause it to wash out. But be careful: being in a large hydraulic with an open canoe can be dangerous if you and it are trading places.

If caught in a hole, rafters should *high side;* that is, move quickly to the downstream side of the raft to keep it from flipping (see figure 3.11). If the raft begins to spin around in the hole the crew may have to move quickly to keep their weight downstream. Sometimes the raft will fill with water and flush out on its own. Other times it can be paddled out or roped out from shore, but a raft full of water is *heavy* and may have a will of its own. You may have to swim out and leave the raft in the hole, especially if there is a risk of hypothermia. Get out by diving out over the backwash of the hole from the downstream tube of the raft.

It is very dangerous, if the raft is caught in a hydraulic, for a crew member to end up underneath it. The swimmer will be recir-

3.11 A raft caught in a large hole. If the raft flips or someone falls out, a swimmer may get trapped underneath the raft. These rafters have moved to the downstream side of the raft to keep it from flipping, while a shore-based rescue party attempts to pull the raft out with a rope.

culated in the usual way but will not be able to breathe if he comes up under the raft. To escape he must either pull himself along the bottom of the raft or be pulled out by a crew member.

Low-head dams form a hazard from which escape by self-rescue is very difficult. A swimmer will surface at the boil line only to find himself sucked back into the water pouring over the dam. The water will force him down to the bottom and then up again at the boil line, and the whole frightening process will start over again. To complicate matters, some dams have exposed reinforcing bars of steel, which can entrap or skewer a swimmer. Debris floating around in hydraulics (logs, for example) can hit a swimmer, though sometimes you can hang on to a piece of debris for additional flotation. If you are caught in a low-head dam, try to take guarded breaths and stay relaxed (see figure 3.12). Save your strength: you can't fight the water. Try to work your way sideways toward the shore while being recirculated. More often than not there will be sheer concrete retaining walls buttressing the sides of the dam, but you may be rescued from the sides if someone can reach you. Sometimes, in smaller hydraulics, it is possible to swim out by diving down and catching the underlying jet of water as you are being recirculated. Otherwise,

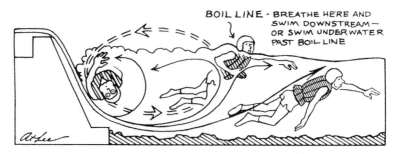

3.12 Self-rescue in a low-head dam.

try to swim downstream only at the area of the boil line, preferably just before you surface. *Do not take off your life jacket* in an attempt to swim out of the hydraulic: if you fail you will be in much worse shape than before.

Cris Leonard tells the story of being vertically pinned in an open canoe on the Gauley River. It's a tale of his own self-rescue efforts, as well as the determined attempts of his fellow paddlers that day.

"My entry into Sweet Falls was too far to the left. Drawing right, I lost forward momentum. The bow of my boat planed out over the pool below, dropped, hit the riverbed with the impact of a sledge-hammer, and stuck fast. I pitched forward hard. Somehow I got my right leg over the thwart in front of me. That thwart caught me in the crotch as my left leg slid under it. The Gauley River was now breaking over my boat and head, pinning me to the thwart. To complicate things further, my boat collapsed partially under the force of the water…enough to ensure that the thwart had a viselike grip across my left thigh. I was trapped and I was scared."

The rescue team was able to lower a line to him but could not extricate him. Cris continues, "My boat had to come out for me to come out. They were hoping they could get the end of the rope to me to tie to my boat (no one else could possibly reach the boat to do it). I remembered that my own rescue line was within reach—it was in the bag tied to the thwart I was braced against. It was a lot of work to tie that rope to the thwart, and I realized that hypothermia was coming on rapidly. I threw the rope downstream and waited.

"Another half-hour passed. Things didn't look too good. I was not in a state of panic or shock. I was going to die that afternoon. The cold water was beating me. It was just a matter of time. I was mentally and emotionally prepared to die, but determined not to give up. There were twenty good men out there pulling for me. After a while, I slumped forward, propping my head upon one hand. I rested, hoping to conserve energy. Time passed, I got a second wind. I know I had been motionless for a long time and thought, 'Those guys think that I am dead!' I sat erect, reached as high as I could and felt my hand break the water. I later learned that this signal was extremely encouraging to my friends.

"The Corps of Engineers had cut the release from Summersville Lake by 300 cfs at one o'clock, so perhaps the water had dropped a little. Maybe the boat had shifted a little, perhaps the group had moved it slightly. They were ready to have the line ferried to river left when Randy Perkins noticed that something had changed. He ran to the water's edge, waving and exhorting, 'Pull!' and pull they did. My boat rolled free. This brought me around in a real hurry. I was able to kick and wiggle loose. My life jacket kept me afloat; and when the group saw that I could hold my head up, twenty men cried."

About the only thing I had learned about canoeing was to head into the part of the rapids that seemed to be moving the fastest, where the most white water was.

James Dickey, *Deliverance*

4

Rescue on the Run

At one end of the river spectrum is the pool-and-drop river. On these rivers, river runners can negotiate one drop at time in a deliberate, controlled fashion. Any mishaps can be picked up in the pools; safety ropes can be set along large bank eddies and chase boats positioned in the runouts. Especially on narrow rivers, this allows for a fairly structured safety plan. At the other side of the spectrum, however, are wide rivers with a steady, consistent gradient. This creates more or less continuous whitewater that can run for miles, and often these rivers are bordered by canyon walls and have few eddies. Some rivers can be both—drop and pool at low water and big and continuous in times of high water.

On big, wide rivers with continuous whitewater, rescue must occur "on the run"; that is, the rescue actually takes place in the current. Shore-based rescue systems are usually ineffective—they lack the reach to get to victims in midstream and usually cannot be moved downstream and reset fast enough to keep up with a moving, dynamic situation. A mishap on a river like this leads to a unique rescue situation—an accident scene moving downstream at ten miles per hour or faster. The victims of the accident must either rescue themselves or be rescued by boats or swimmers in midcurrent.

4.1 On big rivers in fast current, rescue "on the run" may be the only solution.

Safety in numbers is an important concept in bigger, faster whitewater. The people already on the river, in the current, must also be the rescuers. Everyone in the group must be prepared to self-rescue or to assist others. Parties should consist of three to five boats, each staying within sight of another on the river. Larger groups should subdivide, since they are harder to control. Each boater (or boatman) should watch the boat behind them as well as the boat in front. Boats normally run in a definite order with a designated lead and sweep boat, and boatmen/paddlers must develop the habit of frequently looking over their shoulder to keep tabs on "buddy boats." The slower a river party is to retrieve equipment and boats, the greater the consequence to the overall safety of the trip. And, of course, the longer a person is in the water, the greater the exposure to injury, entrapment, or hypothermia, not to mention drowning.

In this kind of whitewater, communications are critical. Hand signals (see appendix A for the ACA/AWA Universal River Signals) are the most common means, although some boatmen now use radios. When the lead boat gives a signal, each successive boatman should repeat it so that it is communicated all the way back to the sweep boat.

Since specific techniques vary widely with the kind of river craft used, this chapter is divided into two general areas: those for the big boats—rafts, catarafts, and dories—and those for kayaks and canoes.

The Big Boats—Rafts, Catarafts, and Dories

Big-water safety for big boats is based on the principle of staying together in the main current in order to render mutual aid. If a boat goes over in a rapid, it takes a long time to ferry out of a bank eddy and chase it down. Another basic principle of rescue on the run is that it is generally faster and easier to have an accident victim come to you by stalling against the current (i.e., rowing upstream) than to chase a swimmer or upside-down raft downriver. Therefore weaker boats should stay upstream; this also allows them extra time to avoid hazards by observing signals from the lead boat.

In any big-water situation, it is imperative that all boats be properly rigged, that is, rigged for a flip. All loose lines (including throw

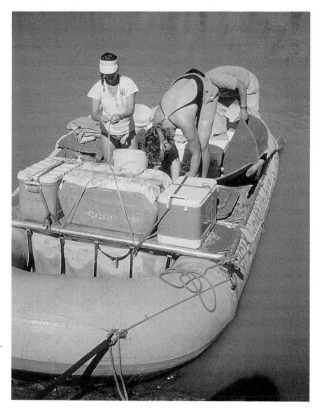

4.2 Always rig for a flip. Pad sharp edges, secure any loose lines, and tie everything in securely.

bags) must be secured and any sharp edges padded. All gear must be thoroughly waterproofed and firmly tied down, since a downriver chase for a flipped raft can be a long one. Loose lines, especially, can be a major hazard.

On the river, boats can run "loose" (far apart), or "tight" (close together). The decision depends both on the situation and the preferences of the boatmen. Tight formations are better for mutual support, but offer less time for reaction to a really big hazard (see the next section for a fuller explanation).

Throwing Zones. Throw bags work equally well when thrown from a raft or from shore. Thus, in a moving, fluid situation, a raft can act as a mobile rescue platform. If a raft is unable to get close enough to a swimmer for a contact rescue, a throw bag is a quick alternative. Throw bags also can be used to rescue swimmers from other rafts. For throw bags to be effective in covering other rafts, however, the boats must run fairly close together.

Barry Miller, who teaches river rescue courses for Canyonlands Field Institute (Moab, Utah), has long been an advocate of rafts running very close together in fast, continuous whitewater. The premise here is that each raft has a "throwing zone" of fifty to seventy feet (15–21 m) in diameter around the raft. As the rafts descend the river the throwing zones should overlap slightly, so that the rafts can offer mutual support without actually touching. All raft passengers are trained in throwing, and throw bags are readily accessible in the bow, center, and stern sections of all rafts (see figure 4.3). Some boatmen favor throw bags worn on the waist, since this allows for a quick toss.

Another advantage of the throw-zone concept is that it allows the option to tow a boat to shore instead of trying to right it in mid-current. Utilizing the zone concept, a throw rope can be attached quickly and the towing process started.

When first trying the zone approach, you may feel that you are running bumper to bumper on some freeway. There are legitimate concerns about mishaps caused by following too closely, like a catastrophic pileup on a riverwide strainer. In reality, as you descend in this fashion, you will find yourself looking past the preceding boat and making your own route determinations as if that boat weren't there. Certainly you don't want to develop tunnel vision while tailgating your way down the river.

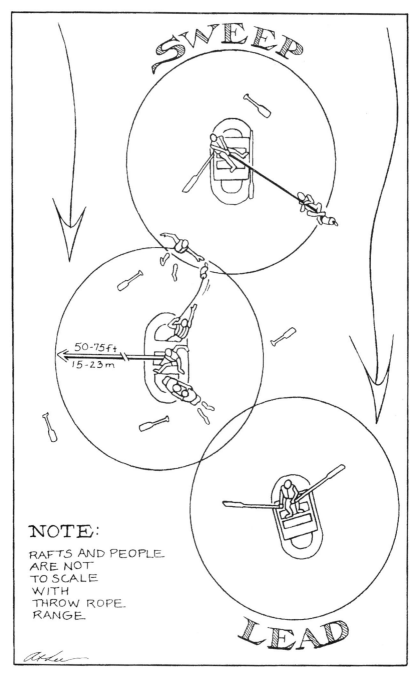

4.3 On big rivers rafts stay close enough together to cover each other with throw bags. The circular "zones" (50-75'[15-25m]) should overlap for best coverage.

Rescuing Swimmers. People fall out of any kind of whitewater craft—it's part of the sport. Sometimes it (oops!) even happens to guides. In most cases, this isn't a serious problem, but passengers can get banged up or, if separated from the boat, go for a long, unplanned swim. It's better to act fast, get them back in the raft, and laugh about it later.

A good start is a thorough pretrip safety briefing: telling everyone exactly what to do if they go into the water. If possible, they should try to grab a hand line, gunnel, or frame on their way overboard. If they have contact with the boat, they can be hauled back in much faster. If they can't hold on to the boat they should try to hang on to their paddle, since it makes a handy extension to reach others still in the raft. If possible, they should try to swim to the raft or at least stay near it. The first few seconds after falling in are the best time for a rescue—before river currents move swimmer and raft away from each other.

Pulling a swimmer back into the raft can be difficult, especially if the swimmer is heavy and has a loose-fitting life jacket. Don't try to pull a swimmer in by his hands or by grabbing an arm—instead, grab the swimmer by the shoulder straps of his life jacket, brace

4.4 *Pull a swimmer into a raft by grabbing the shoulder straps of his life jacket and falling back into the raft, not (as the people on the left are doing) by pulling on his arm.*

your knees against the tubes, then lean backward to pull him in. Keep your back straight and lift with your legs, falling backward on the floor of the raft if need be. Two people can double up if necessary. The swimmer can assist by pulling up on the frame, gunnel, or hand line as he's being pulled in. With practice this is a smooth, fluid motion and works even for big bubbas.

There is some disagreement as to whether the swimmer should face toward the raft or away from it when being pulled in. Proponents of the "toward" school, generally easterners, maintain that this allows the swimmer to see what's happening and assist somewhat. The "away" school (mostly westerners) dismiss this and argue that the buckles of the swimmer's life jacket may catch on the hand line if he faces the raft, so it is better for him to face away from it. In practice, both approaches seem to work equally well.

Boat Righting. Even big boats sometimes flip, and it is often simpler, faster, and safer to right them in midriver than to tow them to shore. This is especially true for dories and lightly loaded catarafts, paddle rafts, and oar rigs in big, fast water. If the boat is well rigged, the crew can right it and continue on their way with little interruption.

If you flip, your first action should be to count noses. Someone might be caught under the boat, either from being snagged or because the buoyancy of their life jacket floats them upward under the raft or the cargo load. Sometimes people will purposely remain

4.5.1 Rerighting after a flip: using the crawl line, the crew gets on top of the raft...

4.5.2 ...helping others up as necessary.

4.5.3 Using the flip lines, they pull the raft back over right side up.

4.5.4 Even heavily loaded rafts and catarafts can be rerighted this way.

under the boat with their head in an air pocket because it seems safe there. Part of the pretrip briefing should be to tell passengers that they must immediately "check in" after a flip, even if this means dragging themselves from underneath the raft by whatever comes to hand. Once accounted for, everyone should move to the upstream end of the flipped boat to avoid getting caught between the boat and a boulder.

To right the raft, one or more people must get up on top of the raft, somehow take hold of the outside tube or outwale of the boat, shift their weight to the other side, and pull it back over (see figures 4.5.1-4). While one or more persons might be able to right an overturned paddle raft or light cataraft, the entire crew may be required for a loaded oar boat, and some rigs will be too heavy to right in midriver. The hard part is getting the people up onto the floor of the inverted boat. With catarafts it is fairly simple to haul yourself onto the inverted frame, but with rafts it can be tough to mount the slippery floor of a boat that is bouncing downriver.

The easiest way to get on top of an overturned raft is to use a "life line" (or crawl line, usually made from 1"[25 mm] tubular webbing) tied across the bottom of the raft from D-ring to D-ring, or from drain hole to drain hole. One crewman can use this to pull himself up on top, then help others up if needed. Since the line can snag or accumulate debris, it is really only practical when the water is high and deep and flipping a possibility. If snagging seems likely, tie the webbing to the raft with fifty-pound test cord so that if you do catch on something, the line will break away.

If no line has been rigged, grab a D-ring or hand line (you might even be able to pull it down far enough to step into it), and pull down with the other hand for balance as you lunge upward. At the same time, swing one leg up onto the raft, as if you were getting out of a swimming pool. Drain holes or the lacing on a self-bailing floor provide convenient "handles" to help. Another method, described in more detail below, is to use the bow line as both crawl line and flip line.

Once on top, you'll have to find a way to grasp one side of the hull while shifting your weight over the other. Again, the easiest way is to have a pre-rigged "flip line." This looks like a tiny throw bag with 6–8'(1.8–2.4 m) of 3/8"(9.5 mm) poly rope pre-tied to the raft's D-rings, normally three to a side. An expedient method is to stuff the line into a short section of bicycle tire tube and clip the end to the

D-rings. If flip lines are in place, the crew merely grasps the lines, extends them, and pulls the raft over.

If no flip lines are available there are other options: you can hook the T-grip of your paddle through a D-ring, drain hole, floor lacing, or hand line on one side of the raft, place your feet on the opposite side, and pull back on the blade, or take your Prusiks and clip them into the floor laces or the hand line, and then pull back. Some waist-mounted throw bags also contain smaller lines that can be used for righting rafts. On catarafts or dories, usually the best place to hook a line is on the oar stands or the oarlocks.

A raft's bow line can be rigged for both a crawl line and flip line, although it requires a good bit of swimming. Free the bow line, then thread it through an amidships D-ring, or oarlock stand, and throw it over the hull. Now swim to the other side where you can grab the rope to haul yourself up and then right the boat. For traditional "bucket" rafts with glued-in floors, this may the only practical method if there are no flip lines rigged.

When righting the raft, instruct your passengers to let go of the boat before you lean back and pull. They have a natural tendency to hang on and can easily keep the boat from righting. However, one or two people may go underneath the raft and bearhug the thwart (see figure 4.7). When the raft flips upright, this crewman is pulled into the raft and can aid everyone else in quickly getting back in. Otherwise, you will have to haul yourself in and then drag everyone else in. The flip is very fast, so the passengers are unlikely to float

4.6 A prepackaged flip line stows neatly out of the way until needed.

4.7 To speed re-entry into the rerighted raft, one or more crew members can either bear hug the thwart or hold the perimeter line, pulling them into the raft as it turns over.

away too far. Like anything else, righting the boat should be practiced in calm water before doing it in whitewater.

Other Options. There will be times when righting just isn't feasible. The boat, especially if it is one of the larger motor rigs, may be just too big. There are circumstances, too, when it is simpler and easier to pull the boat to shore to right it. One method of getting the boat to shore is to have a long bow line or throw bag attached to the boat. If it flips, one of the crew grabs the bag, swims to shore, sets a belay and pendulums the raft in.

Another option is to get on top of the raft and paddle it, still upside down, to shore. This assumes the crew has access to paddles, and this technique usually works better for paddle rafts. There has been at least one instance, however, of a flipped motor rig that was too big to right, even using multiple Z-drags on shore. The boatmen simply inverted the transom and motored it out of the Grand Canyon that way.

The Little Boats—Kayaks, Canoes, and Inflatables

As we saw in the chapter on self-rescue, a reliable roll is critical to a paddler's safety. If a boater can't roll, however, getting the victim out of danger while he is still in his boat makes for a much more controllable situation than if boat, paddle, and paddler must all be rescued separately. As with big boats, rescues of swimmers, equipment, and boats on wide, continuous rivers must be made in the current by other boaters.

Rescuing Boaters. One such method is the Eskimo rescue; it is one of the first techniques a decked-boat paddler learns. When upside down, instead of attempting to roll, or perhaps after several attempts to roll, the boater leans forward and slaps the sides of the boat to signal that he needs help. A fellow boater then moves over and presents the bow of his boat to the submerged boater's waiting hands. It is then a simple matter for the upside-down paddler to roll back upright. A variation of this method is for the rescue paddler to come alongside the upside-down boat, reach across it, grab the cockpit rim, and roll it back up.

4.8 The Eskimo rescue. This is a basic technique of decked boat rescue.

These methods have obvious limitations. The upside-down boater may float into a hazard or into a more dangerous rapid and draw would-be rescuers in after him. A rescue boater may ram his bow into the upside-down boater's hands. Typically, they are used in low-risk places like the deep-water tail waves below a rapid or the eddy just below a hole.

Boats can also be used to rescue other boaters from hydraulics. For small hydraulics the paddler in the rescue boat may stick his bow into the backwash so that the "stuck" paddler can grab it. In larger hydraulics the rescuer may try approaching from upstream with maximum momentum and drop in sideways onto the stuck boat, knocking it clear of the backwash. This technique presupposes a willingness on the part of the rescue boater to enter the hydraulic the stuck boat has just left. Neither of these techniques is for the faint of heart.

Deep-water rescues, similar to those employed by sea kayakers, can also be employed on wide rivers, although they don't work very well in big waves. Two kayakers can run down a swamped boat and empty it over their own boats, then hold it while the swimming paddler climbs back in. This technique works also for open canoes and inflatable kayaks. The rescue boat can come along the capsized

4.9 To rescue another paddler from a small hole, this paddler has given his friend the bow of the boat. By backstroking...

4.10 ...he gets the paddler but not the boat. Results with this method tend to be unpredictable.

canoe, right it, and clasp the gunnels of both boats as the swimmer clambers in from the opposite side. The rescued paddler can then bail his boat while his rescuer holds both boats steady.

Rescuing Swimmers. The most common method of rescuing swimmers with small boats is to have them grab the bow or stern grab loop of the boat, or a painter, and then tow them to safety with an upstream ferry. Approach swimmers with caution: people who think their lives are in danger often act irrationally. If the swimmer suddenly grabs the rescuer's paddle or climbs unexpectedly on his boat, he may turn the rescuer into another victim. If time permits, it is best to approach the victim so that you are just out of his reach and try to get his attention. This way you will be able to make some assessment of his mental and physical condition and give him some instructions. Appear calm and in control, but be on guard for the unexpected. Offer the swimmer the bow or stern grab loop of your boat. If you're going to tow him any distance, a stern hold makes this easier (see figure 4.11.1). Tell the swimmer not to climb up on the boat (there are exceptions to this rule, which we will discuss later) and to help by kicking with his feet.

4.11.1 The basic method of rescuing a swimmer with a kayak is to have the swimmer hang on to the grab loop and kick vigorously with his feet.

Rescue in big waves calls for some extra precautions. The violent up-and-down movement of the boat can easily smash a swimmer's face, even if he is hanging on to the grab loop. In some cases it may be better to follow the swimmer and offer assistance in a calmer section. Having someone nearby in the rapid can be very heartening, but in big, continuous water this is more difficult. A swimmer can climb onto the rear deck of a kayak in big water, holding the cockpit rim. This avoids the problem of the stern hitting the victim's face, makes it easier for the victim to breathe in big waves, and reduces somewhat his exposure to cold water. Having an extra person on the back deck makes a boat heavy and unstable, but the victim can assist by kicking with his legs. Before starting, tell the victim to let go of the boat if it tips over, so you can roll. This is also the most efficient method for kayakers to transport a swimmer from one side of the river to the other.

Another swimmer rescue is the "figurehead." Here the swimmer grabs the bow of the rescue boat, pressing his belly to it with his legs straddling the deck. The swimmer creates a lot of drag this way and cannot assist by swimming, so it should only be done when close to shore with the rescue boat coming to him from downstream.

4.11.2 Towing a swimmer with a decked boat can be difficult. In bigger water the swimmer can crawl up on the rear deck.

Unlike "hard" kayaks, canoes or inflatable kayaks can sometimes shoehorn a swimmer into their boat for rescue or transport. Canoeists may deflate an air bag to make more room (although this is hard to do on the run) and it may be possible to let the victim help by paddling. As with a kayak, the weight of an extra person will make the boat tippier and more sluggish.

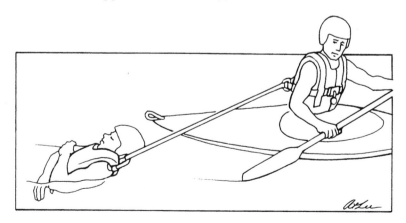

4.12 Towing an unconscious victim.

Unconscious or semiconscious victims present a major problem for little boats, since the victim can neither assist nor hang on, and will quickly drown if left in the water. Canoeists and inflatable kayakers *might* be able to pull an unconscious swimmer into their boat using the deep-water rescue techniques described earlier, but it is very difficult. Tow systems, such as the ones mounted on the decks of some kayaks, can drag an unconscious or very weak victim to shore (see figure 4.12) but it is difficult to ensure that their face stays out of the water. A rescuer may have to exit his craft, contact the victim, and be towed in by other boats or perform a swimming rescue as described in chapter 6. Both these options greatly increase the danger to the rescuer, however.

Retrieving Equipment and Boats. Retrieving equipment is an important task on the river. In an emergency, though, people must come before equipment, so you should decide in advance who is to go after what. If numbers permit, some boaters can go after equipment while others rescue people. Don't risk people, including yourself, for equipment: if you pick up something, be sure you can unload it quickly if need be. Remember to apply the rules of self-preservation: don't run blindly downriver after something without thinking about what lies below.

The same rules of preparation apply for little boats as for big ones: tie or clip all gear in securely, especially things like throw bags that might trail out in the current and snag something or someone. Paddlers should keep hold of their boat and paddle when swimming, unless this puts them in danger.

Finding lost paddles is easier than carrying them once they're found. Paddlers in rafts and open canoes have few problems, but those in decked boats will find paddles a real nuisance. They can be laid on the cockpit rim of a decked boat, but this only works in easy water. A C-1 paddler who carries a spare paddle on the back deck can put a retrieved paddle underneath the spare. One very simple method of retrieval is to grab the paddle and throw it toward the shore, repeating the process as many times as necessary (see figure 4.13). Kayak paddles are even more of a problem, since they're twice as long. One method is to grasp *both* shafts (that is, yours and the retrieved one) and paddle as if they were one. Sometimes it helps to slide the blades out, so that you are only paddling with the blade of one paddle on each side. People with small hands will find this difficult. If your boat has a tow system, you can slide the retrieved pad-

4.13 A simple way to recover paddles on narrow rivers is simply to throw them toward the shore.

dle under the line on the rear deck and keep one blade "chicken-winged" under an armpit (see figure 4.14).

Boat recovery (assuming the paddler can't reenter it) presents another problem. The "bulldozer" technique is the most common method and works well whenever the capsized boat is near shore. The paddler in the recovery boat places his bow on the downstream side of the abandoned boat, sets up as if for a ferry, and then pushes the boat into the nearest eddy (see figure 4.15). Paddlers recovering decked boats should try to put their bow inside the cockpit of the swamped boat, making sure they will be able to withdraw it if the need arises. Open canoes and rafts sometimes have a problem running over the top of the swamped boat.

A decked boat often can be flipped back upright before it fills completely with water, which makes it much easier to handle: if there is not much water in it a good shove often can send it into a nearby eddy. A swamped boat also bulldozes or tows more easily right side up, since the cockpit of a kayak or the open side of an overturned canoe creates more resistance than does the hull.

Towing a swamped boat is more efficient than bulldozing one, especially on a wide river, because the capsized boat tracks directly behind the rescue boat. This presents less drag and allows the tow

4.14 *Paddlers can use the boat's tow system to recover a paddle. One way is as shown: to "chicken-wing" the paddle with the tow line. Another is to clip on a carabiner with a gate large enough to fit over the paddle shaft and tow it with either the boat's tow system or a cow's tail on a rescue life jacket.*

4.15 *Most paddlers use the "bulldozer" method to recover boats. It's convenient but has its limitations. A half-submerged boat, like this one, can be difficult to push. Tow systems work better.*

boat to maintain a ferry angle. Canoeists, when recovering another canoe, can pick up the painter of the swamped craft and tie a slipknot around a thwart. Even under pressure, the slipknot will release when the loose end is pulled. Other boats, as well as many canoeists, may want to consider some other means of towing boats:

Chest Harness. Many life jackets are now available with a built-in, releasable chest harness (see chapter 2 for a description). Many also

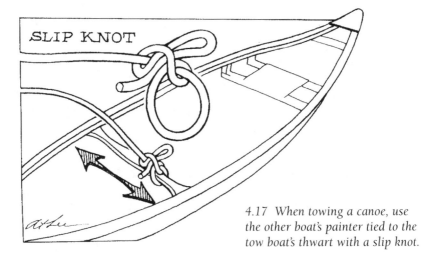

4.16 A tow system can be boat mounted.

SLIP KNOT

4.17 When towing a canoe, use the other boat's painter tied to the tow boat's thwart with a slip knot.

have an attached "cow's tail" tow line, or this can be purchased separately. To employ it, one simply clips the cow's tail to the grab loop of the boat to be towed and paddles with an appropriate ferry angle to shore (see figures below). The better cow's tail designs fit tightly against the body when stowed, but extend far enough under load to let the towed boat clear the stern of the towing boat. This method is quick, simple, and always available, but it does make for a higher center of gravity, and the cow's tail must be restuffed after each use.

4.18.1 and 4.18.2 Another towing option is to use a cow's tail attached to a life jacket. (ExtraSport)

The cow's tail (as well as the harness) must have a quick release for both ends in case of snagging.

Tow Belt. The tow belt resembles a small throw bag worn around the waist, and some models can be used as a throw bag in addition to having tow lines. Most have a small-diameter line 6–8'(1.8–2.4 m) long stuffed into a pouch. It is used in much the same manner as the built-in harness and cow's tail.

Deck-Mounted Tow System. Figure 2.21 shows two types of deck-mounted tow systems; figure 4.16 shows it in actual use. Mounting the tow system close to the cockpit (and therefore close to boat's center of pressure) allows the system to pivot easily to maintain the ferry angle. Tow systems have many applications other than boat rescue; they are easier to hang onto than grab loops if you are swimming; they can be used to haul a boat up an embankment or tie it off in the water; and they can be used to ferry a line across the river for many of the rescue methods described in this book. Canoeists can adapt a similar system by running their stern painter through a cleat mounted on a thwart or gunnel.

Expanding his own river sense, Les describes a "rescue on the run" that occurred in 1986 on the Main Salmon River in Idaho:

"It was my second time down the Main, and the river was pumping a roaring 70,000 cubic feet of very cold water per second. This astonished easterner was amazed at the speed of the water and the lack of eddies. We were scouting a very long rapid called Elkhorn and could see a huge pulsing hole in midriver.

"The river was too wide to set safety ropes, so our group of three oar rigs decided to run it on the right and stay close together. What we hadn't anticipated were the steep diagonal waves coming off the shore and feeding directly into that nasty hole. Two of our boats were able to punch through the diagonals, but the third got funneled directly into it.

"The hole spit the little oar rig skyward—it totally cleared the water and landed upside down. We were within rope-throwing distance, but it still took us about half a mile to gather in the numb swimmers and another mile to tow the raft in. I shudder to think how quickly we could have lost someone, or how far the raft could have gone if we hadn't have been running close together."

*Never travel far without a rope! And one that is long and
strong and light...[it] may be a help in many needs.*
J. R. R. Tolkien, *The Lord of the Rings*

5

Basic Rope Rescue

The most useful single tool in any rescue, from the simple capsize
to the most complicated technical rescue, is the safety rope.
Other ropes may have use in camp or for tying up your raft, but a
safety rope should be used solely for rescue purposes. In chapter 2
we examined the types of ropes available. The choice is up to the
user, but every whitewater paddler should routinely carry a safety
rope and know how to use it. In this chapter we will cover the basic
and most common types of rope rescue and will use the term "rope"
generically.

The Throwing Rescue

Most rope rescues are made with a rescuer standing on the shore,
throwing a rope (usually contained in a throw bag) to a swimmer,
and hauling him in. It sounds simple, but few people can accurately throw a rope—rope throwing requires practice. The goal of a good
throw is pinpoint accuracy at the rope's full extension. The position
of the safety rope is the first consideration. A common mistake is to
stand directly opposite the most likely point of capsize. The best
place is usually farther downstream, because it takes time for the
swimmer to surface, orient himself, and to look at the rope thrower

5.1 A throw bag can also be an effective option when thrown from a raft.

before the rope is thrown (see figure 5.2). How far downstream you position yourself will depend on such factors as the speed of the water, the distance to the next rapid, how many roll attempts may be tried, and the presence or absence of eddies to swing the swimmer into. Remember, if you are too far upstream and miss, you may have a hard time getting back down along the riverbank. It's often better to be a bit too far downstream.

In long or hazardous sections of whitewater, you may need several rope throwers. If possible, they should be positioned above or opposite hazards like large keeper hydraulics and undercut rocks. Consider placing rope throwers on the opposite shore, which means they will have to ferry over to the other side either above or below the drop in question. In sections of continuous whitewater, finding a pool or eddy for rescue may be a problem.

The thrower also must consider what to do once the victim has got hold of the rope. When the rope goes taut with the full force of

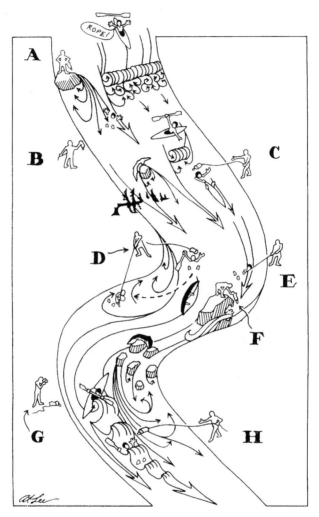

5.2 Setting rope: Position A gives good visibility and has an eddy behind, but is of little use to a swimmer or an upside-down boat in the fast water of the chute; B is a better place to pick up swimmers coming out of the chute or hydraulic, but the rope thrower must get them in before the strainer downstream; C is set close enough to a hole to rescue a swimmer either in or below it. Both C and D are set to swing a swimmer into a convenient eddy; E is set to catch a swimmer who might go into an undercut; F is too close to the undercut for a rope throw, but this would be an effective rescue position if a paddler were trapped there; at G, would-be rescuers must be ready to throw. This rescuer is too close to the hazard and would not be able to hit a swimmer washing out of the hole or a decked boat after several role attempts; H is a better position: below the hazard with an eddy nearby.

the current against the swimmer, the thrower must brace himself to hold the load (belaying techniques are described below). The current will usually swing the swimmer to the near shore like a pendulum. Position yourself so that the swimmer doesn't swing into a greater hazard or get caught out in the full current. Look for an eddy to land your catch in. This may require you to move after the throw has been made, so check your route before you throw. Many rope rescues have failed because the rescuer had lead feet.

Before throwing, always try to get the attention of the swimmer. Yelling ("ROOOOOPE!!!") or whistling will usually get him facing the right way, and establishing eye contact is even better. Once the rope is in the water it may be hard for the swimmer to see. Even though the rope floats, currents will often suck it beneath the surface. Some people, especially those new to the river, will become very disoriented while swimming a rapid and will not respond to you. If you can't communicate before throwing, you must try to throw the rope so that it physically touches the swimmer to get his attention. In case the bag should hit him, never leave a hard object such as a carabiner on your throw bag.

In the excitement of a rescue the throw often is made too soon—while the swimmer is still too far upstream of the rope thrower's position. This increases the distance the rope must be thrown and usually decreases the accuracy of the throw. The throw should be timed so that the swimmer is slightly upstream of your position onshore. This makes the throw shorter while leaving time for a second throw.

Like duck hunting, leading a moving swimmer requires practice. There is some debate about exactly where to throw in relation to the swimmer. If you err slightly to the *upstream* side of the swimmer, as some recommend, the rope will float faster on the surface of the water than will a swimmer who is backstroking against the current. On the other hand, it will land behind him and he may not see it. If the rope lands downstream of the swimmer, he can see it, but may have to swim headfirst to retrieve it and thus compromise his feet-first defensive swimming posture. We recommend that you aim the rope to have it go *over* rather than *to* a swimmer, coming as close to him as possible; a rope thrown directly to a swimmer often lands short.

Ideally, the rope thrower should stand somewhat above the level of the river. Standing on a boulder or up on the bank a bit gives better visibility and allows more time for the rope to pay out while in the air, but too much height will reduce the working length of the rope and increase the time you must allow for it to reach a swimmer who may be moving downstream very quickly.

Never tie off the rope to shore or to yourself when throwing to a swimmer: the rope may become entangled around a part of his body, even his neck, and you may need to let go of your end of the rope quickly to release the tension. You may also need to release the load if it becomes too great for you to hold or for the swimmer to endure.

Swimmers should go for the rope aggressively. (Remember self-rescue? Help yourself!) When you get to it, hold the rope to your chest with your feet downstream. Face upward and do not look at the rescuer: turning over and facing toward the rope may cause you to dive (figure 5.3). Never tie or wrap the rope around any part of your body (except in cold water when the hands may not be functioning well; the rope may be clamped under one armpit and then held against the chest). In the proper position, the victim will plane on the water, and a breathing pocket will form in front of his face, although in extremely fast water the air pocket may be lost. If the swimmer holds the rope with one hand over his head and the other on his chest, his body tends to plane better, and he will be able to breathe more easily. It is harder to hold the rope this way, however, than with two hands across the chest.   A rescuer is sometimes faced with a situation involving multiple swimmers—when a raft overturns, for example. If the swimmers are bunched closely together, throw the rope to the middle of the group. If they are separated, throw to the one farthest away but still within reach of the rope. With luck, some of the others can grab the rope, too. Multiple swimmers should hold on to the rope rather than each other. With more than one on the rope the rescuer will need to create a dynamic belay to bring them in (see below).

Throwing Techniques

There are three primary methods of throwing a rope or bag: underhand, sidearm, and overhand. Each can be effective, but no matter which style you use it is important to throw with your whole body and not just with your arm to get the full extension of the rope. Watch a baseball outfielder or a discus thrower: he uses his whole body, hurling from the legs through the upper torso and following through with the arm. To get the full extension of the rope you must do the same. To make use of your full power potential, you should

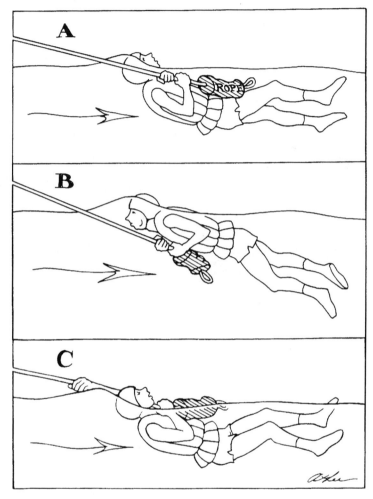

5.3 *Holding a rope in whitewater. (A) The right way is for the swimmer to put the rope over his shoulder, hold it close to this chest, and face away from the rope thrower. This causes him to plane near the surface. The water forms an air pocket around his face. (B) The wrong way is to grab the rope and face toward the thrower. The swimmer gets a faceful of water, which may cause him to let go of the rope. (C) In very swift water the swimmer may want to hold his arm above his head, which causes his body to plane better.*

stand sideways, with your throwing arm on the side away from the river. If you are right-handed and are standing on river right (that is, on the right bank as you face downstream), this means your body will be facing downstream and you will be looking upstream over your left shoulder.

5.4 The correct throwing position for a right-handed thrower—facing slightly downstream, looking over the shoulder.

Before throwing, look for obstacles: slalom-gate wires, bystanders, tree branches, etc. Try to choose a solid spot away from slippery or unstable rocks. With most throw bags, loosen the cord lock closure about halfway, but do not open it to the widest position. Opening it all the way can cause a "bucketing" effect as water flows into the mouth of the bag. Failure to partially open the mouth of the bag prevents the rope from paying out freely when the bag is airborne. If possible, take one or two practice throws to judge your range and the speed of the current. Practice throws also help to work the kinks out of the rope and your throwing arm.

It may seem unnecessary to add that the thrower should hang onto the rope, but many times we have seen even veteran river guides throw the whole rope away. Be sure you have a good grip on the end before you let fly. Hold the loop with your nonthrowing hand, but *do not* put your hand in the loop—if your wrist is in the loop, you may go for a swim yourself. Many boaters retie the manufacturer's loop to be just big enough for a carabiner.

Underhand. This is the most popular and perhaps the most natural-feeling type of throw. The thrower swings the rope back and forth a few times to develop a rhythm, and then releases it (see figures 5.5 and 5.6). The release should be at about a 45° angle to the surface of

5.5　Position for the underhand throw.

5.6　The underhand throw.

the water. A premature release will make the rope hit the water only a few feet in front of the thrower; a late release will make the rope go straight up and then down on the head of the would-be rescuer (much to the amusement of everyone but the swimmer). The underhand is best used for close throws.

Sidearm. Many people, especially smaller ones, find they can improve their distance with the sidearm throw, but this gain often comes at the expense of accuracy. It also requires a fair amount of clear space in which to throw. The sidearm motion, similar to that used by the discus thrower, makes it easier to use your whole body. Wind up by twisting your trunk and bringing your throwing arm behind you, then unwind by throwing your arm laterally. Like the underhand throw, the release should be at about a 45° angle to the surface of the water. In situations where you don't have time to restuff your throw bag, a coiled rope can be thrown sidearm.

Overhand. The overhand throw is superior to the other techniques in that it can be used on brushy banks, over the heads of a raft crew, or in waist-deep water. Both the underhand and sidearm techniques require a relatively obstruction-free throwing zone. The rope can also be thrown with greater velocity over longer distances (see figures 5.7 and 5.8). Like a baseball outfielder, the rescuer rocks backward with the throwing arm behind and then rocks forward hurling the arm overhead. The rescuer throws with the entire upper body as well as with the arm. A variation of the overhand throw is the "quarterback" toss: "pass" the throw bag like a football.

Second Throws. So what do you do if you make a throw and miss? What happens if another swimmer floats by and you haven't restuffed your bag? Second throws without restuffing the bag are notoriously inaccurate. Some throw bag manufacturers suggest heaving a throw bag half filled with water. Our experience suggests it is hard to get the right amount of water in the bag and equally hard to throw it accurately. Not only that, if you hit the swimmer in the head you'll ring his chimes! A better way is to recoil the rope. Starting with the bag end of the rope, make full arm-length coils, laying the coils into your nonthrowing hand, which also holds the bag. Once the rope is coiled, split the coils, and with your throwing hand make a sidearm throw. As the rope sails out, open your nonthrowing hand so that the remainder of the coils pay out, but hold

5.7 *Position for the overhand throw.*   5.8 *The overhand throw.*

5.9 *If time does not permit the thrower to restuff the throw bag, he can coil the rope and throw it. This is slightly faster but less effective than stuffing the rope back in the sack.*

firmly to the bag. A variation of this method for the less adroit is to first step on the bag and then coil the rope for the throw. The best plan, however, is to restuff the throw bag before any other swimmers appear.

Restuffing the Throw Bag. Rescuers can be surprisingly lazy. Quite often you see them make one throw, then coil up the throw rope instead of restuffing it—and wait. Throw bag ropes work best when stuffed in a bag. Stuffing them quickly and efficiently, however, is one of those skills that no one ever seems to teach. Some baggers prefer to grab a handful and stuff it by the fistful into the open mouth of the bag, while others feed the rope into the bag an inch at a time. After many years of practice, we have concluded that the best way is shown below.

This works great with full-size bags but it is a struggle with smaller bags.

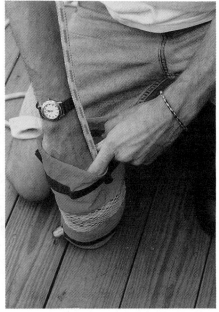

5.10.1 Stuffing a throw bag: hold the bag at the opening and enclose the rope with your thumb and index finger to act as a feeding guide for the rope...

5.10.2 ...then stuff the rope inside the bag a handful at a time.

Belaying. A single rescuer is going to have a hard time holding a swimmer in fast current with only his hands, especially if there is more than one swimmer on the rope. However, he can use friction to assist. Belaying is a technique developed by climbers that enables a rescuer to increase the friction, and therefore the holding power, of the rope to hold much greater loads than can his hands alone. One method is to wrap the rope around his own body or about a convenient object such as a tree to increase the friction. For river use, a belay should have the capacity for variable friction and must be capable of being released, even under load, if swimmer becomes entangled or if the belayer is in danger of being pulled into the water.

There are two types of river belays: static and dynamic.

Static Belay. The static belay is like slamming the brakes on all at once. The rescuer belays the throw rope and holds it. When the rope suddenly comes taut in the current, it puts a considerable load on the rope, the belayer, and the swimmer. Using stretchy poly rope will

5.11 The basic body belay: the rescuer uses the friction of the rope wrapped around her body. The rope should not wrap around the belayer as the victim moves downstream.

5.12 The friction belay uses a quick wrap around a tree or other object to increase the belayer's holding power. The rope can quickly be released if need be.

reduce this load somewhat, but there is still the danger that the swimmer will let go or that the rescuer will be pulled into the water.

The most common belay for throw bags is the body belay, that is, the rescuer uses his body as a friction device. Immediately after making his throw, the rescuer puts the rope around his back and holds it close to his body (see figure 5.11). The more tightly he holds it, and the tighter it wraps around his body, the greater the load he can hold. He should take care, however, that the rope does not wrap completely around any part of his body. The belay should open as the swimmer passes him; that is, the belayer should have the working part of the rope in his downstream hand, and the bitter end in his upstream hand. Sitting increases the security of a belay, especially if the belayer can brace his feet against rocks. If necessary, another person can stand behind the belayer to help hold him. If a tree or boulder is handy, the rescuer can wrap the rope around it, using a simple friction wrap.

5.13 A rescue life jacket can be used as an effective tether to keep a belayer from being pulled into the water.

A second person can assist by grabbing the rope between the swimmer and the belayer and pulling. This creates a vector pull and hauls the victim to shore faster.

Dynamic Belay. The dynamic belay (see figure 5.14) is a more gradual braking process, and so is easier on both swimmer and belayer than the static belay. There are two basic methods of making a belay dynamic. If the belayer has a clear, smooth path, he can move downstream and away from the river after making his throw. This reduces the loading shock on the swimmer and starts him moving toward shore.

The second method is to assume a sitting belay with some excess rope on the upstream side. As the rope comes under load, gradually tighten the rope as it passes around your body to slow down the swimmer. While your life jacket provides a certain amount of protection, you must carefully monitor the speed of the rope to avoid rope burns.

5.14 The dynamic belay. The rope thrower runs down along the bank to decrease the loading shock on the swimmer. The banks must be fairly open for this technique to be used.

Tag Line Rescues

Unlike throwing rescues, which are intended for moving swimmers, tag line rescues normally are used to aid victims who are involuntarily trapped in one place. A tag line is simply a line stretched across the river. It may or may not have a flotation device attached to it. Tag line rescues do require planning and team effort, but they are relatively uncomplicated and much safer for rescuers than in-water rescues. They can be set up quickly, and untrained bystanders often can be used to help manage the ropes from shore.

There are three major types of tag lines:

The **floating tag line**, discussed below, has some type of float attached to keep it on the surface of the water. It is used most often to rescue a conscious swimmer who is being recirculated in a hole or hydraulic.

The **stabilization tag line** is a line across the river that can help an entrapment victim to keep his head out of the water. This method is used primarily to stabilize a victim while extrication efforts are being made. It can be either a bare or floating line. This technique is discussed in more detail in chapter 8, "Entrapments."

The **snag tag** is a bare or weighted tag line meant to be pulled under the surface, normally as part of an attempt to free the leg of a foot-entrapment victim. This technique also is discussed in more detail in chapter 8.

Floating Tag Line. A floating tag line is a very useful technique to rescue a swimmer caught in a keeper hydraulic like a low-head dam. In a hydraulic like this a person can survive for a surprisingly long time if the water is not too cold and if he does not panic. By timing his breathing and clinging to floating debris, the swimmer may gain enough time to be rescued with a tag line.

The first step is to ferry a rope across the river (see next section). Before beginning the ferry, tie a buoyant object like a spare life jacket or inner tube to the middle of the rope for the victim to grasp. Upon reaching the other side of the river, the ferry team gets on shore and manages the far end of the tag line. Both teams then walk upstream or downstream as required and hold the tag line on the surface of the water so it is visible to the victim. The efforts of both rope teams should be coordinated by a rescue leader standing in a position visible to all and directing the action with prearranged hand signals.

Once the swimmer has hold of the rope or the buoyant object, he is either pulled sideways along the hydraulic until he is close

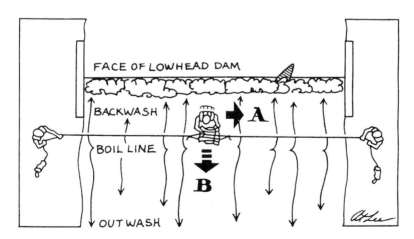

5.15 *The floating tag line rescue.*

enough to the bank to be rescued, or pulled downstream out of the hydraulic by both rope teams. Once clear of the boil line, one rope team can let go and the victim will pendulum to the other shore.

The tag line rescue is premised on the victim's being conscious and capable of clinging to a floating object. What do you do when the victim is unconscious? The Ohio Department of Natural Resources' Division of Watercraft developed a flotation ring with unbarbed treble hooks on it to snag an unconscious victim's clothing. The recreational paddler will have to improvise. A method of last resort might be to use a tethered rescuer wearing several life jackets as the buoyant object. This is a desperate measure, posing great danger to the rescuer, and a rescue team should consider it only if they know the victim is alive and no other method will work (see also the "Tethered Boat Rescue" section in chapter 5).

Rope Ferries. The first step in many rescues is to get a rope across the river. While this may sound simple, it is often the most difficult part of the operation. Next to rope throwing this is probably the most important skill a river runner can master.

The quickest way to get a rope across a narrow river or stream is simply to throw it. Make your throw at the narrowest part, and then move the rope upstream or downstream to the accident site. Rescuers on both sides can wade out as far as possible to reduce the throwing distance, and use a paddle or stick to snare a rope that might be just beyond arm's reach. Another trick is to tie lightweight cord (parachute cord works very well) to a baseball-size rock and throw it across, using the cord as a "messenger line" with which to pull the larger rescue line across. Sometimes the line can be walked across, either by wading across a shallow section or over a bridge near the accident site.

Ferrying the rope with a boat is the most common way of getting a rope across wide rivers or to a midriver accident location. It is also one of the most difficult. The wider and swifter the river, and the larger the diameter of the rope, the more drag there will be when the current catches the rope. The maximum amount of rope drag will occur right about when the ferry craft reaches the opposite bank. Therefore the rope must be ferried across as quickly as possible, secured, and lifted out of the water as soon as it is across. The ferrying craft carries only the end of the rope; the paying out process is managed from shore.

Some tips for better rope ferries are:

- Before beginning the ferry, make sure the rope will feed smoothly. One way is to stack or "flake" it into a pile on a smooth surface it so that it will feed off the top.

- Make sure you have enough rope. A rule of thumb is that you will need about twice as long a rope as the distance to be crossed. If you think two throw bags clipped together will make it across the span, then use three for insurance.

- Position the rope as high above the water you can, and keep it out of the water as long as possible. Hold it high and have the rope handler stand in the ferry boat if possible.

- Use a smaller-diameter messenger line (e.g., parachute cord) to reduce drag, then use it to pull over the main line.

- Make sure you can release the rope if necessary.

The ferry craft must drive into the opposite shore as fast as possible. Time is critical, and the team should attempt to get the rope lifted clear of the water and secured as soon as possible. Otherwise, the ferry craft will be rudely yanked back into the current. If possible, station people on the far bank, ready to hold the ferry craft and grab the rope when it comes over. One trick is to have a throw bag attached to the ferry line. If you cannot make the shore because of the current's drag on the line, you can throw the bag to someone onshore.

An option on wide rivers is the "reverse ferry": start the ferrying process upstream of the rope team (see figure 5.16). That way there will be little drag on the rope until it is directly across the current. Of course, this only works if there are no rocks or other obstructions in the path of the ferrying craft or the rope.

Paddle rafts often are the best craft for rope ferries: they have good crosscurrent power and one person can stand and elevate his end of the rope. The rope handler should stand at the end of the downstream corner of the raft nearest the onshore rope-management team. This produces less drag and thus has less effect on the raft's ferry angle. Keep the upstream end of the raft light, and put a few good paddlers in the raft rather than filling it to capacity. If the ferry fails, pendulum the raft back to near shore and attempt the ferry again.

Canoes, too, can elevate the rope. Tandem canoes have more power, and in larger canoes a rope handler can ride amidships. Solo canoes present more of a problem. Canoeists should paddle on the

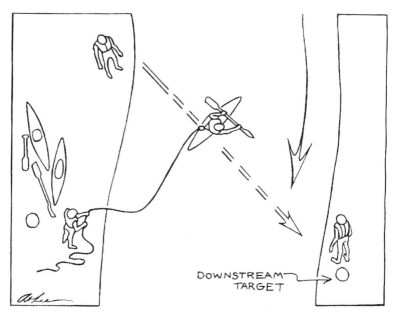

5.16 The reverse ferry starts upstream of the belayer and uses the flow of the water to move the boat downstream across the river.

5.17 Getting a line across the river isn't easy. One method is to attach a line to a rescue life jacket. This keeps the paddler's hands free and allows a quick release in case of snagging. Keep the line out of the water as long as possible. (ExtraSport)

5.18 This kayaker uses a quick and dirty method of ferrying a rope. He wraps the rope once loosely around his body and holds the end in his teeth. This method is not without risk, nor is it recommended for denture wearers.

downstream side while ferrying, and the rope can be attached to the upstream side with a slipknot on a thwart. Attaching the line to a rescue life jacket with a tow system works better and is safer (see figure 5.17).

Kayaks sit low in the water, which makes it difficult to keep the rope out of the water. Here, too, a chest harness or rescue PFD makes the best attachment and does give the rope some elevation. Deck-mounted tow systems work well, too, and can be quickly released. A ferry line also can be tied to a kayak's broach loop with a slipknot. Whatever connection is used, the kayaker must be able to release the rope quickly in case of a capsize or missed ferry.

You do not know how long you are in a river
when the current moves swiftly. It seems a
long time and it may be very short.
Ernest Hemingway, *A Farewell to Arms*

6

Wading, Swimming, and Contact Rescues

Swimming Rescues

A swimming rescue puts a rescuer in the water to make a hands-on rescue of someone in trouble. These rescues are quick to set up and require little special equipment. But by committing himself to the water, the rescuer greatly increases his chances of injury or drowning. A distraught victim in the water may make a desperate lunge for the rescuer or try to climb on top of him. A victim stranded on boulders in midstream, pinned in a boat, or with his foot entrapped may have been in that position for some time—his actions may be difficult to anticipate. If no one's life is in danger, other, and usually slower, shore- or boat-based rescues should be considered first. But sometimes there is no alternative: a life-threatening situation, like that of a paddler entrapped in his boat, demands immediate action, and speed is the major advantage of this method of rescue. Rescuers using this method must sometimes balance the urgent need to rescue a victim against the potential danger to themselves.

6.1 In-water contact rescues are quick to execute, but expose the rescuer to greater danger than other methods of rescue. Here Gordon Grant, secured by a shore tether, wades in to rescue a pinned paddler at Nantahala Falls. (Tony Wilson/ NOC Photo)

To effect an in-water contact rescue, a rescuer must approach the victim, make physical contact with him, and get him to safety. The most common ways of approaching the victim are by wading, swimming, in a boat, or by diving or jumping into the water. In general, jumping into the water feet first is much safer than diving, particularly if the water isn't crystal clear. River depths are often uncertain, and a deep dive is an invitation to a serious cervical spine injury. However, a *surface* dive on the chest with the head held high, in water known to be safe, will get a rescue swimmer out in the current much faster than swimming.

Once in contact with the victim, the rescuer must either swim him to shore or to a boat, or be pulled in by means of a tethering line. Thus the two main variations of this technique are the rescuer as a free swimmer or as a tethered swimmer. A free swimmer has more flexibility to choose the time and place of contact, but it is considerably easier to get a tethered swimmer and victim back to shore.

To intercept the victim, the best position for the rescuer is downstream. Chasing a swimmer downstream can be a lengthy and difficult process. If the rescuer is downstream, however, he can "stall" against the current by swimming upstream. While this will quickly bring the victim to him, it also means that the victim generally will be facing the rescuer, making it difficult to get behind him.

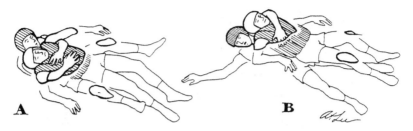

6.2 *For contact rescues in heavy water, use the bear hug (A) to add buoyancy and keep contact with the victim, then use the cross-chest carry (B) in calmer water to swim the victim to shore.*

If the victim is conscious you can ask about his injuries; if the victim is unconscious and breathing, stay on the upstream side of him and keep his head above water. In heavy water, position yourself under the patient with his and your feet downstream (see figure 6.2). Hold him in a bearhug while keeping his face close to yours, in order to provide a little extra buoyancy. Once you reach calmer water you can swim the patient to shore by using a cross-chest carry or by grasping his hair or helmet. Encourage the victim to assist in swimming—hauling someone to shore is a slow and laborious process.

Although these methods have been presented so far in the context of a free swimmer, they are equally applicable in any rescuer-victim scenario, such as with a tethered swimmer (discussed later in this chapter), and when approaching a victim pinned in a boat as discussed in chapter 8.

The Initial Contact—Victim Psychology

At some point in a rescue you must make hands-on contact with the victim. This is the only way to rescue an unconscious person. When approaching a victim in the water it is a good idea to have a rescue plan in mind and to communicate it to him. While a contact rescue in the water does not offer much time for casual conversation or a detailed survey of a patient's condition, lifeguards have found that even a few words of comfort and explanation can work wonders in the subsequent rescuer-victim relationship. Since panic is most often caused by the perception that death is imminent and escape or rescue impossible, it is important to tell the victim exactly what you are doing and planning to do, and what you want him to do.

If the situation permits, approach to just outside the victim's grasp and establish verbal contact. The best position for the rescuer is behind the victim (where he can't grab you), but this isn't always possible. If you are in front, establish eye contact as well. If the victim responds, fine. If not, you will have to make a quick decision: either remain out of reach and continue attempts to establish contact, or move in and make contact, even if it requires grappling with the victim.

Outright panic is relatively rare among paddlers, but not unheard of with rafting customers. Swimming or entrapment victims are usually in one of three states:

- **Survival behavior.** The swimmer is trying to survive. He may not be doing the right thing, but he is capable of following simple instructions. This is the easiest rescue, since he will usually cooperate.

- **Panic.** Random, nonpurposeful movement. A panicked victim cannot be counted on to cooperate, but can sometimes be brought back to survival behavior by the presence of a rescuer. However, *panicked victims can be extremely dangerous* and must be approached with caution.

- **Counterpanic.** The swimmer appears totally unresponsive, and may literally ignore a throw rope dropped into his hands. These victims generally present no direct threat to the rescuer but cannot be counted on to assist, either.

If you are forced to approach a panicked victim, first try to calm him while out of reach. Then move in quickly, grabbing one side of his life jacket to spin him around. If he attempts to grab you, take his arm and use it to turn him around. If a victim lunges for you and attempts to crawl on top of you, roll on your back, plant your feet on his chest and push him away from you. Then try again.

If a victim grabs you and refuses to let go, break his grip by putting your hands under his elbows, digging in your thumbs and pushing up, moving yourself down and back in the process. A stubborn grip can also be loosened by grabbing the subject's thumb and rolling it backwards. Do what you have to do, but get the victim turned around, facing away from you and downstream.

Wading Rescues

Another method of reaching a victim or an accident site, or of crossing the river, is by wading. Although this method has definite limitations, it can be a very effective rescue technique, particularly in areas characterized by shallow, rocky rivers. Generally speaking, groups wade better than individuals, since they are able to stabilize one another. Most rivers have shallow sections suitable for wading, and often accident sites are near enough to shore for this technique to be quite useful. A group of people wading in upstream of an accident site such as a foot entrapment can create an eddy in which rescuers can work.

Wading in swift water is not without its dangers, however. Rescuers must be alert to the danger of foot entrapment and be prepared to swim if they lose their footing in the current.

Single Person. One person can wade in swift water, although this is less stable than a group. It helps to use some sort of staff, such as a paddle, to form a tripod. The wader faces upstream, pushing his weight against the current, and moves sideways across the current. He jams the paddle firmly down into the riverbed, then moves one foot over at a time. Some people prefer to put the paddle blade down on the riverbed, letting the water push it down. Others prefer to use the T-grip end, which has less resistance. A variation of the solo approach is to use a boat as your staff. Point it upstream and lean on it into the current. While it is a challenge to keep it pointed directly into the current, this approach works surprising well.

6.3 A single person wading uses a staff or paddle to make a tripod. He faces upstream and moves sideways across the current.

Two-Person. Two people face each other. Each one grabs the shoulder of the other's life jacket for stability, and the pair begin crab-walking across the river. They can either face up- and downstream or sideways to the current.

Line-Wading. Three or more people can cross with an oar or sapling held by all. If one person loses his footing he can lean on the support provided by his compatriots. This method can be done either upstream or sideways, according to preference.

6.4.1 Another method is to use a staff to stabilize a line of waders abreast...

6.4.2 ...or in line.

6.5 The pivot method also works well. It can be done with as few as two people and as many as a dozen or more.

People Pivot (huddle, triangle of support). Adding more people to the basic two-person configuration adds stability. Each person now holds on to the shoulder of the life jacket of the person next to them, and the entire group moves sideways across the current by pivoting either on the upstream or downstream person (opinions vary as to which is the most effective). As long as the integrity of the chain is maintained, it will often work even if one member's feet aren't touching bottom.

Wedge. Another effective formation is the wedge (see figure 6.6). One person stands upstream at the apex of the wedge, using a staff in the same manner as for a single person wading. Other members are added behind and to the side of the first person, with the wedge facing upstream. The wedge then moves sideways across the river. As the water deepens, the persons behind may have to push down on the lead person to keep his feet on the riverbed.

6.6 The wedge faces upstream, creating a sizable eddy behind it. The lead person stabilizes himself with a staff or paddle.

Human Chain. This is possible when the victim is near the shore and you have lots of people. The rescuers lock arms and wade in at a 45° angle to the current. You simply keep adding more rescuers to extend the chain from the shoreline downstream to the victim.

Tethered Swimmer

The tethered swimmer, or "live bait" (a term borrowed from our Russian friends) uses a rope controlled by a shore- or boat-based team attached to the rescue swimmer. This adds extra security but is more complicated. There is also the possibility that the rescue swimmer will run out of rope before reaching the victim, or that the rope will snag. It is therefore best suited to narrow rivers, although it can also be used from rafts on wider rivers. The rescue swimmer should have a rescue harness or life jacket with an attachment point and a quick-release as described in chapter 2. In an emergency, a *loose* loop of rope passed under the rescuer's armpits will work (see figure 6.7.1), although *this greatly increases the danger to the rescuer.* The loop should be loose enough to pass over his head and shoulders if he needs to escape quickly and should be tied with a noncinching knot such as a bowline. The rescue swimmer also should be equipped with a tightly fitted life jacket, a helmet and wet/drysuit if available, and a knife to cut free of the rope if necessary.

6.7.1 Strong swimmer rescues may be executed with a loose loop of rope tied with a bowline and a stopper. Leave plenty of room for the rescuer to slide free of the loop if necessary.

6.7.2 The preferred method, however, is for the swimmer to use a rescue harness (either separate or built into the life jacket) with a quick release.

For most live-bait rescues, you will need a rope tender/belayer, a rescue swimmer, and a rescue leader, although it can be done with only a tender and a rescue swimmer. The leader should position himself so that he is visible to both the swimmer and the tender and can communicate with them using hand signals.

In practice, the tethered swimmer acts much like a free swimmer. He may use his tether for extra security while swimming or wading, to lower himself in the current (that is, allow himself to float with the current directly to the accident site), or to ferry a line to a rescue site. While the line adds security, it also causes drag in the current and has a finite length. Rescuers should choose the site for live-bait rescues carefully to avoid snagging the line, and be prepared to release or cut the tether rope if necessary.

If the rescue swimmer is intercepting a swimmer, he and the belay team must be aware of the danger of running out of rope. The longer the rope, the more likely it is to snag and the more drag the current puts on it. The rope need not be superstrong, however. Most live-bait rescues are done with 60–70'(15–21 m) of 3/8"(9.5 mm)

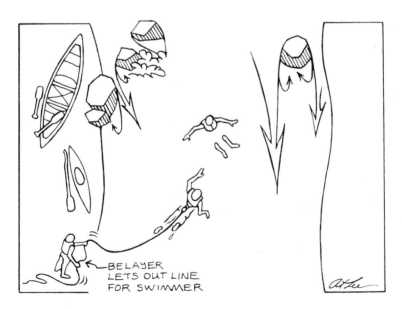

6.8.1 The strong swimmer rescue: tethered swimmer. The swimmer intercepts the victim by swimming upstream, stalling against the current. The line tender gives slack until the rescuer makes contact, then belays both to shore.

6.8.2 *A live bait swimmer deploys. The belayer must allow plenty of slack.*

6.8.3 *The tethered swimmer makes contact with the victim and is then swung to shore.*

poly line. If possible, the rescue swimmer should start somewhat upstream of the tender and swim out in front of the victim, stalling against the current as much as possible to keep from running out of rope. The tender, meanwhile, shucks out rope as fast as possible during the initial phase of the rescue swim in order to avoid having the current catch it. Once the rescue swimmer makes contact with the victim, the tender assumes a belay position and swings both victim and rescuer into shore. This requires practice to do right; the timing for the rescue swimmer to enter the water is critical. Too early and he will be swept downstream ahead of the victim; too late and the victim may get past him.

A strong swimmer may also want to get into the eddy behind the victim. Frequently the hazard that caused the accident or the pinned boat will itself create an eddy. In some cases the rescue swimmer can be lowered directly to the accident site while in others he will have to swim aggressively to reach it. He may be able to wade. In many cases, especially with a rescue life jacket or harness, a swimmer can control his position by angling his body one way or the other in the current.

Once the rescue swimmer has reached the accident scene, he should attempt to free the victim, but his first consideration must be to stabilize the situation and keep matters from worsening. The rescue team could set up a tag line (see chapter 5) to keep a victim's head above water. They could also set up additional lines (pulled over by the rescue swimmer with his own safety line) to keep a pinned boat from moving or to haul it from shore. Once the rescuer and the victim are free, they can be swung in to shore.

Some other types of strong-swimmer rescues are:

Direct or Midcurrent Lowers. Here the lowering point is directly upstream of the accident site on an island, a boulder, a bridge, or a peninsula on a river bend. This method allows more positive control by the belayer (see figure 6.9.1). Ideally, the rescuer is lowered at or near the speed of the current. This is easier on both swimmer and belayer. If held in check in very fast current the rescuer may submerge.

Fixed Line, Wading. The rescue team stretches a fixed line across the river at water level. If the water is shallow enough to stand in, the rescuer holds the fixed line at his waist and works his way out on the upstream side of it. When the rescue swimmer reaches a point

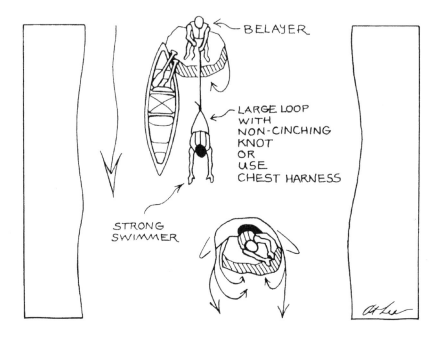

6.9.1 The strong swimmer rescue: midcurrent lower.

6.9.2 The fixed line rescue. The rescuer is held in the apex of the line by the force of the water but is able to swim free by somersaulting over or under the rope.

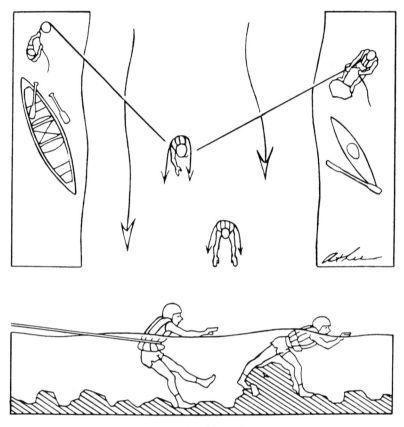

6.10 *The strong swimmer rescue: fixed line.*

directly upstream of the victim the belayers slacken the line to lower him to the accident site. As the lowering process continues, the rescue swimmer is held in the apex of the line and his position becomes more and more secure, and since he is not directly attached to the rope he can escape simply by somersaulting and swimming to safety.

This method is very quick to set up and requires a minimum of equipment. It is excellent for foot-entrapment rescues, which usually occur in shallow water, although it puts the rescuer in potentially the same situation.

6.11 A quick way of getting a rescuer across or out into the current is to have him body surf across on the downstream side of a fixed line just above the water. (Roger Phillips)

Fixed Line, Surfing. A variation of the fixed-line technique, one that works better in deeper and swifter water, is for the rescuer to go out on the rope hand over hand on the downstream side of the rope, letting the current plane his body on the surface rather than trying to stand. The rope is set three to four feet above the surface of the water and must be put in tension with a haul system. Ideally, the line's anchors will be situated so that it will cross the eddy behind the accident site. This method is fairly athletic and should not be attempted by someone with an easily dislocated shoulder.

V-Lower. This variation of the fixed-line method uses a separate belayed line from each shore attached to the **D**-ring of a rescue life jacket. In essence it uses the rescue swimmer as a small rescue craft. Since the loads are considerable, rescuers may want to consider using a belay device (e.g., Münter hitch, etc.). The **V**-lower has the advantage of being able to move the rescuer left or right to the exact location needed. It works best in water shallow enough to wade in or in moderate current. In really swift current the rescue swimmer tends to submerge and breathing becomes difficult.

6.12.1 *The V-lower is similar to the fixed line except that the rescuer uses a rescue life jacket for lowering.*

6.12.2 *The V-lower offers a quick and convenient way of positioning a rescuer in the current. The rescuer must, however, have a way of releasing himself. (ExtraSport)*

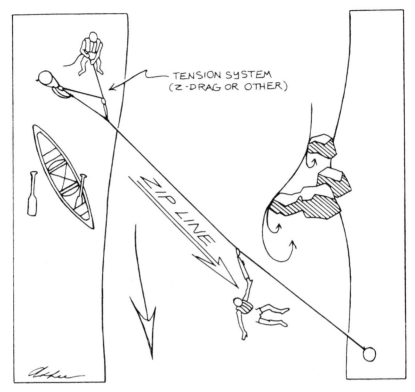

6.13 *The zip line offers a quick way to move people across a river. Both tension and angle are important: a slack line will strand the person crossing in midcurrent.*

Once the rescuer secures the victim, one line is released and they are swung to shore. Since this rescue requires coordination between the belayers, it's a good idea to have a third person in a position to observe and give the necessary signals.

Zip Line (tension diagonal). The zip line is a single tensioned line, stretched diagonally at a 45–60° angle across the river just above water level (see figure 6.13). It can be used for ferrying rescuers and equipment across a river (in setting up a rescue system, for example) with greater security than swimming. It can be used also to get a rescuer to an accident site if it can be set to pass through the eddy of the accident site. The person crossing clips into the zip line with a small loop of rope or webbing attached to a carabiner. A pulley, if available, works even better. He holds the loop (being careful not to

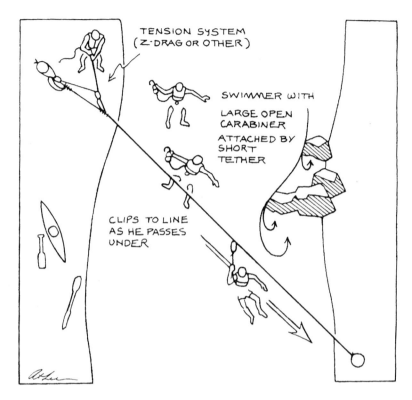

TENSION SYSTEM
(Z-DRAG OR OTHER)

SWIMMER WITH

LARGE OPEN
CARABINER

ATTACHED BY
SHORT
TETHER

CLIPS TO LINE
AS HE PASSES
UNDER

6.14 *The "sky hook": the swimmer uses a large carabiner to clip on to a line angled downstream as he passes under it.*

wrap it around his wrist) and angles his body toward the far shore. The current then pushes him along the line. This technique also works with a raft.

Sky Hook. This is a backup method to help swimmers get to shore. Here the rescuers tension a zip line (as described above) one to two feet above the water downstream of the accident site. If a swimmer floats past the accident site, he can clip into the overhead line and be transferred to shore. To do this, he has a "sky hook" much like the hand loop described above. Swimmers should, as above, avoid attaching themselves to the line or wrapping it around their wrists. They can, however, use a short tether girth-hitched around the quick-release belt on a rescue life jacket or rescue harness, since this can be released under pressure. A large carabiner or small hook makes snagging the line easier, but this isn't a system to try just above Niagara Falls.

Contact rescues are rescues of the heart—the most natural and spontaneous means of saving someone. Les describes one that might have saved his own life:

"It was 1967 and we were four camp counselors doing a canoe trip down the Petawawa River, which flows through the heart of the Algonquin Provincial Park in Ontario. I was soloing a Class III approach rapid to a Class IV drop that we were planning to carry. Like most teenagers, I was braver than I was smart and wasn't wearing a life jacket or helmet at the time.

"Just as I was making the crucial draw stroke for the eddy turn, my paddle shaft snapped loudly and over I went. The next thing I knew I was going down this simply awful drop with an aluminum canoe in my lap. We didn't have air bags in those days and somehow my whole lower left leg got squashed by the canoe full of water. The pain was intense and I was sure my leg was broken. It was all I could do to hang on to the canoe through the rest of the rapids. The canoe ended up stuck in a hydraulic, and I managed to crawl into the boat, and became oblivious to everything else at that point.

"The next thing I remember was Dan pulling me out of the boat and me not wanting to leave it. Later I was told Dan dived in (he wasn't wearing a life jacket, either), swam out, dragged me out of the canoe and performed a cross-chest carry to bring me to shore. I got a severe abrasion and a very fat ankle that got me out of portaging for the next few days. Looking back now I could easily have been trout chow if it hadn't been for Dan's contact rescue."

Man marks the earth with ruin—his control stops with shore.

Lord Byron

7

Tethered Boat Rescues and Telfer Lowers

In chapter 4 we discussed midriver rescues that could be done with various types of boats. Those methods are used routinely on almost any river trip. In this chapter, we will consider rescues in which the boat is tethered, that is, tied to a rope. This gives added security and greater control, and allows the rescuers to position a boat more exactly and hold it in one place in the current. The disadvantage of this type of rescue is that it requires more time, experience, manpower, and resources to set up and use. Recreational boaters, who are used to analyzing rapids and figuring how to safely run them, find that it takes a much different kind of skill to rig a tethered boat as a rescue platform. Anyone contemplating the use of these rescue techniques should try them first in very mild, moving water to appreciate how they work *before* trying them in fast whitewater.

All rafts used in tethered rescues must have bombproof rope attachment points. This can be a rowing frame or beefy (2"[5 cm] or better) metal **D**-rings. Fortunately, most modern rafts have suitable **D**-rings.

Tethered Boat Rescue. The simplest form of boat tether is a security tether. If the boat has to approach a hazard like a low-head dam, the rescuers can tie a rope to it so that it can be pulled back if it gets too near the hydraulic. Otherwise, it acts much like a free boat.

The disadvantage of a tether, as we saw in the section on rope ferries, is that a rope can dramatically increase current drag on the rescue craft. Thus, while it will work quite well in the area just below a hydraulic, where the current is fairly neutral, it is difficult to use this technique in swift current. It is a real concern as to whether the tethered raft will be able to ferry against the current evenly enough to get near the victim. One crew member can try to hold the tether line out of the water during the ferry to reduce the current's drag. Another crew member could have a throw bag ready to throw to the victim in case the raft cannot get close enough to physically contact the victim. If the river is narrow the rescue team may want to use two tethers—one from each bank. This gives more control and is a crude form of the two-point tether described below.

A kayaker or canoeist can also use a tether, but will have to deal with more rope drag than a tether rope elevated from a raft. Rope drag also is much more likely to upset a canoe or kayak than a raft. The paddler can tether the boat, himself, or better yet, both. Clipping the tether line into the rear of a chest harness or rescue life

7.1 A demonstration of the tethered boat rescue in Austria. Both the boat and the paddler are tethered. Note the paddle hook for snagging the victim.

jacket will help keep the tether line higher than simply clipping it on to the stern, and will allow the paddler to be retrieved if he has to abandon his boat (see figure 7.1).

Direct or One-Point Lower. A variation of the tethered boat rescue is a direct downstream lower. This might be used instead of a ferry to get a boat to an entrapment site or to rescue someone stranded on an island. Rescuers can belay the tether line from midriver rocks, or from a riverbank jutting out into the current. They will probably need some sort of mechanical belay device (e.g., Münter hitch, carabiner brake—see chapter 9) or have enough rescuers on hand to lower the rope by hand. The rescuers should put as few people as possible in the raft both to reduce the load on the anchor

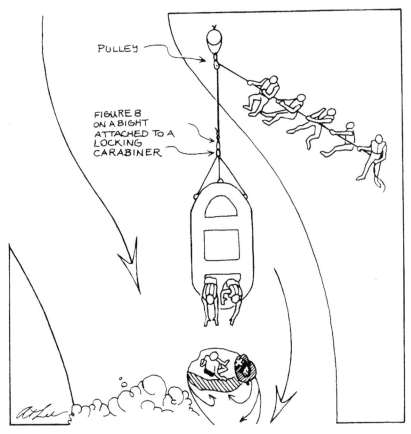

7.2 *If the situation permits, the one-point tether is a simple way to lower a raft to a trouble spot.*

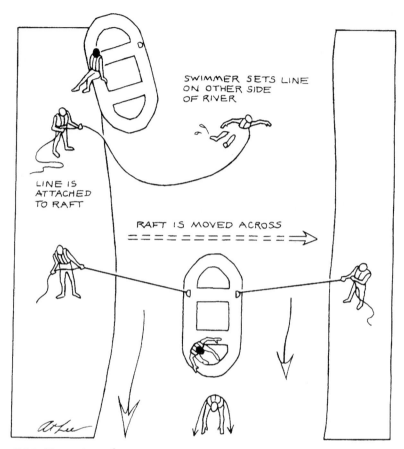

SWIMMER SETS LINE
ON OTHER SIDE
OF RIVER

LINE IS
ATTACHED
TO RAFT

RAFT IS MOVED ACROSS

7.3.1 Two-point tether.

and to minimize the number of people exposed to danger—if one person can do the job, then only one person should be in the raft. In most cases a three-man crew will suffice: one to steer with a paddle or oars to keep the raft from "fishtailing," and the other two to perform the rescue. These rescuers should stay toward the downstream end of the raft; this keeps the upstream end of the raft in a "planing" position and reduces the amount of water piling up on the bow tube.

A kayak or canoe, on the other hand, usually can be lowered with a body belay, since these hard-shelled craft create little resistance to the current. Because of the risk of capsize, a paddler will usually not be able to provide any hands-on support to the victim, but he can take an auxiliary haul line with him to attach to a pinned

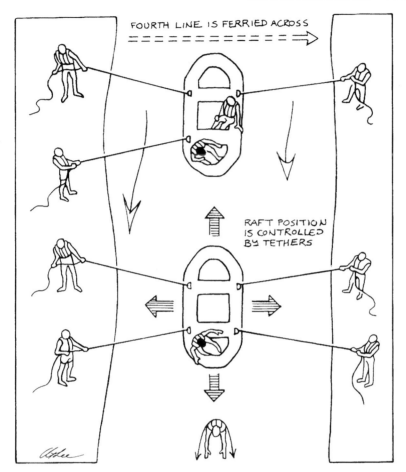

FOURTH LINE IS FERRIED ACROSS

RAFT POSITION
IS CONTROLLED
BY TETHERS

7.3.2 Four-point tether.

craft, or offer his boat for support until a suitable method of extrication can be devised.

Two- and Four-Point Tether. Rescuers can control a raft from shore
by using tag lines from either bank. This lets them hold the raft in
one place and lets the raft crew concentrate on rescue. It is a quick,
easy system to set up and requires little extra training or equipment.
The simplest variation is the two-point tether. Here a tag line is
attached to either side of the bow (normally to the **D**-rings) and
managed from shore. The rope teams hand-hold the rope, and since
there is no belay, the raft can not only be moved back and forth
across the river but also walked up and down along it. It is also quite
easy to move a raft across the river with this system, even with

untrained people in it. For greater control in faster water, add two more tag lines to the stern of the raft for a four-point tether. As with other tethered-boat systems, rescuers should load the boat toward the stern to prevent the bow from diving, and give the crew paddles in case something goes wrong (figures 7.3.1 and 7.3.2).

The two- and four-point tethers have definite limitations. They work well only on rivers narrow enough to allow the tag lines to be kept out of the water, and they cannot be controlled well in really fast current. You can rig these systems to work with mechanical belays in fast current, but if you are going to all that trouble you are better advised to set up a Telfer lower (see below).

Boat Zip Line. In chapter 6 we described a type of strong-swimmer rescue called the zip line. This concept can also be used with a raft. One use of the boat zip line might be to get a raft into an eddy behind an accident site or a rock on which a person is stranded. Another might be to get the raft from one side of the river to the other in a safe, controlled fashion.

The first step is to set an anchor line across the river at a 45–60° angle, one to four feet above the surface of the water (see figure 7.4). This zip line's cross-river anchor line should be both taut and substantial (see the section on Telfer lowers, below, for details). The raft should be lightly loaded so as to put the least weight on the line. The raft's objective is the eddy downstream of the accident site, and the zip line should be positioned to cross that eddy. If the eddy is big enough, the raft will simply eddy out. The raft crew (or boatman, if it is an oar boat) can control the speed of the crossing by adjusting the ferry angle. In a paddle raft, there should be a "guide" on the downstream side ruddering with his paddle; an oarsman can control the angle by the amount of force he puts on his downstream blade.

The raft is rigged with a pulley and a braking Prusik attached to the bow D-ring. On many rafts this D-ring is mounted low, and you should ensure that you can cut the raft loose from both the Prusik and the pulley in an emergency. As the current propels the raft across the river, a rescue crewman holds the braking Prusik loosely on the zip line. If the raft stops in an eddy, the braking Prusik then can be applied to hold the raft in position. If there is no eddy, the crewman releases the braking Prusik when adjacent to or upstream of the accident site. This takes a little experience, since the rope will stretch somewhat when the raft stops, and once set you will be hard pressed to pull the raft up to the zip line enough to adjust the Prusik.

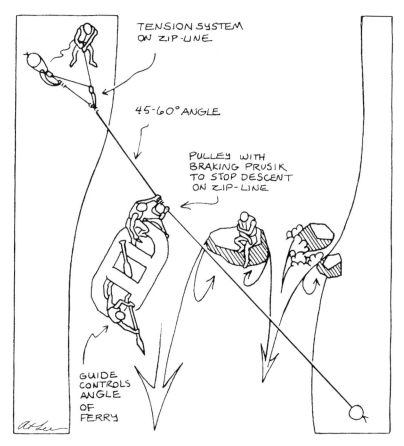

TENSION SYSTEM
ON ZIP-LINE

45-60° ANGLE

PULLEY WITH
BRAKING PRUSIK
TO STOP DESCENT
ON ZIP-LINE

GUIDE
CONTROLS
ANGLE
OF
FERRY

7.4 The boat zip line is a quick way to get a raft in the eddy behind an obstacle.

If possible, err on the upstream side so that the entire zip line can be slackened if necessary to lower the raft.

There is the obvious danger that the person riding across, clinging to the Prusik brake, might get a finger caught in the knot, not to mention that he will be bouncing along hanging over the upstream tube with only one hand. If the raft does stop short, and the Prusik is set, you can always put another braking Prusik on, and release the first Prusik simply by cutting it.

Telfer Lower. The Telfer lower uses a working platform made from a raft or boat floated downstream from a high line stretched across the river to an accident site or into the eddy below it. Tag lines on either shore control the rescue craft's crosscurrent position. The actual

7.5 A raft rigged for a direct lower. The crew sits toward the rear of the craft to keep the bow planing. (Les Bechdel/ Canyons, Inc.)

lowering can be done from either the rescue craft or from shore. It may also be set up with an anchor line just upstream of the accident site, and the rescue craft pulled up to it, or even as a "reverse Telfer," which lowers the rescue craft *upstream* into the backwash of a hydraulic. Even in very swift water it provides a surprisingly stable platform from which to rescue a trapped victim or a pinned boat. The disadvantages of this method are that it takes time to set up and taxes the technical skills and leadership of the rescuers. It also requires a substantial amount of equipment, particularly rope.

A raft works best for Telfer lowers, since it is inherently stable and can carry multiple rescuers. A cataraft may well be the ideal craft for this application, because it provides a stable, unswampable platform. A self-bailing raft does not work as well as the non-self-bailing "bucket" raft. When held in midriver against the current, water sprays into the raft through the drain holes and thus creates more resistance than a non-self-bailer. Two open canoes lashed together catamaran-style make a very stable platform but can swamp more easily than a raft. Three kayaks tied together will work for patient transport on slow sections, but is a bit chancy on fast water.

The same is true for single kayaks and canoes—they tip more easily and tend to fishtail once they are in midriver.

To set up a Telfer, first establish a line across the river. This is usually 20–50'(6–15 m) upstream of the accident site. Allow enough room (and rope) for the rescue craft to float down past the obstacle and come up in the eddy below. The line should be tight and 6–10'(2–3 m) above the surface of the water. Trees usually make the best anchor points, but you can use boulders, car bumpers, or other suitable anchors instead. The line should be angled downstream if possible; this will assist in launching.

Make the high line taut with a simple Z-drag with two or three people pulling it tight. The exact mechanics of rigging the line are covered in more detail in the section on high lines in chapter 10. If using a raft, a 7/16"(11mm) low-stretch nylon rescue rope is a good idea (you should have one in your pin kit).

In rigging a Telfer lower, consider your line ferries carefully. You have not only the main line to ferry, but a tag line as well. If possible, ferry both lines across at the same time, using any of the techniques discussed in chapter 5. A little thought about how and when to ferry the lines across will save a lot of time, as will some practice. Likewise, you also have to think about getting people across the river and how you will communicate with the far shore team and the rescue craft. The rescue leader should remain on shore to coordinate the entire operation.

The heart of any Telfer lower is the pulley system. If you have no pulleys, carabiners will work, but they cause more friction. The upper pulley slides on the anchor line, while the lower pulley serves to lower the rescue craft to the accident site. Be sure that the throat of any pulley you use is large enough not to bind when jerked abruptly to the side. The two pulleys can be linked together with a steel rigging ring, a short loop of webbing, or a Prusik loop. This creates a flexible joint and reduces the chance of the pulleys binding when loaded. Do not use a carabiner here—the side loadings can unhook or break it. Tag lines clipped into the loop control run to either shore (see figure 7.6). If there is enough downstream angle in the high line, you can dispense with the tag line running to the far shore—the current will ferry the raft to midriver. However, a tag line to either shore does give more precise control.

The most critical part of the rescue is the launch, since it is here that the rescue craft is most likely to run into trouble. Make sure the bow of the boat remains pointed directly upstream, because if the

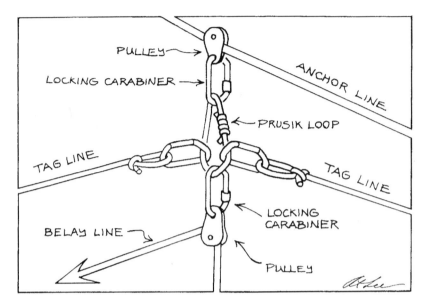

7.6 *Rigging for a lowering system. If rescuers are short of equipment, the pulleys can be eliminated and the tag lines tied directly to the Prusik loop.*

boat swings broadside to the current it is likely to swamp. It also helps to keep the rescue craft directly downstream of the pulley system. Once launched, the rescue craft, whether it is a raft, canoe, or kayak, should avoid hazards like large waves and holes. It is extremely difficult to pull a rescue craft, particularly a raft, up over a wave or out of a hole, and there is a definite danger of overstressing the entire system. If the Telfer craft does start to swamp, the lowering line must quickly be released. There should be paddles (or oars) available for this eventuality. All rescuers should carry knives to cut any fouled lines. A last resort is to cut the anchor line.

So far, all Telfer lowers share the common characteristics already described. We now consider the two major variations of Telfers: shore-based and boat-based lowers. The choice of which type to employ will depend on the number and experience of the people, the number and type of boats, the amount of rope and equipment available, and the distance the rescue craft must be lowered.

Shore-Based Lower. Here the rescue craft is lowered by a shore-based team. This allows the people in the raft to concentrate on rescue but gives them little control over the rescue craft. There may also be communications problems between the two shore parties and the rescue craft. The lowering rope is attached to the bow of the rescue craft and run through the lower pulley to the shore party, who then pay out rope according to instructions from the rescue leader. This method requires a substantial amount of rope. You cannot use two ropes joined together, since a knot or carabiner will not pass through most pulleys. Likewise, there should be no bag on the end of the rope that could become tangled in the pulley system if it has to be released. Once the rescue craft is in position, both river right and river left tag lines must be securely belayed before the lowering of the rescue craft begins.

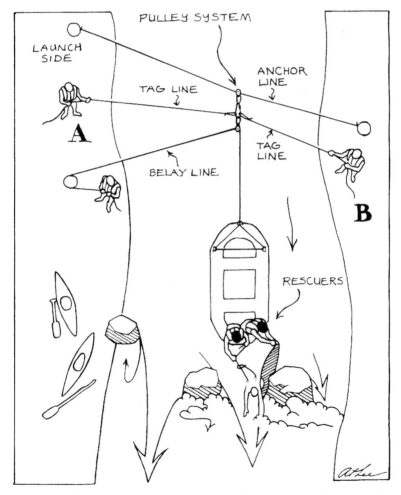

7.7 The Telfer lower: belayer on shore. Tag line B may be eliminated if the rescuers are short-handed.

Boat-Based Lower. Allowing the rescue boat crew to do the lowering makes it easier to position the boat precisely and simplifies communications. It also uses less rope. The lowering rope is attached to the bow of the rescue craft, runs through the lower pulley, and then back to the rescue craft. On the negative side, this gives the crew another task to worry about and exposes another rescuer (the belayer) to the river and the possibility of getting tangled up in the lowering rope. Ensure there are no knots or throw bags that could stick in the lowering pulley if the craft has to release.

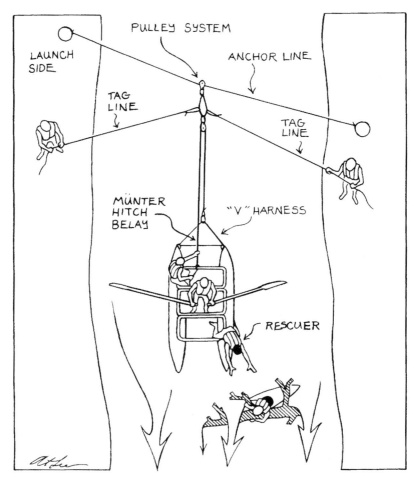

7.8 *The Telfer lower: belayer in the rescue craft. The belayer may hold the line or use the thwart as a belay point.*

Rigging the Rescue Craft

Rafts. Figure 7.9 shows the simplest and most efficient type of raft lower. The pulley system has only one pulley on the high line, and a Prusik loop serves as the connector for the other three lines: a tag line to each shore and the lowering line. The lowering line must pass through the bow (upstream) D-ring to a Münter hitch or other friction device rigged at the center of the raft. The bow D-ring serves as a directional aid to keep the raft aligned with the current. Without it the raft would pivot at the Münter hitch and veer to one side or the other. If the bow D-ring is located close to the water, and short rope or webbing extension with a carabiner may be necessary to raise the lowering line up over the tube.

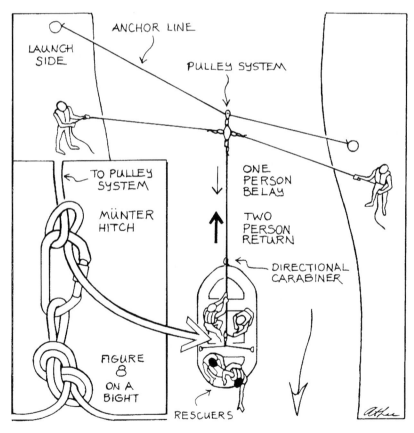

7.9 *The Telfer lower, using a Münter hitch for positioning the rescue craft upstream or downstream.*

Tie the Münter hitch on a locking carabiner centered on a sling on the frame of an oar boat or cataraft. If you are using a paddle raft, a centering line made from rope or webbing can be rigged amidships across the width of the boat. This should be tied tightly from D-ring to D-ring with a figure-eight knot located over the raft's centerline. The locking carabiner for the Münter hitch is then clipped into this knot. Unless this knot is centered, the raft will tend to veer left or right in the current as it is lowered.

Ideally, the belayer can let the raft float down at current speed and apply the "brakes" gradually. The rescuer who has the job of controlling the Münter hitch must be careful not to let any loose items (e.g., hair, parka strings, or fingers) get fed accidentally into it. In practice he can stop the raft by pulling his brake hand upstream toward the pulley system (this is the high-friction position for the Münter hitch). This is enough to hold the raft, and it can be tied off if necessary with a slip knot. As the belayer moves his brake hand downstream, the friction lessens and the raft begins to descend again.

A quick and dirty variation for rigging rafts is to tie the Münter hitch directly to the bow D-ring. This works only with rafts that have the bow D-ring positioned fairly high up on the tube, and since the belayer has to sit or kneel near the bow, this reduces the planing effect and makes the bow dig in.

For catarafts, the lowering line needs to apply an equal force on each tube. Otherwise, the raft will slew in one direction or the other. The solution is to rig a V-bridle on the bow much like that shown in figure 7.8. If possible, tie this line to the upstream end of each tube. Center a double figure-eight or similar loop knot between the two tubes, upstream of the boat. The resulting V should have about a 60° angle. If the "cat" doesn't have D-rings on the ends of the tubes, you can extend a line to the frame or the side D-rings where the frame fastens to the tubes (see figure 7.10). The lowering line leads from the V-bridle up to the pulley system and then back to a Münter hitch centered on the cataraft's frame.

Canoes. Since they swamp more easily than rafts, canoes are not the ideal craft for Telfer lowers. However, they can be used in easier water. To provide maximum stability and a large rescue platform, lash two canoes together catamaran-style. Saplings four to six feet long that lash the hulls a foot or so apart are ideal, but

7.10 *A cataraft rigged for a shore-based lower. The lowering line is attached directly to the frame. (Paul Ratcliffe/ Sierra Shutterbug)*

7.11 *This raft is rigged directly through the bow D-ring for a direct lower controlled by the raft crew. (Les Bechdel/ Canyons, Inc.)*

spare paddles will serve in a pinch. Each crossbar should be lashed at two points on each canoe's thwart or seat to make the catamaran as rigid as possible.

Rig a V-bridle for the resulting rescue craft like that described above for a catamaran, then run the lowering line from the V-bridle up to the lowering pulley and then either back to a rescuer kneeling in the bow (if a boat-based lower) or to a shore team. Since the canoe hull presents little drag, a crewman can control the descent of the boat simply by hand-holding the rope—a friction device is unnecessary. He should ensure that there are no knots or throw bags on the lowering line that might catch in the pulley if the craft needs to be released. If it does, the canoe-catamaran can be paddled to shore (make sure paddles are available for that purpose). The stern paddlers (ideally, one on either side) can control the angle by ruddering with a paddle. These will also be the rescuers who will deal with the victim or pinned boat.

The canoe-catamaran can also be set up to transport a patient from one side of the river to the other. This is a good solution for a patient who is strapped to a backboard, or for a litter that will not fit on one canoe.

A single tandem canoe can be lowered but tends to fishtail badly. The lowering line comes off the bow end, up through the lowering pulley and back to the bowman, who hand-holds it. The sternman rudders the canoe to control the fishtailing. Because this craft is not very stable, this variation works only for such tasks as affixing a haul line to a pinned craft; it can do little to directly assist an entrapped victim.

Kayaks. Because of the kayak's tapered shape it is difficult to construct a catamaran-type rescue platform with two boats. Three kayaks, however, can be rigged as a flexible kind of trimaran by tying a line connecting the bow and stern grab loops of the two outside kayaks, run through (but not tied to) the grab loop of the middle kayak. The lowering line attaches to the middle kayak's grab loop, then runs up through the lowering pulley and back to the middle kayaker. The two outside kayakers brace with their paddles; the middle kayaker holds the lowering line and braces his elbows on the two outside kayaks. The two outside rescuers each should use either a canoe paddle or half of a breakdown kayak paddle, if available, so as to avoid clobbering the middle rescuer.

This trimaran of kayaks is used mainly to get a haul line on a pinned craft rather than to give direct help to a victim. However, it can be used for patient transfer by having the patient lay across the rear decks for a ride across the river. If, for example, you have a patient with a shoulder dislocation, you could place him in the middle kayak and use a shore-based lowering system. Don't tie the trimaran to the lowering system, because the kayaks need to separate from it in case of a capsize.

A single kayak can be lowered with a shore-based system, but like the canoe it is not stable and tends to zigzag unless a paddler does a combination brace and rudder stroke. It, too, is best used for attaching a haul line rather than for rescue. Pass the lowering line through the bow grab loop, then tie a slipknot to a broach loop (see figure 7.13.1) or clip it directly to a releasable chest harness. Any system must allow the kayak to come free if it flips.

7.12 *Evacuating an injured kayaker with a kayak trimaran.* (*Virgil Bodenhamer*)

7.13.1 *This shore-based lower uses a single kayak. The boat is tied to the broach loop with a slip knot. (Les Bechdel/Canyons, Inc.)*

7.13.2 *A kayak trimaran set up for a patient evacuation. (Tom Moore/ Sierra South)*

Under the right conditions boat lowers are very effective, both as a rescue/recovery platform and as a means of ferrying patients across the river during an evacuation.

An example of this was a boat recovery on the Klamath River. A raft was pinned on a boulder that split two chutes of Class IV water. A kayak could catch the eddy behind the boulder, but it was too steep to scale. There were no trees for rigging a Tyrolean. After some discussion, the river rangers settled on a Telfer boat-lower system. Rigging the boat, they lowered it into the rapid and clipped a haul line to the pinned raft. Then the tag lines pulled them to the right chute, where they released the lowering line and ran the chute. Returning to shore, they then used a bumper winch to pull the boat off.

Wherein I spake of most disastrous chances,
Of moving accidents by flood and field, Of hair-breadth
'scapes i' the imminent deadly breach.
William Shakespeare, *Othello*

8

Entrapments and Extrications

A group of expert paddlers went out on North Carolina's Watauga River in the spring. The Watauga is steep, with almost continuous rapids, many big drops, and a fifteen-foot waterfall. "You had to catch every eddy in order to boat-scout the next rapid," one member of the group recalls, "and we didn't know exactly where the waterfall was." As it turned out, the eddy that one of the paddlers missed was the one just above the waterfall. He went down backward over the wrong chute and pinned halfway down the falls on a small boulder.

Fortunately, he was with an alert, experienced group of paddlers. They immediately sized up the situation, got out of their boats, and went after him. The entrapped paddler was able to breathe, but the water was very cold. Though he was dressed for the season, hypothermia was an immediate danger. His legs were entrapped under the thwart seat in his low-volume C-1. The rescuers were able to wade out to the boulder, at some danger to themselves, and hold the victim's head out of the water. "Finally," said one of the rescuers, "we were able to pull him up enough to let him slide his legs out from under the thwart and get free. But it was touchy, and he wouldn't have lasted long in that cold water."

Here we have the classic elements of both a boat pin and an entrapment: a good paddler in hard water making only a small mistake. In this case there was a happy ending, but it was only because of the quick and correct actions of the rescuers.

Boat Pins and Entrapments

People are entrapped; boats are pinned. "Entrapped" means being held in a life-threatening position by the force of the water or by a collapsed boat; a boat is "pinned" when it is held in place against a solid object by the force of the current. Since an entrapment is often a direct result of a pin, we will discuss both in this chapter. Foot and body entrapments are also discussed later in the chapter.

Not all paddlers are entrapped in their boats; there have been cases in which paddlers who bailed out of their pinned boats have had their bodies entrapped by the same obstacle that held the boat. Any kind of swamped craft (raft, canoe, or kayak) can be pushed against a rock and entrap a swimming paddler between it and the rock. Always stay upstream of your swamped boat to avoid being sandwiched.

Boat pins and boat entrapments (of a paddler) fall into two main categories: broaches and vertical pins.

Broaches. A boat broaches when it wraps sideways around an obstacle, usually a bridge piling, a boulder, or a tree (see figure 8.1). There is usually a cushion of water on the upstream side of an obstacle, and the river-wise paddler learns to ride over this "pillow" and avoid a direct collision. Some obstacles, however, such as bridge pilings and undercut rocks, have little or no upstream cushion and are much more dangerous to approach. Paddlers often can avoid a broach by leaning toward the obstacle and pushing off it. Rafters should learn to high-side (that is, to shift their weight toward the obstacle) in order to prevent a broach.

There are other types of broaches beside wrapping. One, the "end pin," occurs when the ends of a kayak bridge two rocks and the boat collapses in the center. If the paddler is lucky, however, the folded boat may flush through the gap. Another type of broach, the "pinch pin," (see figure 8.3) happens when the front half of the boat

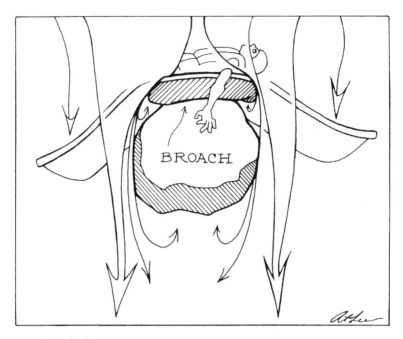

8.1 *A broached boat.*

8.2.1 *A slow high-side led to this pin on Gunsight Rock in Troublemaker Rapid on the South Fork of the American River. (Paul Ratcliffe/ Sierra Shutterbug)*

8.2.2 If pushed into a rock, lean into it and attempt to work yourself off.

wedges between two rocks and the current folds the boat in a down-stream direction.

No matter what the mechanics, the fateful moment occurs when the boat collapses against the obstacle and entraps the paddler. This happens most often to kayakers—the front deck collapses on their legs—but rafts and canoes can entrap people as well.

About the only good aspect of broaches is that they are usually somewhat more accessible than vertical pins. The boulder that has caused the wrap may provide rescuers with an eddy in which to ferry, or a place on which to stand.

Vertical Pins. A boat vertically pins when it runs off a steep drop and the bow slams into the riverbed and sticks (see figure 8.4). This mishap is most common on steep, ledgy, shallow rivers. If the bow wedges into rocks or under a submerged tree, the force of the water will quickly produce catastrophic results: the boat may "pitchpole" and collapse at the fulcrum created by the obstacle, but a more common result is for the water to force the stern of the boat to the bottom too, collapsing it along with the buried bow. Even if the boat does not actually fold, the paddler may be held inside the boat by the

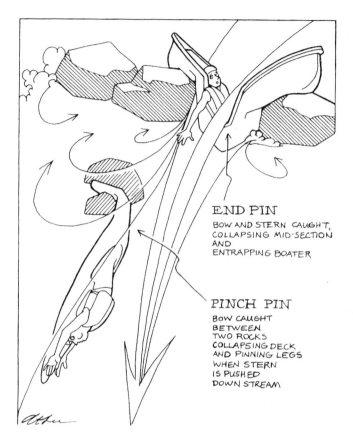

END PIN

BOW AND STERN CAUGHT,
COLLAPSING MID-SECTION
AND
ENTRAPPING BOATER

PINCH PIN

BOW CAUGHT
BETWEEN
TWO ROCKS
COLLAPSING DECK
AND PINNING LEGS
WHEN STERN
IS PUSHED
DOWN STREAM

*8.3 End pin
and pinch pin.*

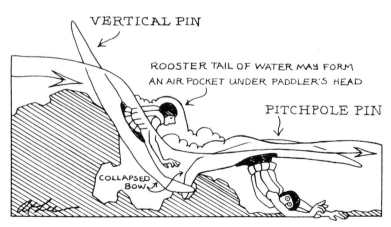

VERTICAL PIN

ROOSTER TAIL OF WATER MAY FORM
AN AIR POCKET UNDER PADDLER'S HEAD

PITCHPOLE PIN

COLLAPSED
BOW

8.4 Vertical and pitchpole pins.

sheer force of the current against his back. If the water is not too deep he may be able to form an air pocket in front of his body by pushing up on the front deck. This is very tiring, especially in cold water, and rescue efforts must begin immediately.

Paddling drops of more than four or five feet invite a vertical pin, but paddling technique and boat design also play a part. A paddler may reduce the risk of pinning by "ski-jumping" the boat off the drop so that it "pancakes" or "boofs" at the bottom of the drop—that is to say, he goes off the drop with a lot of forward speed and leans back radically as the boat starts to drop, causing it to land flat on the bottom of the hull rather than burying the bow. Though this is a useful technique, it can cause back injuries.

On the whole, a low-volume needle-nosed design is more prone to pinning vertically than is a higher-volume blunt-bowed one. Lately a whole class of extreme descent boats has emerged for steep creek runs. These boats are short (usually ten feet or less) and have large cockpits and blunt, rounded bows. Other design improvements include bulkhead-type footbraces, which reduce the chances of ankle injury and entrapment. Another innovation has been the low-volume stern, which allows the stern to sink into the water coming off the drop, allowing the paddler an easier time keeping the bow up for a "boof."

C-1s (decked canoes) often are cited as being less likely to entrap a paddler than a kayak. With low-volume canoe designs, a canoeist's feet can be entrapped by the collapse of the rear deck. Open canoes are less vulnerable to entrapments, but they are certainly not immune. One open-boat paddler spent more than two hours under Sweet's Falls on the Gauley River after pinning in the drop; the boat collapsed, pinning one of his legs between the crushed hull and a thwart. Another canoeist nearly drowned on the Ocoee River after broaching his canoe on a bridge piling. He became entangled in his thigh straps and had to be cut out by a rescue party (see chapter 7).

Foot and Body Entrapments

Foot entrapments happen when a person's foot becomes jammed into a tapered crack in the riverbed, or between two rocks. The force of the current usually prevents him from freeing his foot, and he is likely to drown. This mishap can occur when someone has tipped and is attempting to walk to shore, or as he tries to arrest his downstream progress by pushing against the riverbed. River depths play a critical role here. If the water is less than knee-deep, a foot entrapment is unlikely to result in drowning. Another potential foot-entrapment scenario is when a swimmer goes over a drop. As he goes over, his feet will often drop down and be forced into the riverbed. The swimmer can avoid this by pulling his knees up against his chest. Rescues of foot-entrapment victims are difficult and frequently unsuccessful.

All extremities, and indeed the entire body, can be entrapped by the force of the current; the most likely places are against a strainer or an undercut rock, although virtually any piece of debris (e.g., a barbed-wire fence) will suffice. Tapered sections of rock (such as Left Crack on Section IV of the Chattooga) can produce virtual deathtraps at certain river levels.

Stages of Rescue

Entrapment rescues generally proceed in four stages: assessment, stabilization, extrication, and evacuation. (For a more in-depth discussion of rescue organization and methods, see chapter 11.)

Assessment. This is the critical first step. The most important question is whether it is a "head-up" or "head-down" entrapment: if the victim can breathe you can afford a few more minutes to decide on and use the best and safest method of rescue; if the victim's head is underwater you must react immediately. The amount of time you have will vary depending on the accessibility of the accident site, the force of the current, the skill of the rescue team, and the victim's physical strength and will to survive. All of these factors must be considered in your initial assessment of the entrapment.

Stabilization. The rescuers must first ensure that the victim can continue to breathe; then see that the boat does not shift and make the situation worse. Don't charge blindly into trying to remove the victim before you have stabilized the situation. Be careful about popping the boat's sprayskirt—the boat may shift unpredictably if it fills with water.

If the entrapment site is accessible, the quickest and most obvious way to stabilize the situation is a contact rescue: that is, to physically grab the victim or the boat. Consider whether the rescuers can stand on or at least near the obstacle that created the entrapment, or on the pinned boat itself. If they cannot stand in the current, can they wade out on a fixed line, pendulum, or be lowered down to the accident site with a strong-swimmer rescue and hold the victim's head up? Can a rope from shore or a tag line be rigged to keep the victim's head above water? And should auxiliary lines be tied to the pinned boat to keep it from shifting? The use of rescue ropes is discussed in more detail later in this chapter.

Extrication. Extrication should not start until the victim has been stabilized in a relatively safe position. If he cannot be stabilized, however, as with a head-down pin, you must begin extrication efforts immediately. With a contact rescue (like that described at the beginning of this chapter) one or more rescuers may physically assist the victim in getting out. Try to understand the mechanics of the boat pin. What is the actual cause of the predicament? In foot or body entrapments try to visualize what is physically causing the problem.

Consider also whether the boat can be cut to facilitate releasing the victim. This is difficult with modern boat materials (see the section on kayak-cutting techniques below), but with a raft this may be the logical solution. Likewise, if a strainer is causing the problem, you may be able to cut the tree or branch. Most extrications, however, involve attaching lines to the pinned craft and using shore-based power to pull the boat free.

Evacuation. The final stage of an entrapment rescue is the evacuation of the victim from the accident site to shore. Monitor his condition continuously from the time the rescuers reach the scene and throughout the evacuation. Use CPR and first aid as necessary.

You should give some thought to the evacuation of the patient while you are involved in extricating him. If the patient is coherent and uninjured, you might simply swing him in with a rope; if he is injured but has been rescued from immediate danger, you should use other, slower methods for evacuation. You might pick him up with a raft or another boat, or by means of a Telfer lower. If the situation requires it, he might even be evacuated by helicopter directly from the entrapment site.

Boat Entrapment Rescues

Contact Rescue. The rescue described at the beginning of this chapter is a contact rescue: a hands-on approach with no rope between rescuer and victim. This is almost always the fastest—and the most dangerous—way to reach an entrapment victim if the rescuers are able to wade, swim, or lower themselves to the accident site. If the victim's head is underwater time is critical, and this is usually the first method to consider. If the victim can breathe, consider a safer method first. Contact rescues are best done by experienced paddlers or guides who are used to working in the water. (There is a more complete discussion of contact rescues in chapter 6.)

Broach Rescue. With a kayak, the rescuers must get the entrapped paddler's legs out. This job will be much easier if the boat has a large cockpit and stout walls. Remember that popping the sprayskirt may alter the boat's balance and weight dramatically. In less serious situations the rescuers may be able to grab the victim with a bear hug from behind and pull him free. Rocking the boat up and down, first on one end and then the other, may cause it to wash off the obstacle. If the broached boat is a canoe, the rescuers may be able to cut the thigh straps and release the paddler.

In most cases, rescuers should set a stabilization tag line (see chapter 5) to help the pinned paddler keep his head above water. If the river is too wide they might be able to rig a supporting line from upstream. There have been several cases where rescuers stood in the water and held the victim's head up.

8.5 A rescuer rigs a line to keep the victim's head above the water.
(AWA photo)

If time permits, the rescuers may attach haul lines to the boat and try to pull it free of the obstacle (as described later in this chapter). If the boat is equipped with a broach loop (a loop of cable or nylon webbing positioned just in front of the cockpit), a shore-based haul system might lift the deck enough for the victim to slide his legs out.

Vertical Pin Rescue. In some vertical pins the paddler is not physically entrapped, as in a broach, but rather is held in the boat by a combination of gravity and water pushing against his back. If you want to see how difficult escape is in this situation, get in a kayak, stand it upright on the bow, and try to pull yourself out. A C-1 is much easier to get out of in a vertical pin, since the paddler can simply dive forward.

If the victim can breathe, the rescuers should first stabilize a vertically pinned boat by attaching lines to it so that it cannot shift. A pin is often much more "touchy" than a broach, which means that the rescuers should take the time to set up the best pull and consider the consequences carefully. For the same reason, they should avoid popping the sprayskirt if it has not already blown off. Use a tag line

ROOSTER TAIL

AIR POCKET

8.6 *A stabilization tag line can be set up to keep the pinned paddler's head up while other rescue methods are used to extricate him.*

to assist the paddler in keeping his head up (tag line rescues are discussed in more detail below). In some cases the entrapped paddler may be able to push up enough on the tag line to get free of the boat.

Often the biggest problem with a vertically pinned decked boat is attaching haul lines to it, since it presents a smooth surface with few attachment points (see below). It helps if the boat is equipped with a broach loop and sturdy grab loops. Unfortunately, some commercially produced boats still have grab loops that are inadequate for hauling the boat out. At some point the rescuers must either pull the paddler up enough to get him out of the boat, either physically or with a tag line, or they must pull the boat out of the pin—usually the same way it went in. If they can reach the bow (unlikely in a severe pin) they might try to cut away the pinned part of the boat to get it free.

Give some thought to where the extricated victim might end up. Getting out of the boat doesn't necessarily improve the paddler's chances—he may then swim into a body entrapment. For this reason, if possible, the rescuers should have a positive hold on the victim, either physically or with a rope, during the extrication.

Rigging for Vertical Pin Rescue. In the previous section we posed the question of how we might attach a rope to an inaccessible boat or victim—one that is pinned where there are no convenient eddies or boulders from which to base a contact rescue. Once the line is attached, the rescuers can use any shore-based haul system, from a simple direct pull to a Z-drag, to pull the boat off. Remember that it's a big load to pull: you are hauling the weight of both the paddler and a boat that may be half full of water, and you are pulling against the current.

First the rescuers must get to the pinned craft. For this they might use an overhead or vertical rescue, such as a Tyrolean or bridge lower; a Telfer lower; or even a strong-swimmer. The first two methods require a fair amount of time, equipment, and knowledge to set up, and have definite setup limitations. A faster alternative is to use technical rescue equipment such as paddler-carried throw bags and paddle hooks or "rope tricks" (see the next section). The rescuers might also use the rigging systems described in the next chapter if time permits.

Some European paddlers carry a small throw bag attached to their life jacket or rescue harness to throw out to rescuers if the boat is pinned. This is certainly the fastest method of getting a line on the paddler, and it eliminates many of the problems (like cinching down on the victim's body) associated with the rope tricks. This is the method used by the open canoeist pinned at Sweet's Falls on the Gauley River, at the end of chapter 3: he was able to tie his throw bag onto a thwart and let it float out to his companions.

A quick and simple method for attaching a haul line to a decked boat is to use a carabiner ("rescue" versions, which have a larger opening, are especially good for this) hooked over the cockpit rim, then running the line around the boat. Rescuers may also puncture the boat at the cockpit rim, then thread the haul line through the hole.

Clipping this line to a broach loop might work even better. In many cases a paddler will be able to clip the line to his own broach loop, making it unnecessary for rescuers to directly approach the accident site.

Another method is to use a paddle hook (see chapter 2), which can give the rescuers enough extra reach on a narrow river to get the hook into the grab loop, cockpit rim, or paddler's safety harness. One Austrian manufacturer even makes a harness specifically designed to be "hooked."

8.7 Unpinning a boat using a paddle hook. Here two kayak paddles are joined together with special clamps in order to extend the reach of the rescuers. A haul line is attached directly to the paddle hook, which is then hooked on to the pinned boat's grab loop. Note the rescue harness worn over the rescuer's life jacket. It is designed to have a paddle hook slid in between the two pieces of webbing which go over the paddler's shoulders.

Rope Tricks. Rope trick is a general term that describes methods of using the current to carry a rope around a boat or victim. Often you use rope tricks when you can't get a rescuer to the accident site. Take the kayaker caught in a vertical pin: the boat and the body of the paddler disrupt the current and are frequently out of the water entirely. An appropriate rope trick would be to throw or ferry a rope to the upstream side of the boat and let it float around it. A boat or swimmer could then be used to retrieve the downstream end of the rope and return it to the same shore, thus making a loop of rope around the boat or victim.

In many pins and entrapments the only way to pull a boat and victim out is the way they went in. Similarly, in really inaccessible situations the only way to get a rope to them is often to let the same current that put them there carry the rope. (This was the method finally used to get a rope around Rick Bernard's pinned kayak in the incident described in the prologue, after all other methods had failed.)

Once the loop has been formed, there are several options for cinching down the rope, but the very flexibility of the rope-trick concept prevents showing every variation. If the boat is equipped with a broach loop, the trapped paddler can use one of his carabiners to clip onto the rope to keep it from sliding up. If not, he might be able to catch the rope under the cockpit rim. If this doesn't work, the rescuers should try to cinch the loop around the kayak below its wide point. The distance from the pinned craft, the speed of the current,

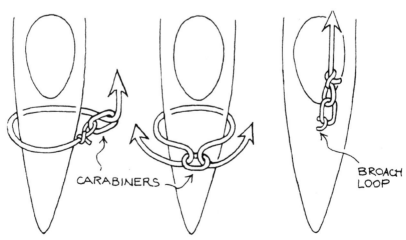

CARABINERS

BROACH LOOP

8.8 There are several ways to attach a rope to a decked boat.

the position of the kayak, and the location of nearby rocks will determine how well these rope tricks work. If floating lines can't be used because the force of the current or the depth of the submerged boat is too great, the rescuers can try a weighted line (the snag tag is described in more detail later in the chapter).

Rope tricks were developed primarily to pull pinned boats. But in some situations there may be no other option than to pull directly on the entrapped paddler. However, this is very likely to cause bodily harm and should not be tried except as a last resort. If the rescuers opt to use a cinching rope loop, the NOC Knot Trick reduces the likelihood of injury (see figure 8.11.2) by using a stopper knot (a double figure-eight) to keep the rope from cinching too tightly on the victim's body. If possible, the rescuers should try to guide the loop around the victim's life jacket to provide some padding. This trick is also used in the cinching tag line (Carlson Cinch) described below.

Cutting Boats. Whittling someone out of a modern plastic kayak is a challenge. It should be attempted only as a last resort—if you are faced with a short-handed rescue attempt or if you can't haul the boat off with ropes. As discussed in the equipment chapter, a knife with a very sharp, thin, fixed or positive-locking blade works best. A serrated edge works best to saw through the triple-layer plastic of the cockpit rim. Saw blades are better yet.

To make an entry cut with a knife, *don't* swing and stab! The knife may bounce unpredictably. Instead, place one palm on top of the handle, then press downward and rock the knife back and forth. That way the blade will slip through the boat in a more or less controlled fashion. With a saw blade, first score a line and saw back and forth in the same groove while pushing downward. Once the blade is through the boat, turn it to a 45° angle to the hull's surface. As you pull the knife or saw the blade, this will cause one flap of plastic to go up and another down. This "scissoring" effect offers much less resistance than trying to pull the knife at a 90° angle to the boat's surface.

The next question is where to cut. In a vertical pin, a careful cut starting at the cockpit rim going toward the bow may release the pressure on the pinned boater's legs, although it may be difficult not to cut the legs. It has been argued but never actually demonstrated that an inspired victim might cut himself out of a vertically pinned boat.

8.9 When cutting a plastic boat, angle the knife in the cut.

For broaches there are a couple of options. If the skirt has blown and the kayak full of water, it will probably want to move around one side of the rock rather than the other. Think of the rock or tree that caused the wrap as the fulcrum point and the boat as a warped lever. If we cut off one end of the kayak, this will create a greater load on the other end, helping it to wash free.

Sometimes the entrapment occurs not only because the paddler's legs are caught, but also because the victim can't move his body to the rear because his butt is wedged into the rear wall and cockpit rim. If rescuers can cut the stern deck and walls away enough, they may be able to drag him out in a rearward direction.

Canoes and rafts also can be cut if necessary to release a victim. Most modern whitewater canoes are made of ABS plastic. This material is virtually impossible to cut with a knife, although it can be cut readily with a saw (see the conclusion of this chapter), as can wooden gunnels and thwarts. Metal gunnels, however, will require a hacksaw.

Rafts can be cut fairly easily with a sharp knife when the need arises. However, cutting through the wood and metal of rowing frames and cargo decks requires saws and hacksaws.

Entrapment Rescues of People

Most of the techniques covered in this section are some form of tag line rescue—stabilization, rescue, and cinching. These work best on narrow streams, and while they are safer than boat-based or in-water rescue options, they do require rope, some experience, and organization.

As a general rule, an entrapment victim has to come out the same way he went in—back upstream against the current. In some cases the victim may be able to free himself if the rescuers can provide him with something that he can push back on (like a tag line), while in other cases the rescuers must physically grab the victim or cinch him with a rope and pull him upstream. If the rescuers can somehow break or reduce the force of the current against the victim, their job will be much easier. There have been several instances in which one group of rescuers waded in upstream of a foot-entrapment victim to create an eddy while another group performed the rescue.

Getting to the victim can be a problem. If the rescuers choose not to use a tag line rescue, they may be able to access the victim by wading or swimming; by lowering a rescue party down to the victim on a raft or boat (e.g., Telfer lower or other boat-based systems described in chapter 7); or by using an in-water technique like the fixed line and V-lower described in chapter 6.

Tag Line. Rescuers can establish a tag line to assist an entrapment victim in much the same manner as described for floating tag lines in chapter 5. It can be established for either stabilization or rescue, and can be applied to foot/body-entrapment victims, or to boat-pin situations. For instance, if a boat has not actually collapsed on the paddler's legs, then a tag line might be able to extricate him from a broached or vertically pinned boat. Likewise, for the foot-entrapment victim, you may be able to pull him far enough upstream, or provide enough of a hold, for him to be able to kick a pinned foot free. While these ideas are valid, we will discuss the tag line here primarily as a stabilization device to keep the victim breathing while we focus on shore-based extrication efforts.

In these situations rescuers normally use a bare line, although they might use a floating line or a weighted line if the situation dictated it. In practice, the rescuers normally bring the tag line up to the victim from the downstream side, so that he can drape his arms over it and lean his chest against it. Even if the victim cannot hear or see under a rooster tail of water, a stabilization tag line will provide a psychological boost by letting him know that someone is out there trying to help.

Because of the force of the water, you probably will need at least two to four rescuers on each shore to get the tag line taut enough to support the victim. Directional pulleys may help, as will body belays, but it takes a lot of muscle to be effective. If the rescue party is short-handed and there are suitable anchors, they may be able to tie off the stabilization line, or a least one end of it.

Snag Tag. Having established a stabilization line, we must find a way to free the entrapment victim. In some cases the stabilization line will also work as a rescue line, and in other cases we can use a surface line or a cinch to pull the victim upstream. In still other cases, however, the line has to be sunk underwater in an attempt to get under the victim or to work his foot out. It may be the only way to get a line under someone for a body recovery.

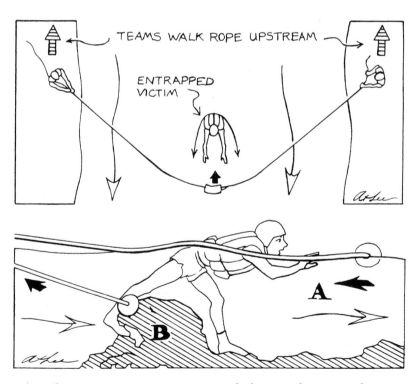

8.10 *The snag tag rescue. Rescuers on each shore get the snag tag line taut enough to support the victin (above). A conscious victim may be able to grab the rope (A). Rescuers may be able to work a second rope under his leg to free his foot (B).*

In this last case, a second line that is run shore to shore can be brought up under the victim's body and pulled in an upstream direction to snag the caught foot. The water pressure will create a **V** in the snag line and the victim (if he is conscious) can help direct the line downward. The victim's body will be fairly rigid as he braces against the stabilization line, so the snag tag will tend to slide downward along his body. Once the rope is at his foot, the rescuers can pull in an upstream direction to free it.

Adding a weighted object to the line may help rescuers to sink the line underwater. However, a weighted tag line takes coordination and a fair amount of physical strength to use effectively, and requires considerable setup time. It is a technique best used in situations where speed is not critical, such as snagging pinned boats or for body recovery. Controlling any snag tag line is difficult, but especially one with a weighted object, which jumps around in the current like a hooked marlin. To control it, each rope team needs a minimum of two people. Position the weighted object approximately 10' (3 m) upstream of the victim, then slacken the rope to allow the object to pass over the victim's head, sink, and land just downstream of him. The force of the current will push the weighted object downstream before it hits bottom. Being hit by it will be the least of the victim's worries.

Cinching Tag Line (Carlson Cinch). The rescue techniques we have described so far have not put a rope around the victim and actually cinched it down. A cinching rescue in swift water carries with it the risk of grave bodily injury, and so should be used with caution and only if other, better techniques won't work. However, a cinch does provide a positive hold on the victim. While most of the other techniques will free a victim, many will not hold him after he is freed.

West Virginia river guide and river safety instructor Glen Carlson developed a cinching variation of the tag line that has been widely adopted. It starts with a stabilization tag line as described above. Once this is in place, the rescuers send a second long line to the far shore in front of the victim. This line is clipped into a control line and passed back over to the near shore behind the victim and clipped back into itself. A second line on the near shore helps to control the tension of the loop around the victim (see figures 8.11.1 and 8.11.2). Using the control lines, the rescuers gradually cinch down on the victim until they are able to pull him upstream.

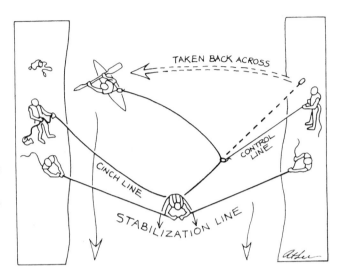

8.11.1 The Carlson cinch. The rescuers first set up a stabilization line, then pass the cinch line under the victim, attach a control line, and pass it back across the river behind him.

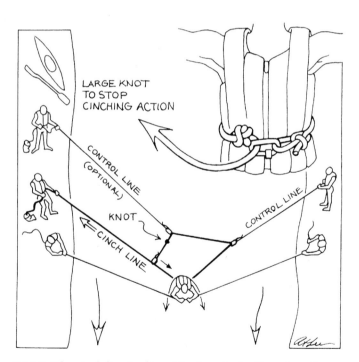

8.11.2 The cinch line is clipped back on to itself, and another control line attached. It is then cinched down on the victim so that he can be pulled back upstream. A stopper knot keeps the loop from cinching down too tightly.

To avoid overcinching and injury, the rescuers use the NOC Knot Trick: a stopper knot pre-tied approximately three to four feet from what will be the victim's end of the rope. As the line cinches down, the carabiner slides down the haul line until the knot stops it and creates a fixed-diameter loop for the victim.

Since we are often asked if there are any actual instances of paddlers being cut out of boats, we will end this chapter with an incident that happened several years ago on the Ocoee River. While cruising down the river, an ABS open canoe broached on a rock, entrapping the paddler. He was in no immediate danger—his head was above water and both the water and the day were warm. But the hull had collapsed on his leg, and had driven two bolts protruding under the seat into his ankle, literally nailing him into the boat.

After several attempts to unpin the boat and get the paddler free, the rescuers flagged down a passing carpenter on the nearby highway, borrowed his handsaw, and cut the boat in half just behind the paddler's seat. It then swung free of the rock, whereupon the rescuers pulled the pinned half of the canoe to shore and freed the paddler.

Bogart: *How'd you like it?*
Hepburn: *Like it?*
Bogart: *Whitewater rapids!*
Hepburn: *I never dreamed...*
Bogart: *I don't blame you for being scared—not one little bit.*
Nobody with good sense ain't scared of whitewater.
Hepburn: *I never dreamed that any mere physical experience*
could be so stimulating.

The African Queen

9

Boat Recovery

Extricating a pinned boat can be an interesting project—so long as there is no victim involved and the safety of the group does not depend upon success. Usually the damage has been done and there is little need for haste. Opinions can be exchanged, options weighed, and the time taken to make sure everyone understands the plan. If you have ten people in your group, you'll have at least twelve opinions about how the boat should come off. Try the simplest and safest methods first; go on to more complex systems if they fail. Often a combination of techniques works best.

Although all pinning situations are different, the recovery sequence is similar to that given for pinned boats in the previous chapter: assessment, stabilization, and extrication. During the assessment phase, think through the entire process. Analyze the forces acting on the boat (see the following section), make a plan, and be sure everyone understands it *before* you start. Organize the

168

9.1 Pinned! And solidly, too. Although the guide was unable to prevent the pin, he has gotten his crew safely out of the river.

9.2 The rescue crew moves in and begins to set up a Z-drag on some rocks in the center of the river. The haul line is attached to one of the submerged raft's thwarts.

9.3 Setting the anchor point on a very strong little tree, they haul away...

9.4 ...until the raft comes off.

site (i.e., upstream spotters to warn other boaters; downstream safety) as discussed in chapter 11. This is particularly important if you have ropes strung across the river that could "clothesline" a boater. Is this a dam-controlled river? Find out the release schedule and maybe all you'll have to do is wait until the water goes off.

While you're doing all this, stabilize the boat by tying it off. Boats have been known to head downstream on their own while their owners are arguing about how to recover them.

The Force of the Current

When recovering a boat, many people fail to consider the force and direction of the current. Time and again we have seen elaborate haul systems based on convenient anchor points or work areas rather than angle of pull. To some extent, of course, the direction of any pull is dictated by where you can anchor it, but the idea is to make the river work for you. First visualize your ideal angle of pull and *then* look for a suitable anchor point. Keep trying: it sometimes takes some trial and error, and often only a small change will make the difference.

9.5 A raft pinned against a bridge piling on Alaska's Nenana River. This photo makes obvious the equilibrium of forces holding the raft against the piling. (Jay H. Power)

9.6 To unpin the raft shown in figure 9.5, the rescuers pulled up on one end, after first cutting a small hole in the floor and passing a rope around the tube. This upset the force equilibrium enough for the water to pull the boat off. (Jay H. Power)

Remember a few simple guidelines:

- Avoid pushing or pulling directly against the current. There is a lot of force out there, and you want it working for you, not against you.

- Try to get the pinned craft away from the water, either by lifting it, by dumping the water out of it, or both.

- The water tends to create a force equilibrium on the pinned craft by pushing more or less equally on the parts of it that are in the water. Think of the boat as a seesaw with the obstacle being the fulcrum. If you can upset this equilibrium, sometimes by even a tiny amount, the craft will often wash off without further effort. If the pinned craft has retained most of its normal shape, it should come off fairly easily. The more deformed the boat is, the harder it will be to unpin.

- Do not blindly trust mechanical devices, no matter how powerful. A common mistake is to assume that the problem is simply not enough pull. Boats are not designed to be tugged on with several thousand pounds of force, and

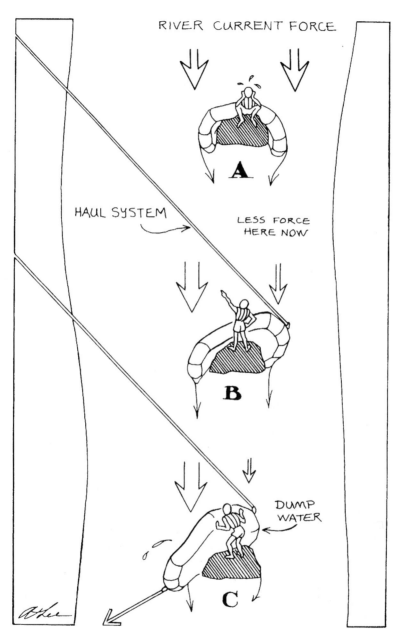

RIVER CURRENT FORCE

A

HAUL SYSTEM

LESS FORCE HERE NOW

B

DUMP WATER

C

9.7 The force of the water: In (A), the current pushes more or less equally on both ends of the pinned boat, wrapping it against the rock. Pulling at approximately a 45-degree angle to the current in (B) reduces the effective force against one side of the boat, causing the current to push the boat around to the other side of the rock (C). Pulling one end out of the water will do the same thing (see figures 9.5 and 9.6) a powered winch or a well set up haul system literally can pull a boat to pieces.

- Give some thought to what will happen once the boat comes off the obstacle. Watch the haul lines as the boat swings free so that they don't take out rescuers or spectators. Make sure the boat is securely tethered. We have seen boats take off downriver after being pulled free, much to the embarrassment of the rescuers. It's very easy to pull a boat off one obstacle only to have it pin even worse farther downstream.

Armstrong Techniques. If you can safely stand at the pin site, then this simple approach to boat retrieval is sometimes the best: grab it and growl! Before starting, study the shape of the rock and figure just how the boat is pinned. This will determine the place and direction for you to push or pull. Since most people's legs are stronger than their arms, it may be more effective to sit on the rock causing the wrap and push with your legs. As the boat shifts, be careful that you don't slip in between the boat and the rock.

9.8 The "armstrong" method will work in a lot of cases. Just grab the boat and start pulling. Give some thought to what will happen after the boat comes free.

In shallow water you may be able to lift one end of the boat up while pushing down on the other. Almost always you'll have to work from the highest end of the boat. With a raft you can sometimes "roll" the high end of the raft toward the low end, dumping the water in the process. Sometimes a simple lever, such as an oar or a tree limb, can be used to pry the boat off the obstacle. Consider sliding the boat sideways off the rock rather than pulling it upstream. It might even be to your advantage to push the boat downward if the rock structure is undercut and angled in a downstream direction.

With a pinned raft consider deflating one of the air chambers in the main tube to reduce the "bucketing" effect of the current and the amount of water trapped inside the raft. You can bleed air valves underwater without getting water in the tubes, as long as you can see a good stream of bubbles. When this stops be sure to close the valve; you do *not* want water in the tubes. If you have a self-bailing raft with a lace-in floor, you can unlace or cut the lacings of the floor to reduce the bucketing effect. With a raft having a glued-in floor, you can cut through it, but this is a last resort—it may free the raft,

9.9.1 Gaining access to a pinned craft can be difficult. The best place to start is usually the eddy behind it... (Glenn Oakley)

9.9.2 ...or the obstacle on which it is pinned. (Wiley-Wales)

but it will mean repair time later. Most pinned rafts can be freed without cutting the floor.

One group did everything possible to unpin a paddle raft at Lost Yak Rapid on the Bío-Bío River in Chile. They were about to give up when they deflated the last remaining thwart tube and, bingo!—the boat came free.

Rigging the Boat

While Armstrong methods will work in a surprising number of cases, in others the rescuers will have to rig a haul line to the boat, either to extend their reach, to get the right angle of pull, or in order to use a mechanical haul system. When we talk about "rigging," we mean how and where to attach the haul line and which way to pull. Often the hardest part of a boat recovery is simply getting the rope attached to the boat. In shallow rivers rescuers may be able to wade to the accident site. On narrow creeks a paddle hook might do the job. In faster, deeper water you will probably have to paddle or row into the eddy behind the accident site. In really steep drops you may have to set up a Telfer lower or a Tyrolean to attach the haul line.

Obvious points of attachment are thwarts on canoes; grab or broach loops on decked boats; and **D**-rings or rowing frames on rafts. These are, by themselves, of questionable strength for the amount of pull sometimes put on them. If possible, it's usually a good idea to spread the load (i.e., to two or more **D**-rings) by using a load-sharing anchor system such as a boatman's eight.

If the boat is severely pinned, it's sometimes better to wrap the haul line around it rather than attach the line to a single point. Two or three wraps work better than a single one. This hull wrap spreads the load over the whole boat. One quick method of encircling the boat or attaching a line to a raft thwart is simply to tie a carabiner to

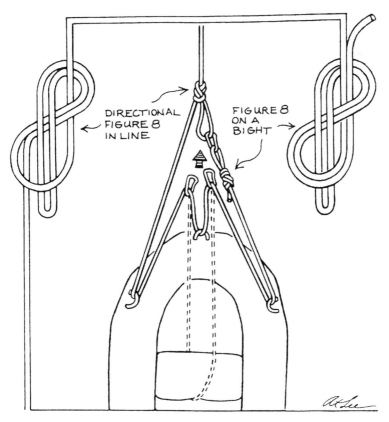

9.10 The boatman's eight makes a rudimentary load-distributing anchor, spreading out the load.

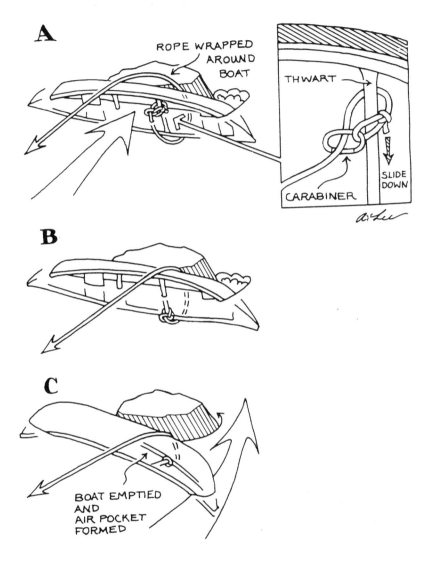

A

ROPE WRAPPED
AROUND
BOAT

THWART

CARABINER

SLIDE
DOWN

B

C

BOAT EMPTIED
AND
AIR POCKET
FORMED

9.11 A carabiner clipped into the end of a line to form a loop is a quick way to attach a line to a thwart.

the end of the line, pull it under and around the boat one or more times, and clip it back into the haul line or under a thwart. With self-bailing rafts, you can feed the rope through a drain hole and tie it around the tube. For rafts with fixed floors, you may have to punc-ture the floor with a hole big enough to feed the haul line through.

If the situation permits, several ropes pulling from different directions may be more effective than a single rope, and this also spreads the load over several attachment points. One solution is to use the main haul line to counteract the force of the current on the boat, and then use a second haul line to slide the boat sideways. Another line might then be used to flip the boat and to dump the water out of it.

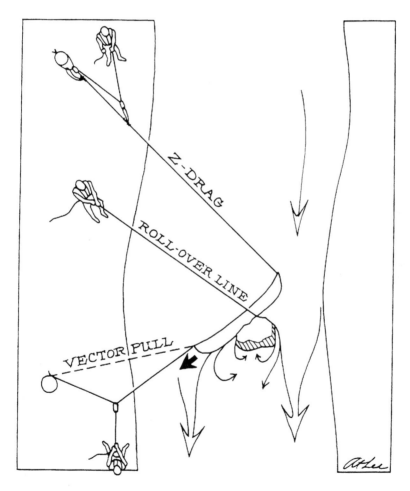

9.12 *Several haul lines are often more effective than a single one. Here a Z-drag is used to pull the boat away from the rock, while another line is used to roll the boat and dump the water. A third line slides along the face of the rock and into the eddy.*

The Roll-Over Effect. There are two forces acting on any pinned boat. One is the force of the current pushing the boat against the obstacle, and the other is the weight of the water trapped in the boat. Since water is heavy (8.33 lbs per gallon/62.4 lbs per cubic foot) and a swamped raft may trap several hundred gallons, this can be a substantial burden. Not only does this weight help keep the raft pinned on the rock, it makes it very difficult to control after it's been pulled off. Therefore it makes sense to dump as much of the water as possible.

Boats typically pin with the open side upstream and the bottom against the obstacle. If possible, you want to try and roll the boat over to dump the water as you pull it off the obstacle. If you attach the haul line to the lower part of the hull (to the low end of a thwart or a **D**-ring) and run it around the bottom of the hull and back to shore in an upstream direction, the craft will turn upside down as it is being pulled, dumping the water. This can also be done with a separate "roll-over" line.

With kayaks, you can clip into the broach loop, and pass the rope underneath and then over the hull. If the kayak doesn't have a broach loop, you can make a cradle rig of two loops of rope, each of which is smaller in diameter than the widest point of the boat. Slip these over both ends of the boat and connect them with a short tether, then attach the haul line to this tether (see figure 9.14).

While it is easy to say "attach the line to the lower part of the hull" it is often extraordinarily difficult in practice. Any watercraft

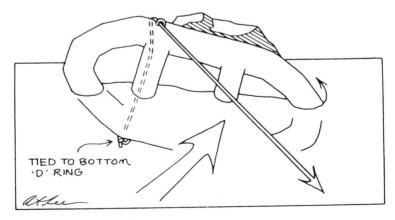

TIED TO BOTTOM
'D' RING

9.13 *Pinned boats should also be rigged to flip and dump the water as they're rolled out. (see figures 9.11 and 9.14)*

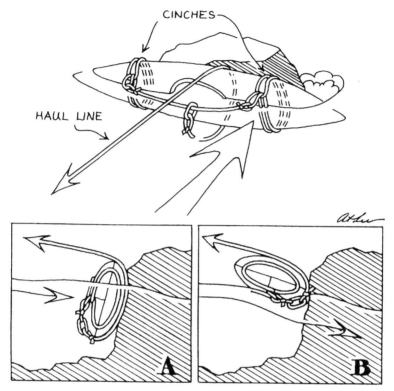

CINCHES

HAUL LINE

9.14 Use a cradle rig on boats without thwarts.

with thwarts (rafts or canoes) can use the Steve Thomas rope trick (see figure 9.15) to get the haul line in position. This ingenious procedure allows you to tie the knots above water and rotate them into position.

Taco Method. Sometimes a pinned raft can be recovered by using the "taco" method. This is a generic description for using one part of a raft as an anchor to pull another part of it either out of the water or far enough up to dump the water (or at least far enough to prevent more from coming in). With paddle rafts, the usual procedure is to pull the raft together end to end. With an oar or motorized raft, you can usually use the frame as an anchor to pull a submerged part of the raft. With really large motorized rafts stuck in the middle of a wide river, this may be the only available anchor.

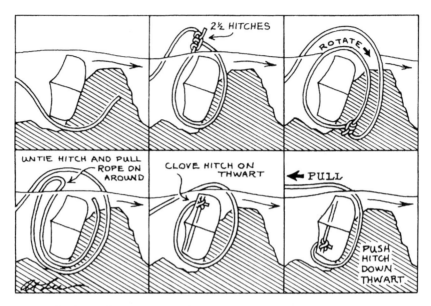

9.15 *The Steve Thomas rope trick.*

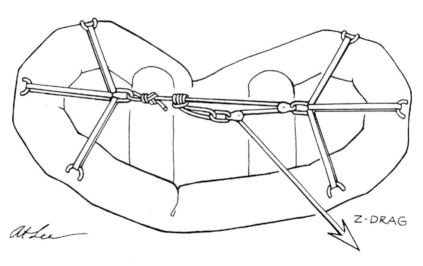

9.16 *The "Taco" method uses one part of the boat as an anchor to pull another part.*

Site Safety

The safety of the rescuers at a pin site must be the main consideration. All normal safety measures apply–the rescuers must wear life jackets and set upstream spotters and downstream safety.

When working around ropes and haul systems, the people on site should see that they do not straddle or get downstream of a loaded line or one that might become loaded if the boat washes off. They should be particularly careful to see that they do not get any part of their body wrapped in a bight of rope.

Working around pinned boats in swift water is risky and demands caution. The boat may shift at any time, but is especially likely to do so under tension from the haul line. Try not to get directly downstream of a boat when it's coming off–people have been run over this way.

When using a haul system, anyone not actually pulling should stand well clear: if a D-ring pops loose it can injure people. For the same reason, the people hauling on the rope should wear life jackets and helmets, and the first person hauling should face away from the load. Rescuers should also consider using a snubbing system on the haul line for backlash protection.

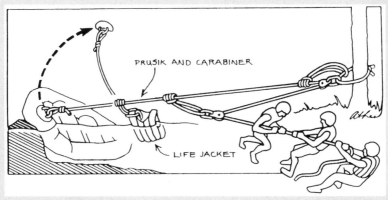

9.17.1 "Snubber" system on a haul line: if a D-ring pops off, attaching a light weight (a life jacket will do) in the middle of the haul line will cause the line and D-ring to follow the dashed line rather than snapping back directly toward the rescuers. The haul team wears life jackets and helmets, and the first hauler faces away from the load.

Basic Rigging Principles

So far we've discussed where and how to haul. Now it's time to look at the specifics of haul systems and anchors. A haul system allows us to put force on a haul line. Haul systems vary from a simple pull to complex mechanical-advantage systems. Integral parts of haul systems are the anchors that hold them and the knots that put them together. This is a complex subject: one we have tried to simplify as much as possible for river runners who use these systems only occasionally. A number of good books on the subject are listed in the bibliography.

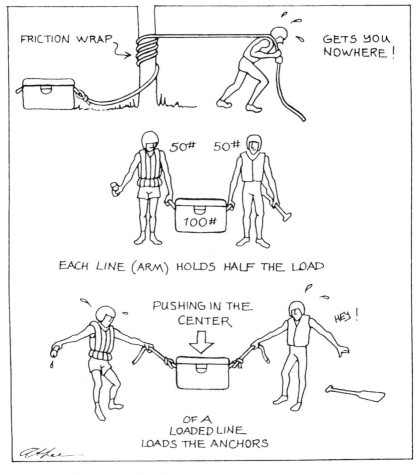

9.17.2 The three principles of rigging.

For our purposes, there are three basic principles of rigging:

- **First principle:** Wrapping a rope around something creates friction and spreads the load.

- **Second principle:** Multiple lines to the same object share the load.

- **Third principle:** Pushing or pulling at the center of a loaded line produces a lot of force on the ends.

Ropes. You should have a substantial rope to haul with. A good-quality low-stretch 7/16–1/2"(11–13 mm) nylon rescue rope works best, but many paddlers may be forced to use the stretchy polypropylene ropes usually found in throw bag ropes. Those who do should take the safety precautions outlined in the sidebar to prevent injuries if something pops loose. Spectra™-core throw bag ropes have also become popular in recent years, since they offer a reasonable combination of strength, low stretch, and compactness.

As a general rule of thumb, the components of a haul system have a safety factor of 4–5:1; that is, the weakest link should be four to five times as strong as the anticipated load. As a planning figure, a group of six adults pulling on a 3:1 Z-drag can generate about 1,000 lbf (454 kgf). River loads, however, are often difficult to estimate.

Knots. Knots keep things together. River runners sometimes can go a whole season without tying a knot. Learn as few as necessary, but well enough to tie them underwater on a howling, pitch-black night—because that's how you'll probably have to tie it. Any knot reduces the strength of the rope, so avoid unnecessary knots.

The figure-eight family of knots fills most river rigging requirements; if you don't learn any other knots, they will probably get you through. They are secure, easy to tie and untie, and easy to identify visually when tied incorrectly. Since variations of the same knot serve many different purposes, learning time is reduced.

FIGURE 8 FAMILY OF KNOTS

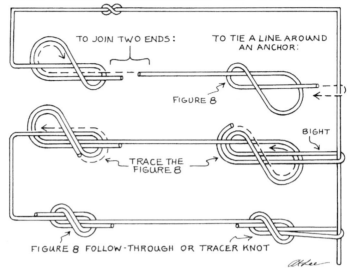

TO JOIN TWO ENDS:

TO TIE A LINE AROUND AN ANCHOR:

FIGURE 8

BIGHT

TRACE THE FIGURE 8

FIGURE 8 FOLLOW-THROUGH OR TRACER KNOT

9.18.1 *The figure-eight follow-through joins two ropes or forms a loop around something.*

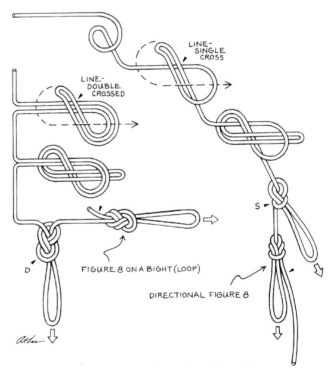

LINE-SINGLE CROSS

LINE-DOUBLE CROSSED

FIGURE 8 ON A BIGHT (LOOP)

DIRECTIONAL FIGURE 8

D

S

9.18.2 *The figure-eight on a bight makes a handy loop for clipping into; the directional eight allows a pull in one direction.*

9.18.3 *The double-loop figure-eight forms two loops for anchor back-ups, and can be used to make a load-adjusting anchor.*

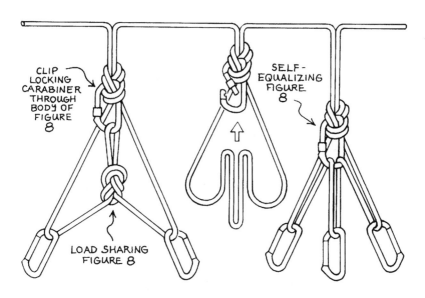

9.18.3 *Clipping a carabiner through the body of a figure-eight on a large bight makes either a load-sharing or a load-adjusting anchor.*

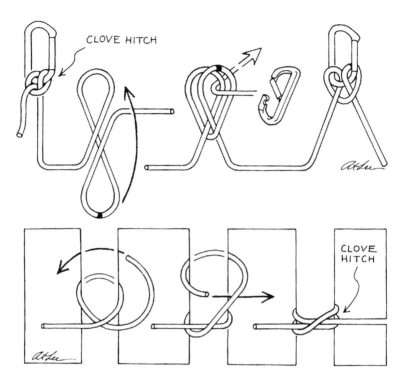

9.19 *The clove hitch makes for a quick tie-off when tied around a tree, a carabiner, or slipped over the wrist of a victim.*

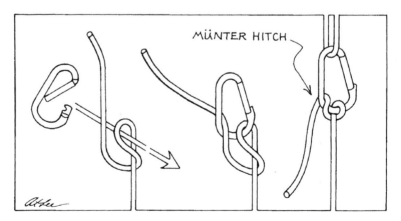

9.20 *The Münter hitch, tied with a large oval, locking carabiner, makes an excellent low-tech friction belay/rappel device.*

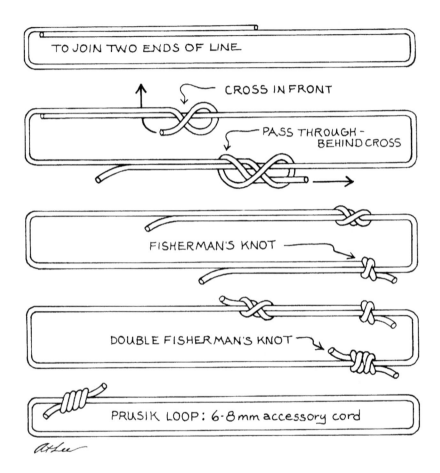

TO JOIN TWO ENDS OF LINE

CROSS IN FRONT

PASS THROUGH –
BEHIND CROSS

FISHERMAN'S KNOT

DOUBLE FISHERMAN'S KNOT

PRUSIK LOOP: 6-8 mm accessory cord

9.21.1 *The fisherman's knot adds security when tying off the end of another knot; the double fisherman's knot joins two pieces of rope or cord, but don't expect to get it apart once you load it.*

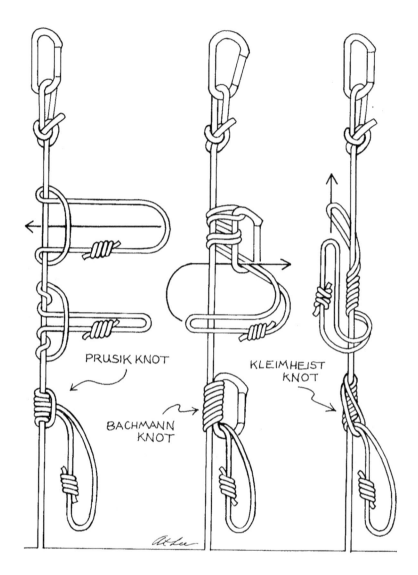

PRUSIK KNOT

KLEIMHEIST KNOT

BACHMANN KNOT

9.21.2 *The Prusik, Bachmann, and Kleimheist knots grip under load but will slide freely when unloaded; they are often used in ratcheting systems. The Prusik grips in either direction; the Bachmann (which incorporates a handy carabiner handle) and the Kleimheist (which can be tied with webbing) work in only one direction.*

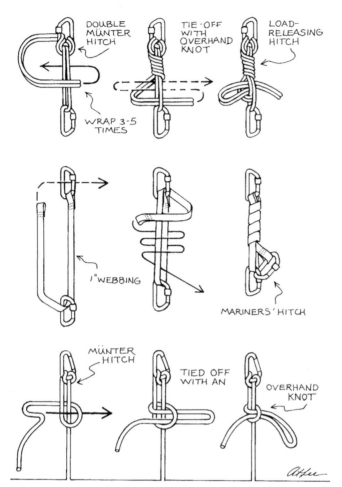

9.22 *If the system overloads you may have to release the load under pressure. The mariner's hitch (tied with webbing) and the load-releasing hitch (tied with 5/16" [8 mm] accessory cord) allow you to do this gradually.*

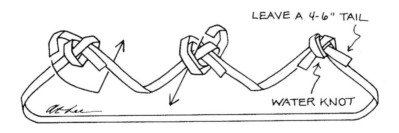

9.23 *The water knot joins two pieces of webbing.*

Anchors. Any haul system needs to be securely anchored, and this is where problems often develop. For example, one group of guides chose a marginal anchor and pulled a boulder over on one of their number.

A detailed discussion of anchors is beyond the scope of this book, but the principle is simple: find something that won't move and tie securely to it. The usual candidates are big rocks (BFRs) or big trees (BFTs). Some river runners carry a selection of rock-climbing nuts and camming devices made to fit tapered cracks. Sometimes you can use a small rock as a chock stone or even jam a knot into a crevice. Whatever anchor you select, ensure that it has no sharp edges, because unless you can clip directly to it (unlikely) you will have to put a sling or rope around it. If necessary pad it with clothing, life jackets, or other material.

An anchor sling can be made of rope or webbing, but it must be tied securely. One-inch tubular nylon webbing is the traditional material for slings: it is abrasion resistant and its flat profile allows it to be slipped through cracks between boulders more easily than rope. If you have enough webbing, several wraps around the anchor point are better than a loose sling. Don't use a girth hitch. Tie web slings with a water knot and place the knot on the inside to reduce the stress on it.

Use a high-strength tie-off for an anchor if you can. To tie it, wrap the rope three to five times around an object like a tree or post and clip or tie it back on itself. Any knot reduces the strength of the

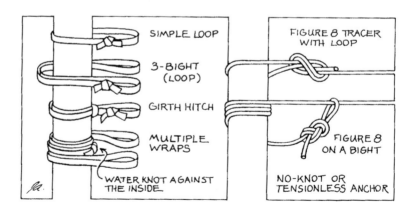

SIMPLE LOOP

FIGURE 8 TRACER WITH LOOP

3-BIGHT (LOOP)

GIRTH HITCH

MULTIPLE WRAPS

FIGURE 8 ON A BIGHT

WATER KNOT AGAINST THE INSIDE

NO-KNOT OR TENSIONLESS ANCHOR

9.24 *Anchors.*

9.25 The high-strength tie-off. (J.E. Weinel)

rope, but a high-strength tie-off (no-knot, tensionless anchor) avoids this by using friction, and so retains the full strength of the rope. If you use a post or tree as an anchor, tie in as low as possible to avoid making it into a lever.

Back up the anchor if possible. Unless you are sure that the anchor is bombproof, you should use two or more anchor points instead of one. Each one should be able to hold the entire load; if one fails the other will hold. Tying each loop of a double-loop figure-eight knot to a separate anchor is a convenient way to do this.

Sometimes you'll have to work with marginal anchors. Back East most rivers have trees on the banks, but out West you often have to anchor off to a miserable collection of sagebrush and loose rock. You'd like each of these dubious anchors to share the load. As stated in the second principle of rigging (assuming the tension to each is equal and the load does not shift direction), each added anchor point shares the load equally. For example: if there are two anchors, each bears half; with three each bears a third, and so on. A multipoint, load-sharing anchor (the cordelette) can be tied very simply by pulling out a loop from each anchor point and tying the loops together in a figure-eight or overhand knot. It is best to keep

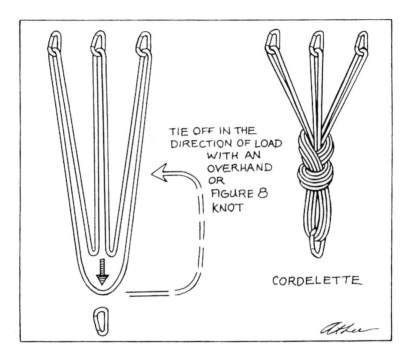

TIE OFF IN THE DIRECTION OF LOAD WITH AN OVERHAND OR FIGURE 8 KNOT

CORDELETTE

9.26 The cordelette can be used as a load-distributing anchor as long as the direction of pull doesn't change.

the cordelette as compact as possible (it takes 15–20'[4.5–6 m] of rope or accessory cord to tie one) and to extend tag lines to the anchors if necessary. Note that this arrangement does not self-adjust—if the angle of pull changes, some anchors will become more heavily loaded than others. Nevertheless the cordelette is quick and easy to tie, and will work in most situations.

There are times, however, when you know the angle of pull *is* going to change and you want a system that adjusts so that the load on the anchors stays more or less equal. If you have some webbing, you can rig a very simple two-point system (see figure 9.27). Be sure to include the twist in the webbing, or the carabiner will come off if one of the anchors fails. A simple multipoint, self-adjusting anchor can be rigged using a figure-eight on a bight with a locking carabiner clipped through the body of the knot. Tie the knot with a very big loop—big enough to clip through all the anchors, with enough left over to pull the rest into the carabiner in the knot (see figure 9.18.2).

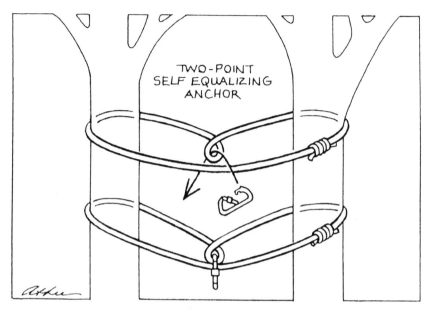

TWO-POINT
SELF EQUALIZING
ANCHOR

9.27 *Two point self-equalizing anchor.*

A FULL PULL ADVANTAGE

120%

120%

120%

60% 60%

120%

120%

9.28 *Pulling power: an adult can pull about 120% of his body weight with a body or shoulder belay, but only about 60% when pulling on a rope.*

One thing to remember with all multiple anchors is to keep the included angles of the anchors small—45° or less. If the angle is too large (120° or more) you'll end up with a vector pull between anchor points (the second principle of rigging), a condition that invites failure.

Use your imagination to create an anchor. On a sand beach, you might dig a trench and bury a "deadman" anchor. Small brush clumps of alder, sagebrush, or willow can be strong anchors if you run a sling around them at ground level.

Haul Systems

"Ten Boy Scouts" Method. This is the simplest haul system: a rope pull with no mechanical advantage. Attach the rope to the boat, find the best angle, and pull. If the boat doesn't move, just add more bodies. This is the most common method of hauling and is usually the thing to try first if you have a lot of people.

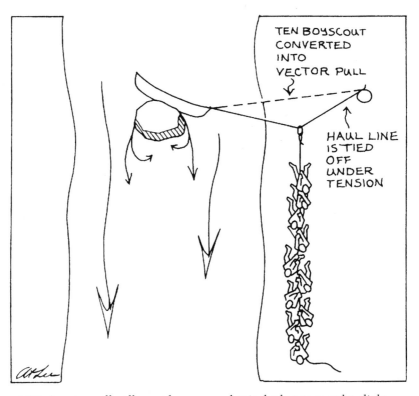

9.29 *A vector pull will provide some mechanical advantage and a slight change of direction.*

After extensive testing, Austrian engineer and paddler Peter Reithmaier found that the amount of pull a person could put on a haul line depended not so much on strength as weight and how they were able to grip the rope. A person who is able to use a shoulder or body belay can pull about 120 percent of his body weight, whereas one who simply grips the rope is limited to about 60 percent of body weight (see figure 9.28). Reithmaier suggests a harness or loop for each person to allow each puller to fully use his body. Another method is to place a series of directional figure eight loops on the haul line to make it easier to grip the rope.

Vector Pull. The vector pull utilizes the third principle of rigging: that pushing or pulling in the middle of an already taut line adds considerable force to the ends. In this case, it gives us "tree" mechanical advantage. The effectiveness of the vector pull falls off rapidly as the angle of the haul line decreases (i.e., from horizontal or 180°) and disappears entirely at 45°. The vector pull is easy to do and is the next logical step if a simple pull fails.

With your "ten Boy Scouts," haul as hard as you can, then tie off the line to an anchor point while keeping tension on it. Next, clip or Prusik a second line into the center of that haul line and pull it at 90° to it (see figure 9.29). You can just grab the line and pull it, but this puts you in a vulnerable position if something fails. The tighter you can get the haul line, the more effective the vector pull will be, which means that it is very effective with mechanical haul systems like the Z-drag. A vector pull also alters the direction of pull slight-

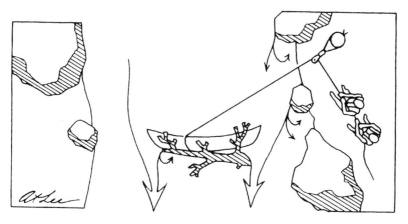

9.30 *A directional pulley will change the direction of pull but offers no mechanical advantage.*

ly. This might help the pinned boat come off, so try pulling in both directions.

Changing Direction. If the ideal path of your pull is blocked, you may have to place a directional pulley. A directional pulley does not enhance your pulling power (in fact it reduces it slightly), but it does change the direction of the pull. Any directional pulley must be firmly anchored, since the load on it may be up to twice that on the other anchors. If you're hauling on a bank, try placing the directional pulley uphill so that the haul crew is pulling in a downhill direction with their body weight.

Mechanical Advantage Systems. At some point in the recovery it may be necessary to use a mechanical advantage haul system. While these increase the force available, they also increase the complexity of the system and the amount of rope needed. It also becomes difficult to stop things from getting tangled when you use complicated systems, especially when using braided rope. For instance, with a 3:1 mechanical-advantage haul system, you will have to pull three feet of rope through the system to move the load one foot. It is often better to try a different angle of pull (or a vector pull) than to increase the pulling power.

It is again time to invoke the second principle of rigging—that multiple lines share the load. This principle applies to mechanical advantage as well as to anchors. If we attach a haul line to an anchor point on shore, then run it through a pulley attached to the pinned boat and back to shore (see figure 9.31), each "leg" holds half the load. Pulling on one leg, in effect, doubles the force of the pull, giving a 2:1 haul system. While this is about twice the power of a direct pull by a team, you must have enough rope to go to the pinned boat and back to shore, and enough acrobatic ability to feed a rope through a pulley on the pinned boat.

Do not confuse the mechanical-advantage pulley with the directional pulley, which offers no mechanical advantage at all. A quick and dirty rule for distinguishing the two is this: if the pulley moves, it provides mechanical advantage; if it does not, it is directional.

The mechanical advantages given here are theoretical; that is, they do not take friction into account. In the real world, each pulley decreases the available pull by 10 percent. A carabiner can serve as a pulley in a pinch, but it has a high friction coefficient. For example, the mechanical advantage provided by a theoretical 3:1 pulley

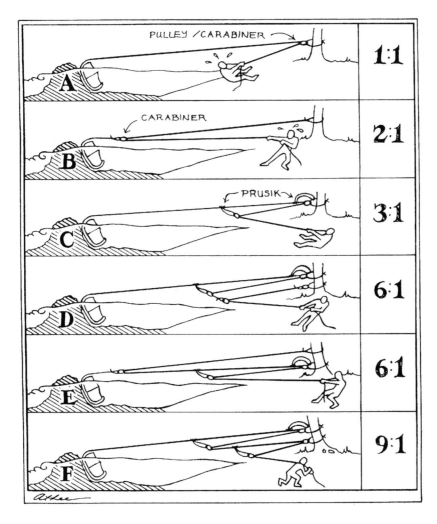

9.31 *Pulley systems can be rigged in various degrees of theoretical mechanical advantage from 1:1 to 9:1.*

system would actually be between 2.5:1 and 2.7:1 with pulleys, but only about 2:1 with carabiners.

Z-Drags. The haul system most familiar to river veterans is the **Z-**drag, a system that may be rigged for several ratios of mechanical advantage. A basic **Z**-drag gives a 3:1 mechanical advantage. It is

When using a haul system, it's often advantageous to set up a ratcheting system on the haul line. This allows team members to pull rope freely through the system when hauling, but holds the load when they stop. The most common way of doing this is to use a brake Prusik attached to the anchor. It's a good idea to attach this brake to the anchor with a knot that can be untied under load (e.g., mariner's hitch, load-releasing hitch).

The brake Prusik must be kept from jamming into the anchor pulley during normal hauling. This can be done either manually by a team member (make sure not to allow any loose clothing, hair, or fingers to feed into the pulley) or automatically with a Prusik-minding pulley. Another expedient solution is to use a Bachmann instead of a Prusik as the brake. Because a carabiner is incorporated into the hitch, it is less likely to jam. You can also use a very short Prusik.

An alternative to the brake Prusik is a separate belay line to maintain tension on the pinned craft.

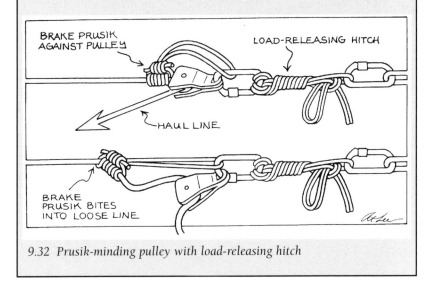

9.32 Prusik-minding pulley with load-releasing hitch

quite flexible, easily integrated with other systems, and can be set up quickly with a minimum of equipment.

To set up a **Z**-drag, first attach the haul line to the pinned boat, figure the ideal angle of pull, and then locate an anchor point. Attach a pulley to the anchor (the "anchor" pulley) and run the haul line from the pinned boat through it and back toward the load.

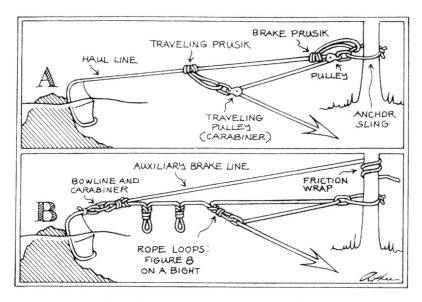

9.33 *Two types of simple Z-drag. Type A uses a Prusik knot to slide down the haul line, while type B uses a series of rope loops. Type B requires a separate belay line to hold the load while the line is reset to the next loop.*

Attach another pulley (the "traveling" pulley) to the haul line with a Prusik and run the rope through this and back to shore. If you need to be able to hold the load between pulls, rig a brake Prusik attached to the anchor (see figure 9.33).

When hauling, pulling in a direct line between the pinned craft and the anchor point greatly improves efficiency. As the pinned craft moves (and your rope stretches) the traveling pulley advances toward the anchor pulley. At some point it will have to be reset by sliding it back down the haul line; the brake Prusik holds the load while this is being done.

Z-drags can be "stacked" or combined with other haul systems. For example, a 3:1 Z-drag pulling another 3:1 Z-drag (the "double Z-drag") gives a 9:1 mechanical advantage. A Z-drag can also be stacked on top of the 2:1 pulley system previously described.

A Z-drag may be improvised with very little equipment. If you don't have Prusiks, tie a series of knots in the haul line, and substitute a carabiner for the anchor and traveling pulleys. In an emergency you can even dispense with the traveling carabiner. Since you don't have a brake Prusik, you'll have to use a separate belay line to hold the load while you reset from loop to loop. This is not the most efficient setup, but it will work after a fashion.

The Z-drag seems complicated at first, but with practice it can be set up and used quickly, and it has other practical applications—like pulling your stuck shuttle car out of the mud on the takeout road.

Piggyback, or "Pig" Rig. The piggyback, or "pig" rig, has been used for some time by search-and-rescue teams. It gives a greater mechanical advantage (4:1) than the basic Z-drag, while using the same amount of hardware. The big advantage of the pig rig is that it can be switched from one haul line to another without losing tension. If you must pull first on one haul line and then another, this is the system to use.

The pig rig is simply two 2:1 haul systems set on top of each other to give a 4:1 pull. To set it up, establish an anchor point and run a haul line out to the boat. Set a belay at the anchor point, (e.g., Münter hitch, friction belay). You will need someone to monitor the belay and take up the slack. Then set up a 2:1 haul system by anchoring the haul line to shore, attaching a pulley to the haul/belay line, and running the haul line through it and back to shore. Now

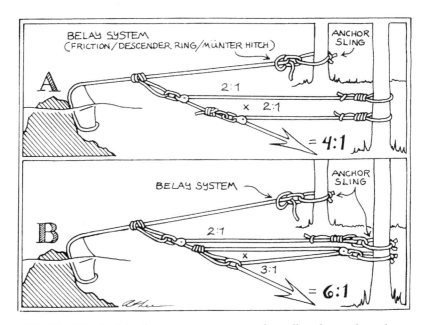

9.34 The "Pig Rig" haul system. System A works well with two throw bags, while B gives a greater mechanical advantage but requires a longer rope. Either can be detached quickly from the haul line and moved elsewhere.

duplicate the system, using the same anchor. The resulting 4:1 haul system and the haul/belay line are completely separate, so the haul system can then be moved to another line if necessary. If you attach a **Z**-drag to the first haul line instead of a 2:1 system, you have a 6:1 system.

Mechanical Winches. Winches are handy gadgets and can save the hassle of setting up a **Z**-drag. Rafters carry them in some areas of the country and they may be available if a rescue unit is on the scene. These include ratchet-type "come-alongs" as well as drum-type sailing winches. These last are expensive, but a single operator can haul loads of more than 2,500 pounds. A typical two-speed rescue winch can develop a high-speed advantage of 15:1; 40:1 at low speed.

Improvised Haul Systems

The Tonsmiere Tug. This ingenious, low-tech haul system was invented under dire circumstances by two veteran Idaho river run-

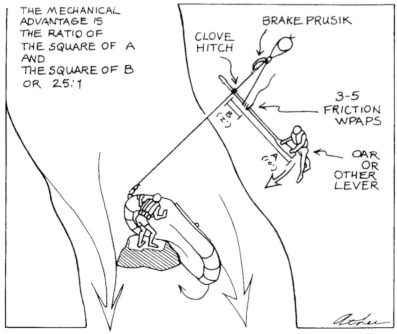

9.35 *The Tonsmiere Tug, born of necessity, is elegant in its simplicity.*

Passing a Knot

If you don't have a long rope, you may have to join two ropes (e.g., throw bags) for your Z-drag. If so, you will probably have to pass a knot through it. This is not an insoluble problem if you prepare for it. First, use a secure, compact knot like the double fisherman's to join the rope, even though you'll probably have to cut it apart when you finish. Second, have an extra long Prusik and anchor sling ready.

When the knot reaches the traveling Prusik, you'll have to hold the load with the brake, undo the traveling Prusik, and move it past the knot. Then pull again until the knot reaches the brake Prusik. Put the long

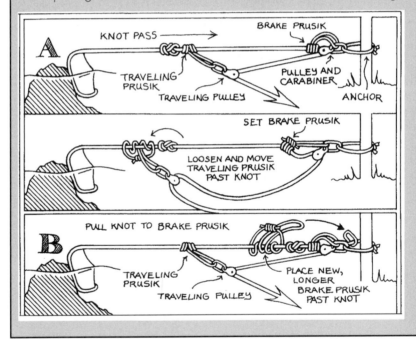

ners whose boat was severely pinned on the Owyhee River. Their choice was simple: free the boat or walk a hundred miles.

Establish an anchor point with a brake Prusik (the original model used vise grips) coming off the sling to the haul line. Attach the haul line to the boat, then tie a clove hitch near the handle end of the lever (an oar or stout pole) between the brake Prusik and the boat. Run the haul line through the anchor pulley (or carabiner) and wrap the tail of the haul line several times around the lever. As seen

Prusik on the haul line behind the knot and remove the old brake Prusik. Haul the knot down against the anchor pulley and set the brake Prusik. Now tie the new (longer) anchor sling. Move the pulley past the knot and clip it to the new anchor sling. The new anchor sling must be longer to get the pulley past the knot. Now pull tension again until the knot moves past the brake pulley. Pull again until the knot reaches the traveling pulley, set the brake, and move the pulley past the knot.

You're done!

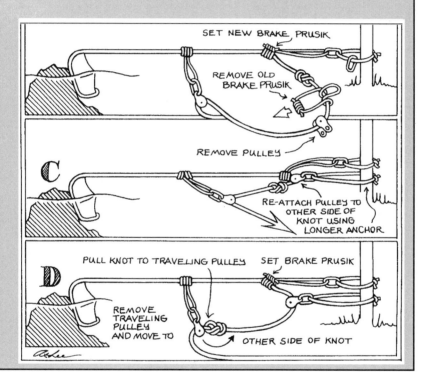

in figure 9.35, the oar becomes a powerful lever. The greater the distance between the wraps and the clove hitch, the longer the effective lever and the bigger the mechanical advantage. For example, if you use a ten-foot oar and the distance from the clove hitch to the wraps is two feet, this gives a 25:1 advantage. As the boat advances, or the rope stretches, set the brake Prusik to hold the load, then reset the wraps and start again. Beware of breaking oars with this system!

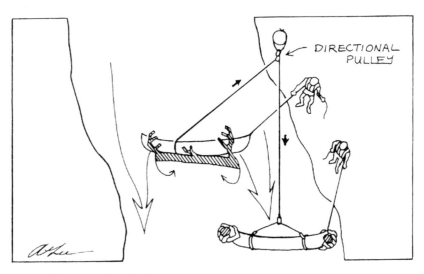

DIRECTIONAL PULLEY

9.37 The sea-anchor haul system.

Sea-Anchor Haul System. This ingenious haul system was suggested to us by an Alaska wilderness guide. It utilizes the power of the river on one boat to unpin another. Attach a haul line to the pinned craft, then rig a directional pulley upstream of it to give the correct angle of pull. Note that this directional pulley will have to hold *double* the system load.

Run the line to where the sea anchor will be set up. Originally, this was a swamped open canoe. Attach the boat to the haul line with a cradle rig so that the hull holds the load. If you tie to the thwarts, you will probably break or bend them. The rescuers will have to wade out and maneuver the overturned canoe into the current to load the system. If the current on the sea-anchor canoe is equal to or greater than the current holding the pinned boat, the boat should come off the obstacle.

A variation of this system is to use an oar boat instead of a swamped canoe. The current hitting the greater surface area of a raft, pushed farther down in the water by the extra weight of the cargo, generates a lot of force. Passengers and crew can stand in the upstream end of the raft so that current is hitting the tubes as well.

Both the pinned canoe and the sea-anchor craft should have backup belay ropes to ensure their timely return to shore. Since

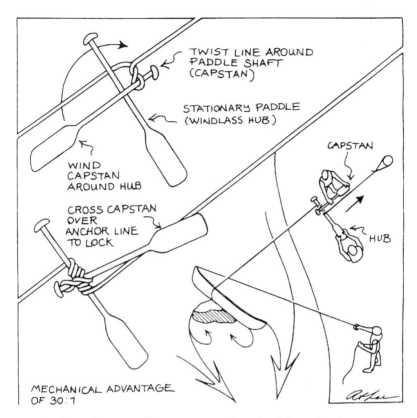

TWIST LINE AROUND
PADDLE SHAFT
(CAPSTAN)

STATIONARY PADDLE
(WINDLASS HUB)

CAPSTAN

WIND
CAPSTAN
AROUND HUB

CROSS CAPSTAN
OVER
ANCHOR LINE
TO LOCK

HUB

MECHANICAL ADVANTAGE
OF 30:1

*9.38 The paddler's windlass generates a lot of pull but is hard on paddles.
It is not well suited to long pulls.*

there is some danger of losing or pinning the canoe serving as the
sea anchor, try other boat-retrieval methods first.

The Paddler's Windlass. This is a capstan-type winch that has been
used since ancient times. One paddle is needed to stand in a vertical
position to serve as the hub, or capstan. The **T**-grip of a second paddle is fitted into a bight on the haul line. The haul line is then pulled
tight and tied off to an anchor. The second paddle is held parallel to
the haul line and is cranked around the shaft of the capstan. This
windlass creates a theoretical mechanical advantage of 30:1.

Oh to be rescued
from above,
On the wings
of a dove
Traditional

10

Vertical Rescue

In a vertical rescue, the rescuer is lowered to the accident site rather than approaching it from river level. This is usually a technique of last resort, because of the time required to organize equipment and manpower, and because of the exposure to the rescuer.

Yet there are times when a vertical rescue is best. If the water is too heavy for boat-based or swimming rescues, or if there are no eddies, a high-line traverse may be the only way to reach a victim. For accidents on bridge pilings, a simple rope lower can be a very fast and effective rescue method.

Helicopters may also be used for vertical rescue, but these, too, must be considered a last resort, for reasons that will be discussed later in this chapter.

Safety Considerations

We will cover a number of techniques in this chapter normally associated with climbing and mountaineering. Because of the river orientation of this book, and because there are a number of excellent books already written about them, we have deliberately limited the

10.1 A direct bridge lower on the Ocoee. The victim is given a rope loop and pulled up by simple manpower. A backup belay line would have been a good idea. (Helen Mary Johnson)

depth of treatment here. This chapter is intended to orient rescuers to existing techniques and show how river applications differ from conventional practice. Before attempting any of these techniques on your own, we strongly recommend that you get professional training.

Many of the techniques covered in this chapter involve using a lifeline; that is, a rope with a live person (maybe you) hanging from it. Because of this, considerably more caution is in order when setting things up, and the choice of equipment, particularly rope, becomes much more critical than for simple hauling or lowering tethered boats. With the ropes recreational paddlers normally have with them on the river, safety margins for vertical rescue are likely to be less than ideal.

There are many things that cause a rope to lose strength—knots, wear, age, and ultraviolet deterioration, to name only a few. Since it is difficult to figure all these things directly, riggers customarily build in a safety factor—an arbitrary ratio to the rope manufacturer's stated maximum load at failure—to account for all the negative variables. For lifelines, it is usually 10:1. In practical terms, this means that the working load of the rope should be no more than one-tenth its rated maximum. In the case of the 3/8"(9.5 mm) Spectra™-core rope now carried by many river runners, the rated maximum is 4,500 lbs (2,041 kgf), so the working load would be no more than 450 lbs (204 kgf). This is adequate, however, for raising or lowering two people at a time.

High lines or Tyroleans are even harder on rope. When we stretch a tensioned line across the river and hang someone from it, it creates a vector pull (the third principle of rigging) that really loads the rope and anchors. While short high lines can be set up with a braided polypropylene rope (we've done it), a much better choice is to use a good low-stretch nylon rescue rope.

Vertical rescues on the river do tend to be somewhat less dangerous than those in climbing, however, since the rescuer is generally operating over water and is rarely more than fifteen feet off the surface. Riggers must, however, give some thought to what will happen if a rescuer ends up in the water. He must be able to get free of the rope, either by cutting or releasing it.

Rappelling

Rappelling is a quick way to reach a victim below you. He may be entrapped at the base of a cliff or in a boat wrapped around a bridge piling. While rappelling can be done with just one person and a minimum of equipment, it is dangerous and requires training and practice. There are a number of rappelling accidents every year in the rescue and climbing communities. One of the most common problems is the rappeller's hair or clothing getting pulled into the friction device. This being the case, paddlers should reserve "free" or "hanging" rappels for emergencies or leave it to those with a rescue or climbing background.

Rappelling can be quite useful, however, to safely control your descent down a steep embankment. If the bank isn't too steep, a simple "scurry line" will suffice for people to hold when they go up and down the bank, but if it's really steep you may want to use a rappel when going down the bank.

The simplest method of rappelling is the Dülfer wrap (hot seat, body rappel; see figure 10.2). It is easy to set up and requires no extra equipment, but it is not very secure—the rescuer can unwrap

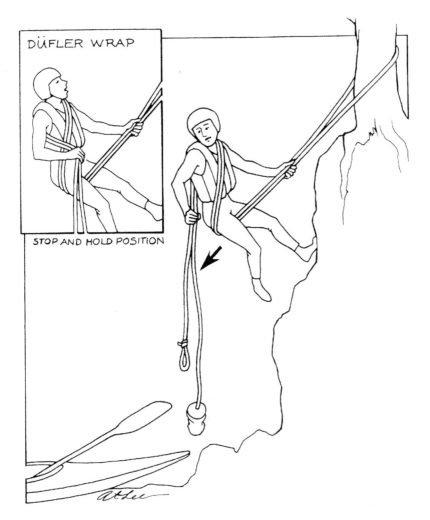

10.2 The Dülfer wrap, while uncomfortable and somewhat chancy, requires no special equipment other than a rope.

and fall. The Dülfer is not recommended for free (or hanging) rappels, but works well to assist someone down a steep bank.

You can use a throw bag rope for the Dülfer, but a thicker rope is easier on the body. Pass the rope around an anchor point (such as a tree) and then back down to where you're going. Double the rope if possible: it increases friction and comfort, and you can retrieve the rope by pulling on one end after you reach the bottom. Run the rope between your legs, around a thigh to the outside, and then diagonally across your chest, over the shoulder, and down across your back to the side of your waist. The uphill hand guides the rope and helps you maintain your balance while the downhill hand acts as the brake and controls the rate of descent. Pulling the right hand into your stomach will stop you. Face uphill, spread your legs in a wide stance, and slowly walk backward down the hill. Wear your life jacket and wetsuit (and gloves if you have them), to reduce friction burns. Your helmet will protect you against rockfall.

To increase control, add a friction device to the rope; to increase your security, use an improvised sit harness (see figures 10.3, 10.4, and 10.5). The friction device lets you control the amount of friction on the rope—and therefore the rate of your descent. You can use one designed for the purpose (i.e., figure-eight descender) or you can improvise one. A Münter hitch will work, as will a brake bar descender made from carabiners (see figure 10.15). The amount of available friction can be increased by doubling the rope, or, with the brake bar, by adding another carabiner across the path of the rope.

10.3 Three steps in tying a simple seat harness. First, make a loop of rope as long as the distance from one shoulder to the opposite outstretched finger, and tie it with a double fisherman's knot.

10.5 *Finally, clip the three loops together, using a locking carabiner or two carabiners with the gates reversed.*

10.4 *Then pull it into three loops, one around each hip and one under the crotch.*

Rescuers can add greatly to the safety of rappels by using a separate backup belay rope to the rappeller. However, this does require more rope and people, and the belay rope can twist with the rappel rope on long free rappels. Another common safety measure is for the rappeller to use a Prusik coming from his harness to the rappel line. He holds the Prusik with his guide hand to keep it from gripping. If he loses control, he releases the Prusik, which then grips the rope and (hopefully) stops him. This technique, while useful, is not foolproof.

There are a couple of other tips for improving the safety of rappels:

- Tie a "stopper" knot at the bottom of the rope to keep from rappelling off the end.

- Keep spectators away from your anchor point so they are less likely to kick debris on you.

- Keep a Prusik (or two) in your pocket in case you have to unweight the descender to get hair or clothing out of it.

- Carry a safety knife (beware, however, of using an open blade around a loaded rope).

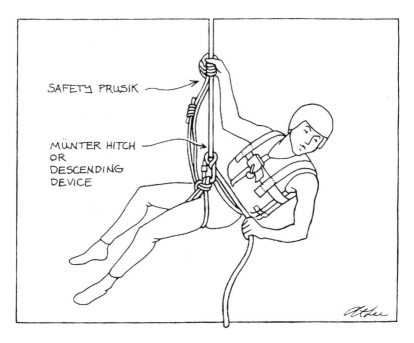

SAFETY PRUSIK

MÜNTER HITCH
OR
DESCENDING
DEVICE

10.6 A Münter hitch set up with a large, locking, pear-shaped carabiner, makes a simple improvised rappel device. A safety Prusik offers some back-up, but is not foolproof.

Bridge Rescues

A good example of a bridge rescue is one that occurred at Powerhouse Rapid on the Ocoee River in the fall of 1982. A paddler broached his open canoe on the central bridge support (which has since been removed). As the boat wrapped, his left foot became entangled in the webbing of the thigh straps. He could not free himself, although he was able to breathe periodically by doing pull-ups on the gunnel. The force of the water made this difficult and he was tiring rapidly (see figures 10.7–10.12).

By good fortune, a group of professional river guides were just upstream and quickly responded to the situation. A rescuer tied herself into a rope and climbed down the bridge girders to the victim. She was belayed by a friction wrap around the bridge railing. The rescuer's first action was to tie off the victim with another line from above to keep his head out of the water. Next she cut the tangled

10.7 *Ocoee Bridge rescue, October 1982. John Norton, an Atlanta canoeist, was rescued by Karen Berry and a group of guides from High Country, an Atlanta-based outfitter. Norton's left foot became entangled in the thigh strap webbing of his canoe as it broached on the bridge piling at Powerhouse rapid. Norton could breath only by pulling up on the gunnels. (Photo sequence by Jeff Ward)*

10. 8 *The rescuers first attempted to free Norton by lowering a rope to him. When this failed they lowered Berry to the broached canoe.*

10.9 *First, Berry tied a stabilization line to Norton's wrist, to ensure that his head would remain above water.*

10.10 *Then she cut the thigh strap, releasing Norton...*

10.11 ...who was then pulled up on a shelf of the bridge piling in the eddy
behind his pinned canoe.

10.12 Finally, Berry rigged a sit
harness for Norton, who was
then raised by simple manpower.

thigh strap to release the paddler, who by this time was becoming disoriented from fatigue and incipient hypothermia, and moved him onto a small shelf on the lower part of the bridge piling. She then rigged a leg-loop harness for the paddler, and he was pulled to the top of the bridge by sheer manpower. The elapsed time of the rescue was about fifteen minutes.

The rescuers could have used other methods, but in this case a direct vertical lower was faster and more expedient, since there were plenty of people available to haul on the rope. As with most river rescues, speed was the overriding consideration. Fortunately, the rescuers were professional guides used to working together, and this made the organization of the rescue much easier.

Raising and Lowering. Vertical raisers and lowers use many of the techniques already discussed. Raising is done with the same haul systems used in boat recoveries. If there are not enough people for the Armstrong haul mentioned in the above example, consider a **Z**-drag or other haul system, such as a winch. An automobile might also provide the necessary power, but must be used carefully. How you rig a bridge raise will be dictated to some degree by the design of the superstructure of the bridge and the number of people available to help. Since most accidents occur on the upstream side of the

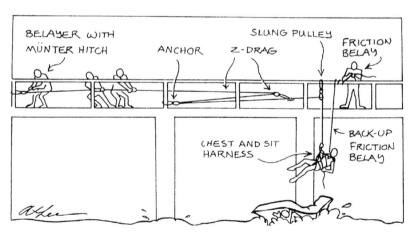

10.13 This bridge lower system uses a Z-drag belayed by a Münter hitch. The distance between Z-drag anchor and the slung pulley should be as great as possible in order to avoid having to reset the Z-drag. A backup belay line provides additional security.

bridge abutment, you will probably want to rig the haul system on the downstream side of the bridge to provide some working room.

When raising and lowering a live load, a few extra precautions are in order. If possible, always back up the haul line with a separate belay line to the rescuer. You can use a simple friction wrap or Münter hitch for belaying, rigged on the upstream bridge railing so that the belayer can observe the dangling rescuer. Have the haul team raise slowly so that a rescuer can work the rope back through the Münter hitch or friction wrap as he comes up. Try to keep slack out of the belay line.

Edge protection is critical: a rope can easily be damaged or even cut if loaded and drawn over a sharp or abrasive surface. The heavier the load, the greater the concern with edge protection. Some bridges have smooth railings over which a rope will slide smoothly; others have sharp edges that must be padded with life jackets, clothing, or anything else that will keep the rope from abrading or cutting. An even better solution, if the bridge structure allows it, is to sling a pulley for the haul line. This protects the rope and reduces friction at the same time.

Lowering is done with a friction device. Sometimes part of the bridge structure itself, such as a railing, can be used for a friction wrap to make the lower smooth and slow. If not, a suitable friction device like a Münter hitch or a carabiner brake can quickly be improvised. Depending on the amount of friction needed, the carabiner brake can be either single or double.

When organizing a bridge lower/raise, consider also the following:

- The rescuer to be lowered should be one of the lightest and most athletic of the party. A climber would be a good choice. He (or more likely, she) should have a knife, helmet, and life jacket as well as appropriate thermal protection.

- Rig a simple sit harness for the rescuer. This can be fashioned from rope or webbing. While not particularly comfortable, it is quick to tie and relatively secure. A chest harness increases both comfort and safety (see figure 10.16), but don't lower a rescuer by a chest harness alone. Some life jackets have integral chest harnesses and can be used with a sit harness.

10.14 The bridge lower. The rescuer uses the sit harness shown in figures 10.3, 10.4 and 10.5. The lowering rope is run through a slung pulley (actually two carabiners with the gates reversed) on the bridge structure. She is lowered by running the rope around the bridge railing to provide enough friction for a smooth descent. Ideally there should be a backup belay rope. The rescuer carries an auxiliary line with her.

OPPOSED
CARABINERS

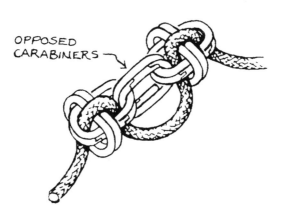

10.15 Carabiner brake. Depending on the amount of friction needed, a carabiner brake can be either double (shown here) or single.

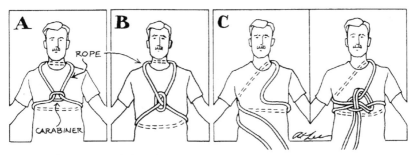

10.16 *Three types of chest harness.*

- Teamwork is critical, since the haul/lowering team often can't see what's going on. Make sure that someone can see the entire operation, and that a leader is in place to direct the various groups.

Once the victim has been freed, both he and the rescuer must be raised to safety. Since most of the systems mentioned here are suitable only for raising and lowering one person, it's best to raise one at a time. Unless the patient needs constant attention, he should be raised first. If the victim is seriously injured and needs to be raised in a litter, you probably will have to wait for a rescue unit.

Tyrolean and High Line Rescues

The terms Tyrolean and high line describe overhead rescues based on a rope stretched above the river. These shore-based rescues can be used to get a rescuer near enough to attach a line to the victim or the boat; to move a rescuer or victim across a river; or to pick up a victim from a midstream position and move him to the banks.

These rescues are dangerous: if the rope or another component breaks, or if an anchor point fails, it means a fall onto the rocks or into the water. Even if the water cushions the fall the rescuer still may become entangled in the ropes. Because of the danger to the rescuer, the time and training required to set it up, and the amount of equipment and manpower involved, the Tyrolean is a technique to be considered only if simpler methods aren't feasible.

The quality and strength of the rope are more critical for Tyroleans than in any other rescue application. A good 7/16–1/2" (11–13 mm) low-stretch nylon rescue rope is a must. Rafters or rescue squads may have these, but what do kayakers do? If the situa-

10.17.1 A cross-river high line or Tyrolean. (Glenn Oakley)

tion dictates, they might choose to use a 3/8"(9.5 mm) Spectra for emergency, short-span situations.

As in bridge lowers, the rescuer going out on the Tyrolean should be light and athletic, and if possible have climbing experience. In addition to the necessary harnesses, he should be equipped with a helmet, a life jacket, and a knife.

Rescuers should avoid overtensioning a high line. Remember that pulling on the center of a tensioned line (a vector pull) produces a heavy load on the anchors. A very rough generalization is to keep a sag (that is, the amount the line droops below horizontal) of at least 10 percent. For a hundred-foot line, this would be a sag of ten feet. The anchors on a high line must be high strength (e.g., a tensionless hitch around a tree) and located as high as possible to allow adequate sag for the main line.

Ranger Crawl. This is the simplest form of a Tyrolean—and the most dangerous to the rescuer. It is quick to set up and requires a minimum of equipment. The rescuer simply crawls along a tensioned line. A variation of the ranger crawl uses two parallel lines. In both cases, others in the rescue party can slowly release a belay wrap or

10.17.2 A single line ranger crawl. (Roger Phillips)

10.17.3 A dual line ranger crawl. (Jay H. Power)

Münter hitch at one end of the line to lower the rescuer into position (this means he must crawl uphill to get back to shore). Use the ranger crawl only when falling means no more than getting wet.

Drooping High Line. The drooping high line is extremely simple. Here the rescuer is attached directly to the overhead track line with a pulley. He is pulled into position over the accident site by tag lines, then raised and lowered by slackening and retensioning the track line. This system can be simplified even further by eliminating the tag lines and having the rescuer pull himself out along the track line in the same manner as the Tyrolean traverse used in mountaineering.

There is a fixed anchor on one side, and on the other a fixed anchor with a haul system integrated into it so the track line can be tensioned. To allow the track line to be locked off and provide a safety belay, there is a secondary anchor system on the track line with a tandem Prusik setup. During raising and lowering, a team member "minds" the Prusiks, keeping them from gripping. If the track line starts to drop, he jams the Prusiks tight, holding the track line. The rescuer wears a sit harness and attaches himself to the main line pulley with a short webbing or Prusik cord loop. The tag lines are clipped into this loop.

In operation, the line is tensioned by the haul team until it's high enough, the Prusik belay is set, and then the rescuer is pulled out over the accident site. When raising and lowering, the tandem Prusik setup provides a *backup* safety belay, but the track line is actually held in tension by the haul team. When the rescuer reaches the right position, the haul team pulls enough tension to allow the Prusik belay to be loosened, then gently slackens the rope. To bring the rescuer back, the process is reversed.

When tensioning a drooping high line, use the following approximations:

- Six people can pull a 1/2"(13 mm) rope with a 3:1 Z-drag without overtensioning it.

- With a 7/16"(11 mm) rope, six people should pull with a 2:1 system. These figures assume a steady pull by average adults using gloves, with no jerking or "heave-hos."

Rope Ladder Rescue. This variation of the Tyrolean uses a fixed track line of 7/16"(11 mm) or greater, and includes a rope ladder for the

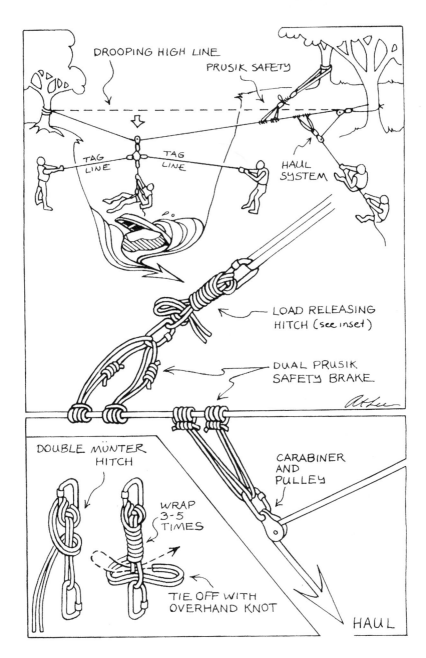

DROOPING HIGH LINE

PRUSIK SAFETY

TAG LINE

TAG LINE

HAUL SYSTEM

LOAD RELEASING HITCH (see inset)

DUAL PRUSIK SAFETY BRAKE

DOUBLE MÜNTER HITCH

WRAP 3-5 TIMES

TIE OFF WITH OVERHAND KNOT

CARABINER AND PULLEY

HAUL

10.18 *The drooping high line. The rescuer is moved up and down simply by tensioning or slackening the main line with a haul system. The dual Prusik brake acts both to set the tension on the line and as a safety when raising and lowering. Tag lines move the rescuer back and forth.*

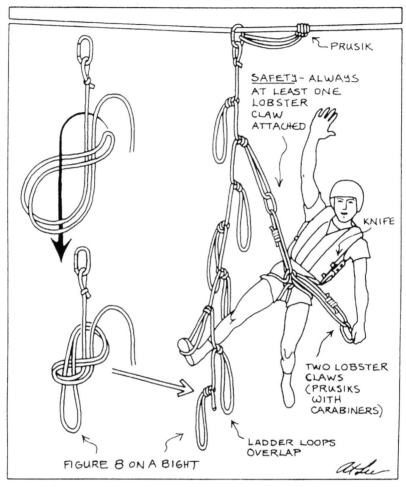

PRUSIK

SAFETY - ALWAYS
AT LEAST ONE
LOBSTER
CLAW
ATTACHED

KNIFE

TWO LOBSTER
CLAWS
(PRUSIKS
WITH
CARABINERS)

LADDER LOOPS
OVERLAP

FIGURE 8 ON A BIGHT

10.19 The rope ladder rescue.

rescuer to climb up and down on. The track line is set up and tensioned much as in the previous example, but left tensioned and locked off with the double Prusik brakes and the hauling end of the Z-drag tied off.

The ladder can be made from a good-quality throw bag rope and is made by tying a series of double figure-eight knots. Each loop should be big enough to step into and should overlap the next one. The rescuer clips directly to the anchor line, pulls himself out over the accident site, clips the ladder into the anchor line, and then climbs down the ladder to the victim. The rescuer can use a Prusik on the anchor line to keep the ladder in position, or he can rig tag lines going to either shore. The rescuer's sit harness has two short tethers (called "lobster claws") with carabiners on each. He keeps one of these always clipped into a loop to protect him as he climbs up and down the rope ladder.

Helicopters

Helicopters are wonderful tools for rescue and evacuation—if used correctly. Like anything else, however, they are subject to physical laws and have their limitations. Many of the problems that arise in helicopter rescue have stemmed from ignorance of those limitations. Most people, and this includes many rescue professionals, are not familiar with the capabilities of helicopters.

The advantages of the helicopter are mobility and speed. It is sometimes faster than other systems and is especially good for cutting evacuation time to a minimum. It can hover over an accident site where there are no nearby bridge pilings or anchor points and can rescue victims from the middle of rivers too wide for ropes to reach

10.20 Helicopters can dramatically reduce evacuation time. They are much better suited to this task than that of actual river rescues. (Paul Ratcliffe/ Sierra Shutterbug)

across. Some helicopters, especially military ones, are equipped with powerful winches, which can be used for vertical rescue.

The disadvantages of the helicopter are many and should be carefully considered before employment. Helicopters are fast in flight, but are often slow to respond. Even in areas where they are used frequently, the tasks of the getting the required clearances, scrambling the crew, and other administrative details may use time precious in a river rescue. Once the helicopter is on the scene there are often communication problems: unless the group on the river has a radio (unlikely) and can talk to the helicopter (even more unlikely), they must use ground-to-air signals, which are slow and inexact (see appendix D). Helicopters also need a lot of room in which to operate, which limits their usefulness in narrow, tree-lined river gorges. If a helicopter snags a rotor and crashes, an already tragic situation becomes much worse. Furthermore, the rotor back-wash from a helicopter hovering over a victim can dramatically increase the possibility of hypothermia.

There is an almost universal tendency to overestimate the capabilities of helicopters, which has led rescuers to try to lift water-filled kayaks or to unpin rafts with them. Probably the worst problem with the use of helicopters in river rescue, though, is the temptation to put off rescue attempts "because the chopper will be here any minute." Rescue attempts on the river *must not be put off for any reason,* unless it is absolutely clear that there is no other alternative.

In May 1980 a kayaker became pinned on the upstream side of a boulder on the Kern River in California. He could breathe, but he could not get out of the boat. There were several delays in assessing the situation, and it was nearly half an hour before help was summoned. A deputy sheriff on the scene concluded that a shore-based rescue was too dangerous and prohibited a group of commercial rafters from making any attempts. One guide and a private kayaker did swim out anyway and held the victim's head up.

It was crucial to the deputy's thinking that he had radioed for a helicopter and expected it to be there within fifteen minutes. He did not know, as Charlie Walbridge comments in the *Best of the River Safety Task Force Newsletter,* that "it would take 25 minutes to get the necessary clearances and 35 minutes to scramble the crew before the 15 minute flight could commence." Nor could he communicate with the helicopter's radio, which was on a military frequency.

What followed was a near-tragedy. When the helicopter arrived the victim was nearly hypothermic, having been in the water almost two and a half hours. The helicopter had been called one and a half hours before. The helicopter lowered a horse-collar rescue device to the victim, who was still in his kayak, and tried to lift both to the shore, but the helicopter lost lift and almost crashed in the process. Fortunately, in spite of this and more bungling in treatment and evacuation, the injured kayaker escaped from both accident and rescue with only minor bruises.

Walbridge comments that "the people in the helicopter had no idea how much water was in the kayak, or if they had enough lift to do the job, much less if this could be done without injuring the victim." He concludes that "river rescues are not like other kinds. Time works against you and a helicopter is, at best, a back-up."

The lessons of this incident are clear: communications, capabilities, and time must all be considered. Does this mean that helicopters should never be used? No. Helicopters are used routinely in many areas for evacuation, and the following incident on the Cheat River in West Virginia (reported in the *Best of the River Safety Task Force Newsletter*) shows how they may be used to advantage.

An outfitter's raft flipped on the Cheat at high water. Everyone was rescued except one person, who was stranded on a midstream rock. The river was already beyond the "safe" level for trips and was still rising. The victim was shaken, and although the outfitter was able to get a kayak over to the rock, a huge strainer downstream made the ferry a real risk for a raft. The river was too wide and swift for a Telfer or Tyrolean system, but it was relatively unobstructed. The local rescue squad called a helicopter, which was able to execute a single skid landing on the rock and pick up the victim. In this case the helicopter, which was already in the area, was the best choice.

Helicopter Evacuation

On the whole, helicopters are better used for evacuation than for rescue. However, even if a helicopter has been called, the rescue and evacuation should proceed as if it were not available. Meanwhile, the rescuers should look for a suitable landing zone for an evacuation. It is much safer, unless the patient's injury is so serious that he can't be moved, to use a proper landing area than to force the pilot into making a dangerous pickup at the accident site.

Communication with the helicopter, as already mentioned, can be a problem, and radios will seldom be available. Several pilots have told us that the best way to get their attention is with a signal mirror, which works even on cloudy days. Other ways to mark the accident site include pocket flares, smoky fires, and waving brightly colored clothing.

Landing Zone (Helispot). Set up the landing zone or helispot in a flat, clear space with no obstructions around it. Telephone wires or power lines are a special hazard, since they are hard for the pilot to see. An isolated knob or hill is ideal. The landing area should be flat, however, since helicopters cannot land on a slope much greater than 8–10°. A landing zone for the widely used Bell 205-series helicopter should be a minimum of thirty-five paces wide. A pilot can set a helicopter down in a circular area this size, but he will find it difficult to take off or turn around. The landing zone therefore should be three or four times as long as it is wide, and the long axis should face into the wind (see figure 10.21). If there are obstacles like trees and power lines at the end of the "runway," this distance must be greater. Although helicopters can take off and land vertically, it is much easier for them to take off into the wind, just as it is for airplanes. Clear the landing zone of all loose debris and brush, leaving no obstacles higher than one foot. Mark it clearly, and if possible arrange for some indication of the direction of the wind. Paddle jackets or brightly colored clothing laid in a T or H pattern will serve as markers, but you will have to stake or weigh them down to keep them from blowing away. Indicate wind direction with smoke or a streamer made from clothing or by standing with your back to the wind and holding your arms forward.

Evacuation Techniques. Do not rush out to the helicopter when it lands because the pilot may want to move it around first. Instead, make sure you have the attention of the pilot or crew chief and wait until he indicates he's ready. Approach the helicopter only from the front or side—stay away from the tail rotor. If the ground slopes, approach from the downhill side only and duck as you pass under the arc of the rotors. Once you are at the helicopter, a crew member will instruct you where to put the patient. If it is a medevac ship, there will be a doctor or flight paramedic aboard; if not, a first-aider

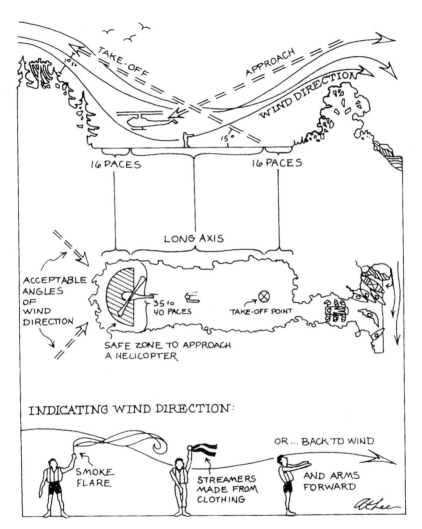

10.21 Helicopter landing zone.

should accompany the patient to the hospital if there is room on the aircraft.

Tim Setnicka, who has worked extensively with rescue helicopters in Yosemite National Park, reminds us in *Wilderness Search and Rescue* (Boston: Appalachian Mountain Club Books, 1980) that rescuers "must always consider the negative impact of any one of these factors: bad weather, malfunction, darkness. We therefore want to stay *helicopter independent* in SAR planning and thinking, in spite of the seductiveness of constant reliance on helo support."

Vertical rescues are a specialized branch of river rescue. They are more dangerous than other methods of rescue and require special training and equipment. They should usually be considered last, but there are times when a vertical rescue may be the only means to reach an accident site. Les relates a Tyrolean boat-recovery story:

"It was one of those crazy Fourth of July holidays on the Nantahala River. Everyone and his brother decided to run the river that day. About midday, several rafts had come in to our rental shop with ripped floors before we finally figured out that a very wrecked aluminum canoe had gotten lodged in the middle of Nantahala Falls. Fortunately no one had been hurt yet, but it wouldn't take long considering the traffic.

"The canoe was barely visible in this very steep, fast Class III drop. There was no eddy. The only way to get at the canoe was by Telfer Lower or via a Tyrolean high line. Because we didn't want to stop all the river traffic to do a Telfer, we opted for high line Tyrolean. The Nantahala is very narrow at this point, and within fifteen minutes we had a high line up and a gung-ho raft guide dangling from a rope ladder. He was able to clip on a haul line and then pitch it to a crew on river left. A quick Z-drag was rigged and canoe came right off.

"I was trying to act nonchalant in front of the hundreds of spectators. But, when the applause went up I was grinning ear-to-ear. It was my first Tyrolean under the gun and I was delighted that it came off so well."

Training is everything. The peach was once a bitter almond;
cauliflower is nothing but cabbage with a college education.
Mark Twain, *Pudd'nhead Wilson*

11

Organization
for Rescue

The moment of rescue—from the time the need for rescue is recognized until it actually begins—is critical. The most important
part of that time is devoted to the organization of the rescue. Because
of the very limited time available, organization and timing are vital.

Because of the shortness of time available in most rescues and
the need to work together, there is no substitute for organization and
leadership. Reaction time in a life-threatening situation is critical:
seconds and tenths of seconds count. This is no place for arguments
or democratic discussions: the directions of the leader must be followed. We realize that some will condemn us as safety fanatics for
trying to organize a very individualistic sport, but experience has
shown that organized groups perform better in a rescue. The rescue
leader must take charge of the situation *immediately,* assigning
responsibilities and directing rescue efforts. If the crisis should
involve the trip leader, the leadership role must be assumed by the
most-experienced paddler in the group.

However, while organized groups with designated trip leaders
are the norm on commercial raft trips, these are rare for groups of

paddlers. Instead, most paddlers subscribe to the so-called "common adventurer" concept; that is, a group with members of approximately equal ability who agree to share the risk of the enterprise. This also spreads the responsibility (and presumably, any liability) equally throughout the group. With groups of experienced paddlers, this is a perfectly acceptable arrangement. A less-experienced group, however, may lose precious time organizing themselves while trying to respond to an accident. Even with common adventurers, it is still often a good idea to designate someone, usually an accomplished paddler with rescue knowledge and experience, as "rescue leader" if something goes wrong. This can save critical minutes in an emergency.

For these reasons we suggest that any organized group take the steps described below.

The Rescue Process

What factors should you consider when organizing a rescue? You must first assess the situation, then *communicate* the problem, determine the best *method* of rescue, and organize the rescue. Let's look at each factor in turn:

Assess the Situation

- Where is the victim? Is he entrapped? Does he have a means of self-rescue?

- Can the victim breathe? Is it a "head-up" or "head-down" entrapment?

- How many people are involved? Where are they? What are their skills? Are there other people nearby who can help or go for help?

- Can the situation get worse? How? Can the boat shift? Is the water rising? Is hypothermia a consideration? Can you stabilize the situation until a method of rescue can be worked out?

- How much time do you have? Consider the time left for the victim, the time for rescue, the hours of daylight remaining, and the time needed to summon help.

Communicate the Problem

- To the victim. What is the rescue plan? Can the victim be talked into a reasonable means of self-rescue? The person being rescued will need assurance and certainly will want to know what is being done to help.

- To others in your party and to other parties on the river as possible, so that everyone knows what the problem is.

- To outside resources, such as a dam keeper, rescue squad, or emergency medical services.

Determine the Best Method of Rescue

Consider the mnemonic *RETHROG*. First, can you *RE*ach the victim for a contact rescue? If not, can you *TH*row a rope to him? Can you *RO*w or paddle to him for a boat-based rescue? Can you *GO* to him with a swimming rescue?

- Consider the time available to set up and use the rescue system. This is vital if the victim cannot breathe or is in extreme danger.

- What danger will each method pose to the rescuers? This is a question too often overlooked. A reasonable risk might be accepted to save a life, but the safety of the rescuers must come even before that of the victim.

- How many people will be needed? With some methods, untrained bystanders can assist.

- How much equipment is required? Some otherwise desirable method may have to be eliminated if critical hardware is not available.

- Can different methods be used concurrently or as a backup? Can a quick-to-use method like a boat-based rescue be tried first while another team readies a slower method like Telfer?

Organize the Rescue

- Appoint individuals to rescue teams if enough people are available. Designate team leaders and tasks. In small groups each paddler will form a team of one.

- The most important thing is to stabilize the patient's condition and start the extrication. The most skilled paddlers

11.1 When possible, combine rescue systems. Here a group of rafters recovers one of their number after a spill. They are backed up by a chase boat and a rope farther downstream.

and river-wise people should be appointed to the extrication team.

- While the extrication is in progress, prepare for medical treatment (first aid, CPR, and hypothermia) as necessary.
- Send for help. Notify local rescue agencies. Prepare for ambulance pickup at the nearest road. If on a dam-controlled river, notify the authorities to shut off water. Call the nearest emergency medical service and give a description of the patient's injuries (see chapter 12 for the recommended format) so that proper medical facilities can be made ready.

That's a lot to think about, isn't it? How much time do you have to get going? Because of the life-threatening nature of many river emergencies. you must be able to begin the rescue *within fifteen seconds* of the time of the accident. Experience, river sense, and presence of mind count for a lot here: if you have been following the course of events leading up to the accident and automatically analyzing them (the "what if" factor), you should be propelled into action almost instinctively. And though we cannot overemphasize the importance of time in a river rescue, there is no substitute for the moment of reflection before starting: it is no rescue at all to hurry into an ill-considered attempt that endangers the lives of the rescuers and is doomed to failure because of poor and hasty organization.

Leadership

As a rescue leader you must concern yourself with clear, unemotional thinking. This isn't always easy, particularly if the safety of a friend is involved. If at all possible, you should not become directly involved with any of the individual tasks of the rescue. It is important to have someone who can oversee the whole operation and not get distracted by any single problem. Obviously there will be times when you can't do this; you may be the only one qualified in a certain skill, for example. Remember that your duties as rescue leader are to *observe, organize,* and *direct* the efforts of the entire rescue team.

Rescue Priorities

One of the most important factors on the river is always time—the time it takes to set up and use a rescue system and the time a victim may have left. Almost inevitably, time must be traded off against the danger to which a rescuer must be exposed. If the victim's remaining time is measured in minutes or even seconds, a rescuer may be prepared to accept greater danger to himself in order to save a life. But this trade-off must be carefully considered and the attempt skillfully made, with all possible safety precautions taken for the rescuer, or he can end up as another victim.

The rescuers' most important priorities are as follows: First, they must be able to rescue themselves, and not to commit themselves to a rescue unless they can reasonably assure their own safety. Second, they must be able to back each other up and rescue each other. Third, they must rescue the victim. Unfortunately, there may be times when a rescue cannot be attempted because it is too dangerous for the rescuers. Generally, if the situation is immediately life threatening, the fastest system consistent with the rescuer's safety must be used, with safer but slower systems as backups; if people must be rescued but are not in immediate danger, slower and safer systems should be used; if only equipment is involved, choose the safest system for the rescuers.

System Selection

Rescue systems vary greatly in effectiveness, speed, safety for the rescuers, and resource use. What is effective and appropriate in one situation may be useless in another (for example, the most expert chase boater is of little use in a vertical-pin rescue). When selecting a system, consider the three S's: *safety, speed,* and *simplicity*.

- *Safety.* How safe is it for the rescuers? The safest place for the rescuer is on the shore, the next safest in a boat, and the least safe is swimming in the water with the victim. Safety must sometimes be balanced with speed, but the safety of the rescuers must be the first consideration.

- *Speed.* How long does it take to set up? Throw ropes and chase boats are usually the quickest to employ; strong-swimmer and tag lines are next, then tag lines and mechanical rescues, then Telfer lowers. Tyroleans and high lines take the longest.

- *Simplicity.* How many people does it require? How much equipment is needed? Use the simplest systems first: they are faster to set up and have less to go wrong. Use more complex systems for backups. The choice of the correct system is an important one, and often will weigh heavily on the minds of the rescuers. When selecting the correct system consider the following characteristics:

Throwing Rescues and Tag Lines. These are safest for the rescuers, require little special equipment, and are quick to set up. They require minimal training in rope use and safety.

Chase Boat. It is quick to react and set up and requires little special equipment, but is less safe for the rescuer and requires paddling ability equal to the situation.

Telfer Lower. It is less safe for rescuers but requires little paddling ability. It requires practice for quick setup and is slower than above methods. Telfers require a fair amount of specialized equipment (ropes, carabiners, and so forth) as well as organization, leadership, and manpower.

Strong-Swimmer Rescues and Contact Rescues in General. Least safe for rescuers but very quick to employ in situations in which rope throws and chase boats are not appropriate, such as pins and broaches. Minimal equipment and manpower are needed.

High Lines. Slow to set up and employ, and it requires specialized equipment and training, leaders, and manpower. Dangerous for the rescuer.

Rescue Organization

It would be impossible to set out here exactly what organization you will use for a rescue. Each rescue is different, and the equipment, experience, and number of people available will vary greatly. One primary goal is to make the best use of all available manpower, and the most effective way to do that is to organize people into teams. Our intention here is to provide a guide to the functions or areas of concern that you might have in an ideal situation. Normally teams or individuals perform these tasks, and in some cases one person may have to do them all.

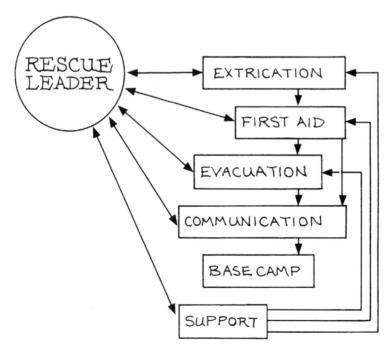

11.2 *Rescue organization*

The organizing should be done by the rescue leader, except when he is deeply involved in an extrication or other rescue task (for which he may be the only one qualified), or in the case of a small group of experienced paddlers who, thanks to experience and instinct, react instantly. If for any reason the trip leader cannot organize the rescue, someone else, preferably the next most experienced person, must take over. The following functions are usually needed:

- *Extrication.* Most needed in pin or entrapment, more often than not this group is not appointed but consists of the people nearest the scene of the accident. Because speed and efficiency are critical, these should be the most-experienced and water-wise paddlers.

- *Medical.* The medical team prepares to treat the patient while the extrication is going on. It should include the medically best-trained people present and is responsible for the treatment of the patient. The team must determine whether and where CPR will be performed, who will do the compressions and who the breathing, what first aid is needed and where, and whether a litter or backboard is necessary.

- *Evacuation.* The "evac" team coordinates with the medical personnel to determine the best method of evacuation, then selects the evacuation route. They also construct or locate litters or backboards and perform the evacuation.

- *Communications.* Someone must go for help by the best means available (on foot, paddling, hitchhiking) to make contact with such outside agencies as dam keepers, search-and-rescue teams, ambulances, and hospitals. Contingency plans should be discussed before leaving. It is a good idea, if possible, to send out people in pairs, in case one is injured. Well-equipped commercial trips may have radios or cellular phones, or it may be possible to signal aircraft or helicopters.

- *Logistics/Base Camp.* Someone must support the people performing the rescue. The rescuers may need more equipment, and eventually will need food, water, and perhaps a place to warm up. Someone should also look after the other group members, who may be having their own problems with shock, grief, or hypothermia. If the group needs to keep moving down the river or split up, who will be the new leader? The support people may have to prepare a fire, a meal, or a campsite. It may be necessary to set up a base camp with someone to receive and coordinate information and resources, comfort friends and relatives as needed, provide continued support with food and clothing, and deal with the media. Finally, someone should be taking notes and, if possible, photographs so that a record of the incident can be made.

Site organization

In addition to organizing the people, the rescue site must also be organized. The rescue leader's primary concerns must be to keep anyone from interfering with the rescuers, and to safeguard them as much as possible. If the accident occurs near a road, someone will need to control curious onlookers. Other organizational considerations are:

- Someone should be stationed upstream of the accident site to warn off other paddlers and rafts, especially if ropes are being stretched across the river. Upstream spotters also provide warning to the rescuers if dangerous debris comes floating down.

- Other rescuers should be positioned downstream of the accident site in case one of the rescuers or the victim gets loose and comes floating past. They may be in boats, or have backup throw ropes, or other rescue capabilities (e.g., rescue swimmer) as the situation dictates.

- Establish a secure way for rescuers to get up and down the riverbank. A good way is to put up a fixed "scurry line," a rope people can grab to keep from falling.

If the First Attempt Fails

What happens when the first attempt fails? Obviously you can't just give up while you have the means in your power to rescue someone.

If enough people are available, some should be working on an alternative method of rescue while the primary method is being tried. For instance, if a paddler is pinned in a boat in midstream, you might first try sending the rescue team out in a canoe or raft. While this is being done, a second team can be stretching a rope across the river to prepare for a Telfer lower or Tyrolean rescue.

Reassess the situation, using the same criteria you did the first time. Don't give up! Was there something you missed? Has the situation changed? Are there other alternative methods you haven't considered? Solicit suggestions from others. Are the rescuers getting tired or otherwise endangering themselves? In your concern for the victim do not ignore the effects of hypothermia or shock on the rescue party. Has someone been sent to notify others, such as a search-and-rescue team, who might have equipment you don't have?

Keep trying, and keep thinking. Keep the rescuers safe, but don't give up until the situation is clearly hopeless. Remember that apparent victims of drowning have been revived after more than an hour's immersion in cold water.

The Professionals

By "professional" we generally mean someone who makes his living on the river—that is, a guide, instructor, or boatman. These are the river professionals. By guiding for hire, the whitewater professional assumes an added responsibility for the safety of his customers, who are therefore entitled to rely on his expertise, training, and judgment. But there is another important type of professional: the search-and-rescue squad member, the firefighter, or the park ranger whose duty it is to rescue members of the public in trouble. This large category of "rescue professionals" includes both amateurs and professionals, in the sense that some are paid to do their rescue work full time and others, such as those belonging to volunteer fire departments and rescue squads, are unpaid part-timers. Representing a variety of federal, state, and local agencies, these people try to prevent accidents and save lives, but their level of training and expertise in swiftwater rescue varies greatly.

The skills the rescue professional needs are much the same as those of the river professional. The rescue professional will have more and better equipment and support, but this is wholly or partly offset by the greater experience and knowledge of the river professional. All too often, pride is a factor on both sides: members of the search-and-rescue squad resent the amateurs in life jackets trying to tell them how to do their job; the whitewater outfitters are often reluctant to call for help because they prefer to handle their own problems. The only solution lies in increased awareness of the abilities and skills of each team. The search-and-rescue community must become more aware of the special problems and skills needed for whitewater and swiftwater rescue; river professionals must improve their own skills and actively work to promote good relationships with local public-safety professionals. Training together, and identifying problem areas in advance, will help achieve the common goal of safe, effective rescue.

For most public-safety professionals, river rescue is a secondary aspect of the job. Because they do not normally work with whitewater they often lack an appreciation of its dangers and can unknowingly risk their lives in an emergency. In addition to training, having the right personal equipment is essential. A good life jacket and wetsuit should be considered mandatory for river rescuers: firefighters should not wear "turn out" coats and boots. Everyone should know the basics of swimming in whitewater, rope throwing, and mechanical rescues. In general, public safety professionals should use shore-based rescues if possible, and avoid going into moving water in a boat or for a swimming rescue unless they have had specific swiftwater training.

Liability

In these days of the "sue everybody" society, the question of liability frequently comes up. Unfortunately, there is lot of misinformation about it, even in the legal community. In the simplest terms, you are liable to a person when, through fault or omission, you cause injury to that person or his property. After that it gets complicated, and discussions of this subject have filled many law books.

What happens when you see someone in trouble on the river? Are you under an obligation to help? And what happens when you do? Many states have "Good Samaritan" laws, which protect a would-be rescuer who acts in good faith. Some even make it a crime not to render aid. What's good faith? It just means that you are really trying to do the right thing within the limits of your knowledge and capabilities. You are not expected to endanger yourself or attempt the impossible.

Still, it is impossible to have a lawyer on every trip, and in some cases the river you're on may even be the border of two states with different liability laws. As a practical matter, there are too many things to think about during a rescue—you don't need to add liability to the list. Your knowledge will protect you; if you know river rescue and first aid, use good judgment, and try to prevent accidents before they happen, your chances of being sued as a private boater are very slight.

The Media

If the accident is near a road, you may be visited by members of the media. This might mean anything from a part-time newspaper reporter to a full "action news team" with cameras, lights, and sound. Media people can be distracting and sometimes obnoxious, but they have a right to be there *as long as they don't interfere with the rescue or evacuation.* If the sheriff or a search-and-rescue outfit is on the scene, one of them will usually take care of media relations. If not, one of your group will have to do it.

Probably the worst thing you can do is to try to keep the media away altogether and refuse to comment. This invariably will raise suspicion that you are trying to hide something. The best policy is to give a general statement ("Yes, there's been an accident here, and we're in the process of attempting to rescue that fellow over there"). Most reporters respect this and will be satisfied with the basic facts. The details can wait for later.

You are well within your rights to keep reporters and bystanders out of the immediate rescue and evacuation work area. A rope run around the work area works well to define it.

There is one thing, however, that you should *never* tell any reporter: the name of the victim, particularly if he is dead or seriously injured. That information is not to be made public until the victim's next of kin can be notified. Notification is the job of a clergyman or a close friend and is not the sort of thing for someone to hear about first on the five o'clock news.

Thinking the Unthinkable—The Failed Rescue

In a book, all rescue attempts can be successful, but in real life you must be prepared to deal with those that fail. An unsuccessful rescue means someone is dead. Death is not a pleasant thing to think about, but it's something you must consider as a logical extension of organizing for rescue.

As we have said, the rescuers must keep trying to save or revive the victim until the situation is clearly hopeless. What then? If there is no doubt that the victim is beyond help, a decision must be made as to whether to continue efforts to recover the body. Because of the emotional attachment of people in the rescue party to the victim, this may be a hard decision to make, but you should continue recovery efforts only if they are not compromising the safety of the rescuers.

Consider the condition of the rescuers. They are almost certainly tired and emotionally upset by what has happened. Is the

11.3 Rescues save lives, but sometimes they fail. What would your reactions be to the death or serious injury of one of your party? (Cindin Carroll/Nantahala Outdoor Center)

party near a road or takeout? How much daylight is left? Should the party continue or abandon the trip? The safety of the living must come first. If the group is near a road or town and recovery attempts have been fruitless, it may be better to leave the attempt to a sheriff's department or a search-and-rescue unit. If you are on a multiday wilderness trip, the victim may have to be left for a later search party. It is well known among mountaineers that a party will tend to abandon an expedition after a death, regardless of the actual difficulties. Certainly the death of a companion affects any undertaking, but the risks and rewards of continuing must be evaluated realistically.

Suppose the rescue is unsuccessful, and the victim has been recovered. What do you do with a dead person, especially a friend? If all attempts at revival have failed, remove the body to a safe place until you can either evacuate it or arrange for that to be done. If you are in the wilderness and far from help, you may have to bury it, either temporarily or permanently. In either case the grave must be marked.

In most places in the United States a person must be pronounced dead by a civil official, usually a coroner or a medical examiner. The coroner must file a report and, if he thinks the circumstances warrant it, order an investigation. Any death must be reported to the local police department or county sheriff, along with the circumstances. These authorities will want specific information. To be able to provide this information, the people involved in a rescue, whether it involves a fatality or even a near miss, should debrief as a group as soon as possible. It is surprising how quickly people forget details and how subjective impressions of time are. The only way to be sure is to write things down as soon as possible after the event. Try to specify exactly what happened: who did what and in what order. If possible, take photographs of the accident site, the rescue, the evacuation, and the victim. It may seem morbid to take pictures at a time like this, but they are invaluable in trying to piece together events later. A photograph will not forget details. Another reason for setting all this down is to pass on the experience, good or bad, to others who might at some time be in a similar situation. Write down a summary of the accident and send it to the Safety Committee of the American Canoe Association (see introduction).

Reactions

We have talked about successful and unsuccessful rescues and some of the administrative considerations involved in both, but what really happens in your mind when there is a fatal accident on the river?

At the beginning of the emergency there is faith, a certainty that the victim will be saved. This is replaced by disbelief that the accident is really happening, and then by hope that a miracle will occur. Inevitably, there is the realization that the accident actually has happened and the anger and frustration that go with that realization. This is often coupled with a strong sense of personal guilt, regardless of the circumstances. Finally, there is the acceptance of death, which leaves a numbing feeling that lasts for some time.

Situations like this can lead to critical-incident stress; a long-term adverse psychological reaction (also called post-traumatic stress syndrome) that can appear months or even years after the event. Common symptoms include survivor guilt, sleep disorders, anger, and problems with interpersonal relationships. Any time you have been exposed to a traumatic incident (i.e., a drowning or a near miss), critical-incident stress counseling is a good idea. It is also beneficial for the entire group of rescuers to debrief as a group immediately after an incident.

As a conclusion to this chapter, here is Les describing some of his feelings after a drowning death on the Bío-Bío River in Chile:

"It was to be my last trip on the Bío-Bío. After four seasons there I had come to love the beauty of this rugged river and its whitewater. We were running Lost Yak rapid and my raft was first. We took on a lot of water and went through the next rapid, Lava South, as well. As I returned to Lost Yak on foot another raft was coming through, and then I saw Ted in the water away from the raft. Because of the width of the river we were unable to use safety ropes to reach him, but John approached him in a kayak. Ted grabbed the boat, and they began to struggle toward shore. I had *faith* in John's ability, but a lot of cold, fast Class IV water lay between them and safety.

"My mind flashed back to a similar incident two years before [the rescue described in the prologue]: We were at the bottom of Lava South, and a person from another company, who had fallen out of his raft in Lost Yak, was forced to swim through Lava South. That time we were lucky to be in the right place at the right time.

"Ted died only a few feet from shore. Caught under a rock, he was still clutching the kayak's grab loop. *Disbelief.* This can't be happening. I watched helplessly from the opposite shore as Ted disappeared face-down into Lava South. John had lost his paddle in the struggle to free Ted and was trying to follow him on foot. All our other rescue attempts, some foolish and some brave, ended without success.

"Somewhere during all this my hopes crashed. *Frustration* had been growing during the pursuit of Ted's body and it ended in anger. It wasn't fair. We had done everything by the book, taken every precaution. He was an experienced paddler. I had to turn my *anger* and despair into something else. We had to start thinking about ourselves. As I walked back to the rest of the group, waves of *guilt* washed over me. We should have portaged around Lost Yak. I should have been able to do something to save Ted. It was my fault that he was here. And now he was dead.

"Getting the group together that night wasn't easy. Each of us had his own way of dealing with the grief. We didn't know whether to quit or go on. We knew we had to get out of the canyon; after that we would take it one day at a time. We finished the trip and took out four days later at Santa Barbara. The authorities found the body the next day.

"My trip lasted longer. We sent Ted's body back to West Virginia, and it was there at his funeral that I accepted the reality of his death. His mother asked me if the river was beautiful and I said that it was. She said, 'At least he died doing something he loved the most...paddling whitewater on a beautiful river.'"

Eventually, all things merge into one, and a river runs through it. The river was cut by the world's great flood and runs over rocks from the basement of time. On some of the rocks are timeless raindrops. Under the rocks are the words, and some of the words are theirs. I am haunted by waters.

Norman Maclean, *A River Runs Through It*

12

Patient Care and Evacuation Techniques

Basic medical training should be considered an integral preparation for any outdoor activity or sport. Some whitewater aficionados spare no expense when buying equipment or attending a paddling school, but rarely spend the time or money to take a wilderness medical course. One of the worst feelings in the world is to see anyone, but especially a friend, in pain and not know what to do. Until this point our concern has been with rescuing the victim of an accident. When rescued, however, the victim becomes a patient, and in this chapter we will be dealing with the person who is now your patient. It is not our intent to teach medical protocols, but we do feel it is important to highlight some thoughts on accident prevention and postrescue care that should concern any river rescuer, as well as some areas that are specific to river rescues.

Outdoorspeople frequently find themselves engaged in an active sport where injury in a wilderness setting is a distinct possibility.

Professional help can be hours, days, or even weeks away, which means that some training in dealing with medical emergencies is a must. Most common medical protocols were developed for an "ambulance" context, meaning that the treatment standards and techniques were based on the assumption that advanced life-support treatment was no more than twenty to thirty minutes away. Treatment in a "wilderness" context requires some modification of accepted procedures and techniques, however, as well as some knowledge of conditions (e.g., long-term-care protocols) not thoroughly covered by conventional first-aid training.

The Wilderness Medical Society has developed a series of wilderness medicine training programs that address emergency treatment in remote areas, including such issues as prolonged transport, severe environments, and improvised equipment. These have been widely adopted and form a common training standard. The best bet for most paddlers and guides is the Wilderness First Responder, but rescuers and trip leaders should consider becoming a Wilderness Emergency Medical Technician.

The Initial Contact

When approaching a victim it is a good idea to have a rescue plan in mind. Communicate it to him. Tell him exactly what you are doing and planning to do, and what you want him to do. Ask his name. Ask about injuries: "Where does it hurt?" Try to get as much information about the accident and the patient's condition as you can. If the patient is conscious but not responding to your inquiries, be cautious.

If you have witnessed the accident and know the patient, use his name. Be calm and reassuring. Be honest about the situation, remain positive, and try to inspire trust and confidence. The first few seconds of interaction may make the difference between a patient who remains cool and one who goes off the deep end. A patient's mental condition is critical and should be monitored at all times. Rescuers should be aware of psychogenic shock (sometimes called ASR—autonomic stress response, or acute stress reaction), which can easily be confused with true shock. An otherwise insignificant injury or even a seemingly innocuous remark ("God, he looks terrible!") overheard by the patient may be enough to trigger this event. This is true even of unconscious patients. The patient may then appear "shocky," causing the rescuers to misread the urgency of the situation. Make sure you have properly assessed the patient's physical condition (see below) before you conclude that he is in shock.

If the patient is stationary and out of immediate danger, your primary concern should be to assess his condition correctly and stabilize it so that it doesn't get worse. We have previously discussed strategies to use in pins and entrapments, so the emphasis here is on assessing the nature of the patient's injuries and his emotional state. Do not aggravate the patient condition by hasty, unnecessary movement. First, make a quick survey of the patient's condition. You will need to do this in a systematic way, as if following a pilot's checklist; otherwise you may not know where to begin, or of worse, you may forget an important step. We have outlined the process below; a more complete Patient Assessment System is reproduced in appendix F. Neither is intended to replace the appropriate training courses.

- Survey the scene: Is there danger to the rescuer? What was the mechanism for the injury? How alert is the patient to your questions?

- Conduct a primary survey, using the **ABC** system: Is the Airway clear? Is the patient Breathing? Is the Circulation intact? (Is he bleeding?) If there is a problem with any area in the primary survey, you must deal with it before continuing.

- Conduct a brief secondary survey of the patient's head, eyes, ears, nose, mouth/throat, neck, chest, abdomen, pelvis, genitalia, legs, arms, back, and buttocks. Look for injuries that might not be obvious on first inspection.

- Check the patient's vital signs: pulse, respiration, and skin color. If you are equipped to do so, take blood pressure and temperature. Note the time and the patient's consciousness and mental status (**AVPU**): Is he Alert; not alert but responds to simple Verbal questions; nonverbal but responds to Pain; or Unconscious?

If the patient is conscious, get a history, including any allergies, any medications and when last taken, any past medical problems that might affect treatment, the time of the last meal, and the patient's recollection of the accident. Especially if you are faced with a lengthy evacuation or must communicate with medical support, write down all the above information. This will prevent confusion and allow supporting rescuers to have the right equipment ready. Use the **SOAP** note format:

- What are the patient's Subjective complaints?

- What are your Objective findings?

- What is your overall Assessment of the situation and anticipated problems?

- What is your Plan for treatment and evacuation?

Continue to monitor your patient's condition, including vital signs, and note the times. If possible, record all of this information. Often a problem will become obvious only after looking at the pattern of a patient's condition over time.

Common Injuries

One of the most common injuries for river runners is damage to the lower extremities: sprained and broken ankles; cuts and injuries to the feet. Most people are used to walking in an urban environment with manicured lawns and flat sidewalks, and not on slippery rocks that move. Cuts, dehydration, bruises, sunburn, and poison oak and ivy can also be an unplanned and unpleasant part of one's river experience. These problems generally can be avoided if people think and act with some caution. In this sense almost any river is a wilderness area. Other injuries often associated with whitewater sports are tendinitis and shoulder dislocations.

Tendinitis. This is the inflammation of a tendon, the fibrous tissue that connects muscle to bone. It is an overuse syndrome, often aggravated by poor paddling technique, and usually (for paddlers, at least) affects the forearm tendons and extensor tendons of the hands. A common cause is the combination of an overfirm grip on the paddle, cold water, and poor conditioning. A looser and more relaxed grip, more body rotation, and better preparation usually avoids the problem. Immediate treatment for tendinitis is to apply a cold compress, take an anti-inflammatory drug (e.g., Ibuprofen), and cut back on paddling. Like most other medical problems, it is best caught and treated early.

Shoulder Dislocations. A shoulder dislocates when the ball of the upper arm bone pops forward out of the socket of the shoulder. It can happen to any type of paddler and it is always painful. As with

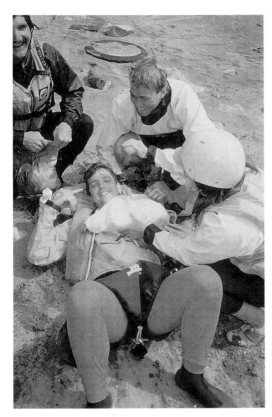

12.1 Shoulder injuries, including dislocations, are fairly common among kayakers. Proper paddling technique can reduce the likelihood of having one.

tendinitis, a shoulder dislocation is often caused by poor paddling technique. It typically occurs when the paddler extends his arm away from his body, rotates it rearward on a brace or roll attempt, turns his head in the opposite direction, and receives a jarring blow on the paddle (see figure 12.2).

First-aid field treatment is to put a sling on the arm and then tie a swath bandage around the body to keep the arm immobilized. The position of comfort (and indeed the only one that most people can tolerate) involves propping the bent arm up in front of and away from the body. Prop it by fashioning a wedge from a SAM™ splint or ensolite pad and placing it between the arm and the chest and stomach before applying the sling and swath bandage. Check to see if the patient has a good pulse and feeling in the arm. The patient should be evacuated, and although he can usually walk he should not be sent out alone. If the evacuation time is lengthy the shoulder probably should be "reduced" (put back in place) by a doctor, since this

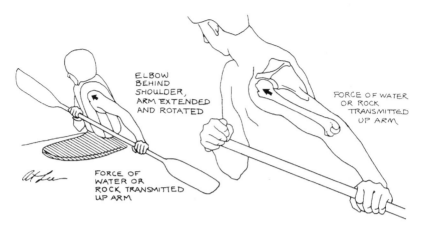

ELBOW BEHIND SHOULDER, ARM EXTENDED AND ROTATED

FORCE OF WATER OR ROCK TRANSMITTED UP ARM

FORCE OF WATER OR ROCK TRANSMITTED UP ARM

12.2 This is how a shoulder dislocation happens.

can dramatically reduce the pain and secondary injury. Paddlers venturing into remote areas may want to learn methods of reducing a shoulder dislocation themselves. Some people have a history of shoulder dislocations and know exactly how to reduce it. Though methods of reducing shoulders in the field are beyond the scope of this book, this training is available in many wilderness medicine programs. If his shoulder is reduced in the field, a paddler should not be allowed back in his boat until he is examined by a doctor.

Hypothermia

Few paddlers die of hypothermia, but it is very often a contributing factor in drowning. Hypothermia occurs when the cold challenge of the environment (that is, low temperature, wet conditions, and wind) overwhelms the body's ability to maintain a constant temperature. The body's ability to do this is affected by its size and shape, insulation, percentage of body fat, fluid status, and the available "fuel" stores of glycogen. The body's immediate response to the cold challenge includes reducing the circulation to the shell areas (that is, the extremities and surface areas of the body) and increasing blood flow to the core. The body also produces heat by burning more fuel and by exercise. Shivering is involuntary exercise, as the body tries to generate heat and is the body's best way initially to rewarm itself.

Subacute hypothermia, often called "mountain" or windchill hypothermia, is a long-term process in which the body gradually loses the contest with the cold. The onset is measured in hours or days. Of more concern to the paddler, however, is acute or "immersion" hypothermia, caused by sudden immersion in cold water. This generates a very high cold challenge that can overwhelm the body's response in a matter of minutes. It is characterized by sudden onset and a radical temperature differential between the body's core and shell. Frequently the body's stores of fuel are almost intact. This is often how paddlers drown: the shell (that is, arms and legs) quickly loses strength and coordination, which makes the victim unable to perform even simple self-rescue tasks like swimming or holding a rope.

Hypothermia is usually classified as mild/moderate or severe, depending on whether the body's temperature is higher or lower than 90°F/32°C .

The best way to deal with hypothermia is to prevent it. Wear the proper clothing and have the skill to paddle the water you've chosen. Know the warning signs of hypothermia and take action to keep matters from worsening as soon as you recognize the signs. Hypothermia affects judgment and coordination and is insidious in its effects. A good example is that of the paddler who swims once and gets cold, then starts missing his roll and swims again and again, becoming colder and more exhausted each time until finally he becomes hypothermic. Keep an eye on people after they swim. If it happens again right away and they are shivering, it is time to suggest a warm-up.

Early recognition of hypothermia is important. Generally a victim will be shivering and uncoordinated, and may experience mild to noticeable changes in mental status. What is the best treatment for hypothermia on the river? One group's recommendation for mild/moderate hypothermia (body temperature above 90°F/32°C) is to "feed 'em and beat 'em" (that is, food and exercise). In the early stages the patient can walk, and that's exactly what he should do. Walking will rewarm him and get him away from the probable cause of his hypothermia—the cold water. Consider walking out from the site, but don't let the patient do it alone; hypothermia is notorious for clouding a person's judgment, and people have gotten lost on simple trails because of it. At least one and preferably two people should accompany the patient. An often overlooked treatment is to have the patient replenish his food and fluid supplies.

Symptoms of Hypothermia

Body Temperature: The hypothermia victim has a core (internal body) temperature that is lower than normal. The following list shows the successive stages of the condition:

Moderate
Above 95°F. The victim is conscious and alert and may have vigorous shivering.

90-95°F. The victim is conscious but has mild to moderate clouding of mental faculties. Shivering is present but diminished.

Severe
86-90°F. The victim has severe clouding of consciousness, may even be unconscious. Shivering is replaced by muscular rigidity.

Below 86°F. The victim is unconscious, with diminishing respirations.

Below 80°F. The victim has barely detectable or nondetectable respirations.

Blood Pressure and Pulse: Blood pressure is lower than normal (frequently less than 100 mm mercury systolic). Pulse is generally slow and often irregular; it may be difficult to find it at all in the extremities because of blood vessel constriction—measure the heart rate in the neck at the carotid artery or in the groin at the femoral artery.

General Appearance: The victim is pale in appearance and his skin is very cold to the touch. In fact, his skin and subcutaneous tissues are often at the temperature of the water he was immersed in. The victim's pupils begin to dilate at temperatures around 92°F and are fully dilated and poorly reactive to light at around 86°F.

Cold
Water
Survival
Chart

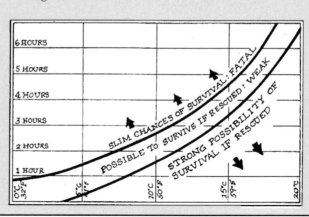

When walking, do not ignore windchill, rain, and other factors. Several fatalities have occurred when paddlers have tried to walk out in very poor conditions and never made it. If you carry basic survival gear (including matches), it may be better, especially if you can find a protected spot, to try to rewarm a moderately hypothermic patient on the spot while someone goes for help. Build a fire, and if possible get the patient into dry clothes or a sleeping bag. If these aren't available, use extra clothing from other members of the group. Give the patient a warm, nonalcoholic drink. You may also choose to use body heat from the other members of the group in a skin to skin "human sandwich." Another solution is to heat damp life jackets in front of a fire and wrap them around the patient, exchanging them for freshly warmed ones as they cool.

If conditions permit, you can try the "steamy jungle" approach. Erect a tent, insulate it from the outside with extra sleeping bags, then boil water on a camp stove inside the tent. Obviously you have to guard against carbon monoxide poisoning, but the warm, moist atmosphere is pretty effective. If no stove is available, rocks heated in a campfire and then brought to the tent and splashed with water will create a sauna atmosphere. Remember to have first-aiders inside the tent as well to monitor the patient. The more advanced the hypothermia, the less effective field rewarming techniques will be.

Field rewarming is impractical and medically unsound with severe hypothermia (core temperature below 90°F/32°C). Hypothermia becomes critical here; the body can't rewarm itself without outside help, even in a dry sleeping bag, and there is a danger of cardiac arrest if the patient is suddenly rewarmed or handled roughly. This stage of hypothermia is on the whole easily recognized: the patient is unconscious or has severe mental status changes, and has stopped shivering. To measure body temperatures in this range (below 94°F/34°C) you will need a special hypothermia thermometer.

Severely hypothermic patients must be evacuated to a hospital. Insulate the patient as well as possible to retain remaining body heat (a vapor barrier works well) and handle gently (a hypothermic person's heart is subject to ventricular fibrillation, or uncontrolled beating, if handled roughly). Ventilate the patient if he appears to have stopped breathing, but remember that the body is now in a "metabolic icebox," and pulse and breathing may be barely perceptible. This is a protective response: people have been revived with a core

temperature of 64°F/18°C and no heartbeat. The use of chest compressions in a hypothermic patient is a controversial question
because of the urgent need for evacuation and the danger of ventricular fibrillation. Many experts recommend that rescuers ventilate
severe hypothermics as long as possible, and reserve chest compressions for patients who lose pulse during an evacuation. They further
recommend that no chest compressions be given if doing so will sig-
nificantly slow the evacuation or if it puts the rescuers at risk.

Paddlers should be aware that a protective survival response
sometimes occurs when the body is suddenly immersed in cold water
(70°F/21°C or less). The heart rate slows and circulation concentrates
between the brain and heart. All body functions are slowed to a barely discernible point; the body is sustained on the oxygen present in
the blood and tissues at the time of immersion. To an observer the
victim may appear dead: he has very slow and shallow respiration;
weak, slow pulse; fixed, dilated pupils; and clammy, white skin.
Victims have been revived without brain damage after being submerged for as long as one hour. While opinions vary as to whether
this is due to MDR (mammalian diving reflex) or hypothermia, the
point is not to give up on rescue efforts or CPR just because four minutes (the old standard of "clinical death") have passed. If the victim
is young, the water cold (below 70°F/21°C) and clean, and the sub-
mersion time less than one hour, you should start CPR as soon as
possible. Acute hypothermia produces symptoms similar to death.

Drowning

The primary threat to a paddler's life is respiratory failure in a fluid
environment, or drowning. Drownings can be divided into two
types: dry and wet. In the dry drowning a spasm of the larynx clos-
es the airway and prevents water from entering the lungs. This probably happens in about 15 percent to 20 percent of the cases.
Although the spasm will ultimately relax, persons in this condition
have a much better chance of survival with basic life support procedures (that is, CPR), particularly if the victim's metabolism is also
slowed because of hypothermia. On the other hand, a wet drowning
means that a substantial amount of water has entered the lungs.
Water in lung tissue causes pulmonary edema and other harmful
effects: the effects may be delayed up to twenty-four hours. There
have been several cases in which a near-drowning victim has been
revived, only to die several hours later in a hospital. This is often

called "parking lot" or delayed drowning. Any person who has aspirated water, been given CPR, or been revived after a near-drowning must be taken to a hospital immediately, no matter how well he or she might feel.

Cardiopulmonary resuscitation, or CPR, is a proven life-saving technique that every whitewater paddler should know. For a drowning victim, the most important thing is to start it as soon as possible, even if this means doing ventilations in the water when you first make contact. Your first step, assuming there is no mechanism for cervical-spine injury, will be to open the victim's airway by pulling up on his chin with one hand and pushing down on his forehead with the other. This tilts the head back and may cause the patient to start breathing again on his own. If conditions permit, look into the victim's mouth to see if there are any obstructions such as mud, vomit, or vegetation. Leave the mouth open during resuscitation efforts, and note the position of the tongue, which has a tendency to fall back into the throat or to stick on the roof of the mouth, obstructing breathing. Although you can ventilate a person in the water, you cannot perform adequate chest compressions. However, many drowning victims will simply be in respiratory arrest and will not require chest compressions. For effective chest compressions, get the patient to the nearest hard surface: this could mean boulders in midstream, gear boxes on a loaded raft, or even the hull of a canoe. Do not spend precious moments hauling the victim up a river embankment if you can find a flat place at the water's edge. If you are alone, initiate one-person CPR until help arrives. (For details on CPR, see appendix E).

Start CPR if the victim has been underwater for less than one hour. After that, most experts agree that CPR has little, if any, chance, of reviving a drowning victim. After starting CPR, continue until the patient starts breathing on his own, is transferred to a medical facility, *or the rescuers are at risk.*

What does this mean to the rescuer in the field? Do the best possible CPR before attempting to transport the patient: you cannot perform effective chest compressions while moving. In an emergency like this you will feel urgently that you want to get the patient to an ambulance or hospital, but don't jeopardize the quality of your CPR in a rush to evacuate. In remote areas, when the patient has not responded and no medical assistance is nearby, the safety of the group may outweigh the need to continue CPR.

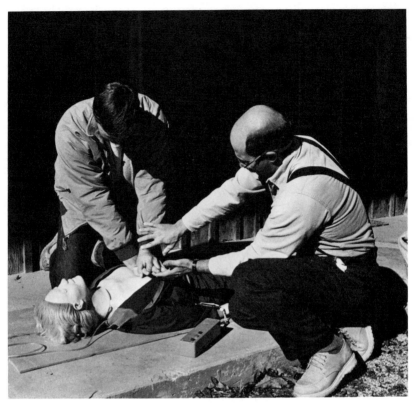

12.3 CPR is an important skill for any paddler.

If CPR is successful and the patient begins to breathe on his own, rescuers must stand by to restart CPR at any time. Keep the patient warm and quiet, and evacuate him. Under no circumstances allow a paddler who has undergone CPR to get back in his boat. If you are forced to spend the night in the field, the patient's condition should be continuously monitored, preferably by at least two people.

Evacuations

As the first-aider, you must decide whether the injured party should be evacuated or not. This is not always an easy decision, and it should be made only after considering all other alternatives. Some considerations are:

- What is the patient's medical problem or problems? Do any of the present or anticipated problems need advanced

12.4 Deciding whether and how to evacuate a patient is not always easy.

levels of medical treatment? What time factors must be considered?

- Considering the difficulty of the river versus that of the surrounding terrain, what is the most expedient route of evacuation—over land or down the river?

- Can the patient walk or paddle himself safely? Or, must he be evacuated by litter?

- If by litter, do you have the tools and materials to construct one? If not, how can you get one to the scene? How many people are necessary for the evacuation? Will they be endangered?

If the patient's condition cannot be stabilized and serious consequences will result from delay, speed must be the overriding consideration. This may justify faster but more hazardous evacuation methods such as helicopters.

On the other hand, if the victim needs advanced care but can be adequately stabilized (for example, he has a simple fracture), a slower, more controlled evacuation is in order. This would be true if road access is not too far, or perhaps there is a nearby landing strip or helispot. If the injury is not disabling, the patient can often walk out on his own, and this is certainly easier than carrying him. But his condition could worsen, or he could become disoriented or lost. As a precautionary measure, at least two people should be sent out with the patient, so that if his condition does worsen, one can stay with him and another can go for help.

Lightly injured people can be carried for short distances with one- or two-man carries: the clothes drag (figure 12.5) is for emergency use only; the fireman's carry (figure 12.6) and the cross-shoulder carry (figure 12.7) are often effective for transporting people from the water to shore; the piggyback (figure 12.8) is really only practical with lightweight patients; the two-man carry (figure 12.9) requires a wide path. One of the most comfortable ways to carry someone is the rope coil, a technique borrowed from our climbing friends. You must have a rope long enough (sixty feet or longer) to put into a climbing coil (see figures 12.10 and 12.11). The coiled rope then goes around the rescuer's shoulders so that the patient can sit in it.

12.5 The clothes drag.

12.6 *The fireman's carry.*

12.7 *The cross-shoulder carry.*

12.8 *The two-handed carry (piggyback).*

12.9 *The two-man carry*

12.10 and 12.11 Two views of the rope-coil carry.

12.12 Splitting the coils of a throw rope also makes an effective carry.

Injuries of a more serious nature require a litter. Ready-made litters are ideal if available (some day-trip outfitters place them near potential trouble spots ahead of time). If not, you can construct them from all kinds of materials—all it takes is a little imagination. Here are some examples:

- A rope litter can be improvised from two throw ropes. "Weave" it with a series of slip knots (see figure 12.13).

- Life jackets can be rigged on saplings or paddles.

- A canoe with the flotation removed can be used as a litter. A canoe slid crosswise along railroad tracks, using two rescuers as "dog teams," makes an excellent evacuation vehicle (see figure 12.14).

- A self-bailing inflatable kayak makes an improvised litter if you thread web or rope carrying straps through the drain holes. You can remove the walls, seat, and foot braces of a "hard" kayak to make a coffinlike sled to drag

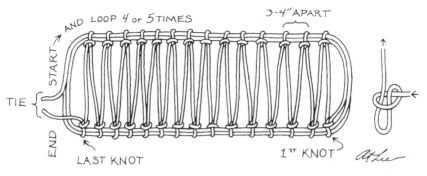

12.13 *Woven rope litter.*

12.14 *A canoe can be used as an evacuation litter by towing it sideways along a railroad track. Many rivers have railroad tracks alongside them.*

12.15 *Decked boats can also be used as improvised evacuation litters, although the walls and seat must usually be removed first. It's helpful to have someone stay with the boat to keep it from flipping over.*

out a victim. It is a bumpy ride but works well in short-handed evacuations (see figure 12.15).

- Your imagination is the limit. Debris such as car hoods, lumber, and billboards have all been used in emergencies. Test any litter first with a healthy person before transporting the patient.

Moving the Litter

Evacuations are hard work. The primary goal of the litter bearers is to keep the patient horizontal and to make the movement of the litter as smooth as possible. Designate one of the litter bearers as captain. This person will coordinate lifting, lowering, and movement. You should have selected and scouted the evacuation route by now, but it is still a good idea to have a scout in front of the litter team to pick the exact route around boulders, trees, and other obstacles.

More than six litter bearers will generally get in each other's way; other team members should stand by to relieve the bearers from time to time. The safest way to switch bearers is to put the litter down, but this takes time. A more expedient method is to switch one person at a time "on the fly." Relief bearers walk alongside and take over from the litter bearers when they start to tire. Only one bearer should switch at a time, and litter bearers should switch frequently so that they don't get so tired they might drop the litter. Shoulder straps help distribute the load (see figure 12.16). If the litter team is faced with an obstacle the bearers cannot step over, the bearers stay in one place and pass the litter to another team on the other side with a caterpillar pass (see figure 12.17). In very rough terrain the litter's movement may be by a continuous series of caterpillar passes.

In rugged terrain the patient must be secured to the litter. Foot straps, groin straps, and underarm restraint straps will keep him secure. Pad the straps, especially around pressure points, and check the patient occasionally to see that everything is comfortable. Comfort is not the only issue here—an extremity without circulation, a nerve with too much pressure on it, or anything that changes mental status or the perception of sensation may be reported as discomfort when actually it may be a sign of something more serious needing prompt adjustment. Periodic questions and evaluations during the evacuation may be the only way to pick up on problems in circulation or nerve function that do not result in pain. If the

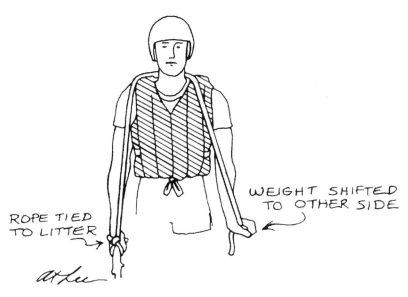

ROPE TIED
TO LITTER

WEIGHT SHIFTED
TO OTHER SIDE

12.16 A shoulder strap makes litter carrying easier.

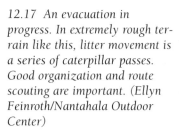

12.17 An evacuation in progress. In extremely rough terrain like this, litter movement is a series of caterpillar passes. Good organization and route scouting are important. (Ellyn Feinroth/Nantahala Outdoor Center)

patient is conscious, don't tie his arms: he can fend off branches, scratch itches, and generally not feel so helpless.

If the patient has a cervical-spine injury, *this must be stabilized before moving him,* otherwise permanent paralysis may result. The mechanics of packaging a cervical-spine injury are beyond the scope of this book, but suffice it to say that if one is diagnosed or suspected, an improvised litter will not be adequate. Unless it is a grave emergency or no other alternatives are available, you will need somehow to get a metal litter (e.g., Stokes basket) or a sturdy backboard and package the patient in it so that his cervical spine cannot shift.

When moving a litter up a steep bank (something you often have to do in a river evacuation), a Talus belay is a useful technique. Tie two of your longest ropes to the head of the litter, then send a team member up the bank to select a belay point like a tree or boulder. The belayer should keep slack out of the rope as the litter is moved, so that if it falls the rope will keep it from bobsledding back down the bank. When the litter gets to the first belayer, a second belayer should repeat the process from the next belay point up the

12.18 The Talus belay alternates belay points to provide security against the litter's slipping back down the bank. The litter should not be moved without one of the ropes on belay.

bank. In this way, the litter is always secured and you lose little time. This technique also can be used for moving a litter downhill.

In many cases, the most expedient means of transport is simply to travel downriver to the planned takeout point. Most patients with serious injuries are not anxious to get back on the water, and the flexing of an inflated boat can be painful even to the best-splinted fracture, but this may be the best alternative. If you do choose river evacuation, keep the following considerations in mind:

- Always have the patient wear a life jacket and helmet unless the nature of the injuries preclude it.

- Do not tie a patient into a raft or onto a litter in a raft unless absolutely necessary. In addition to the real danger of drowning if the raft flips, it is important to consider the patient's subjective feelings of fear.

- Two canoes can be lashed together, catamaran-style, for increased stability. The two-point tether and Telfer lower (see chapter 6) are excellent methods for transporting a patient across a river.

- You can always line the easier rapids and carry the patient around the more difficult ones.

- If you must cross the river above dangerous rapids or falls, rig a belay line or a Telfer lower.

If possible, the primary first-aider should stay with the patient all the way to the hospital. He is familiar with the injuries and vital signs and can monitor change more accurately. Perhaps more important, he and the patient will have developed a rapport that should not be interrupted.

Your responsibility to your patient doesn't automatically end when the evacuation team reaches an ambulance or rescue squad. In remote areas (particularly outside the United States) you may find volunteer rescue squads or ambulance personnel whose hearts are in the right place but who lack up-to-date training. Do they look organized, well supplied, and medically competent? Most squads and ambulance drivers should be EMTs (emergency medical technicians) and should be trained and equipped for patient care. If the medical authorities do not appear competent, you must continue the care of your patient until you find someone who can provide adequate care. This may require you to be direct and insistent about the manner of treatment, and this can be difficult if you are dealing with a legally constituted civil authority like a local search-and-rescue squad.

Slim relates an incident at the Chattooga's notorious Seven Foot Falls. "A kayaker had been pulled off the bank while trying to belay a swimmer and had smashed his knee on a submerged rock. He had shattered his kneecap, so we immobilized his leg with an air splint. There were not enough people for a litter party, so we decided to walk him out. With one of us supporting him on either side, it soon became obvious that three people abreast was just not going to work on the narrow evacuation trail. The two outside people were crashing through the brush, and the hopping was painful to the injured paddler. After a quarter of a mile we were all exhausted.

The solution was surprisingly simple: since the weather was warm and the injured paddler still had his life jacket on, we put him back in the water and pulled him by the back of his life jacket upstream through the eddies, helping him from one to the next. The air splint kept his leg floating on the surface. This was much easier for us and far more comfortable for him, and we soon made it back to Woodall Shoals."

Appendix A
Universal River Signals

Stop: Potential hazard ahead. Wait for "all clear" signal before proceeding, or scout ahead. Form a horizontal bar with your outstretched arms. Those seeing the signal should pass it back to others in the party.

Help Emergency: Assist the signaler as quickly as possible. Give three long blasts on a police whistle while waving a paddle, helmet or life vest over your head. If a whistle is not available, use the visual signal alone. A whistle is best carried on a lanyard attached to your life vest.

All Clear: Come ahead. (In the absence of other directions proceed down the center.) Form a vertical bar with your paddle or one arm held high above your head. The paddle blade should be turned flat for maximum visibility. To signal direction or a preferred course through a rapid or around an obstruction, lower the previously vertical "all clear" by 45 degrees toward the side of the river with the preferred route. Never point toward the obstacle you wish to avoid.

Appendix B
Useful Knots

Double Fisherman's Knot: Also used to tie together two pieces of rope, this knot is good when the ropes are substantially different in diameter, but it is very difficult to untie after being put under tension.

Simple Prusik: Named for its inventor, Dr. Karl Prusik, this knot has many uses in river rescue. Its main virtue is that it will grip when under tension but stay loose when not.

Simple Bowline with Stopper: Easy to tie, this knot must be tied off or backed up in some way so that it will not loosen when not under tension. Feeding the free end back through the eye of the knot works well as a safety. This knot is not difficult to untie after use.

Figure-of-Eight Family of Knots: The Figure Eight knot is strong, simple to remember, and easy to untie and to verify visually that it is tied correctly. The four variations shown below will serve almost any purpose on the river.

> *Figure Eight Follow Through:* a strong knot to tie two lines together. Use this rather than a Double Fisherman's if you want to untie the lines later. Both this and the next knot are sometimes called "tracer" knots.

> *Figure Eight Follow Through Loop:* Climbers use this knot for tying into a sit harness, and it can be used for any situation that requires a loop around something. It is less likely to untie when not under tension than a bowline.

> *Figure Eight on-a-Bight:* A quick, easy, and strong way to put a loop at the end of a rope, or anywhere along it.

> *Double-Loop Figure Eight:* Use this when you want to double a line for increased strength, such as for a doubled haul line, or for two anchor points.

FIGURE OF EIGHT FAMILY OF KNOTS

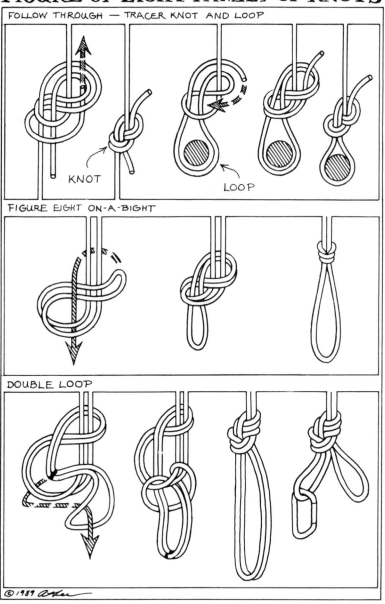

FOLLOW THROUGH — TRACER KNOT AND LOOP

KNOT

LOOP

FIGURE EIGHT ON-A-BIGHT

DOUBLE LOOP

© 1989

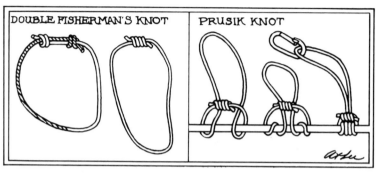

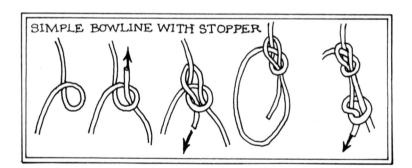

Water Knot: A simple overhand knot to join pieces of webbing.

Münter Hitch: A simple and effective belay system which uses the friction of the rope against itself, the Münter works best on a large carabiner with a smooth radius. The hitch will work in either direction and requires only a carabiner to function.

Bachmann Knot: A cinching knot similar to the prusik except that it works only in one direction, the Bachmann uses a prusik loop

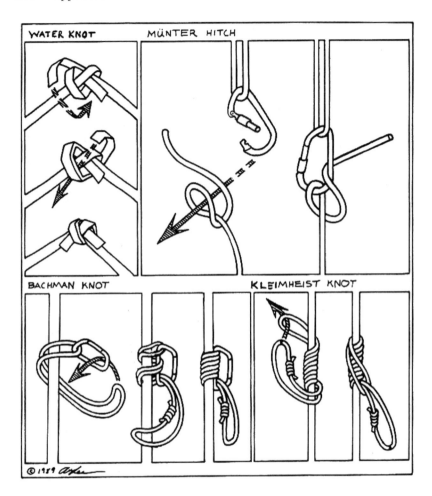

wrapped around a carabiner, which provides a convenient handle. The Bachmann knot's best application is as a substitute for a brake prusik. The carabiner will not pass through the anchor pulley/carabiner of a Z-drag and so does not need to be monitored.

Kleimheist Knot: This is another cinching knot that can be used in place of a prusik if you are using webbing rather than cord. Like the Bachmann, it works in only one direction.

Appendix C
First Aid Kit

1. "Ouch Pouch" for Day Trips

Ten 1" adhesive bandages
24" of half-inch adhesive tape
8 gauze pads (four 4" x 4", four
  2" x 2")
Roll of gauze (2" wide)
10 aspirin or aspirin substitute
Sunscreen
Lip balm
Butane lighter

Pocket mask
Sterile gloves
Anaphylaxis kit (injectable
  epinephrine)
Trauma scissors
Povidone-iodine ointment or
  solution
Triangular cravat (1)

2. Group Kit for Day Trips
(divided into three parts}

Quick-access bag

20 aspirin or aspirin substitute
Ten 1" adhesive bandages
Roll of adhesive tape
4 large safety pins
Sunscreen
Povidone-iodine ointment or
  solution
Anaphylaxis kit (injectable
  epinephrine)
Glucose (oral)
Sterile gloves (2 pair)
Pocket mask
Trauma scissors

Trauma bag

Ten 1" adhesive bandages
20 gauze pads (ten 4" x 4", ten
  2" x 2")
2 rolls of gauze strip (2" wide)
Trauma dressing (gauze)
2 triangular cravats
2 tampons
4 elastic roller bandages (2")
Roll of adhesive tape
Chemical cold pack
Bottle of eyewash solution
Hand towel
Combine dressing (2)

Materials bag

Tweezers
Snake-bite kit (suction)
2 finger splints
Butane lighter
Small flashlight
Emergency "space blanket"
3 ammonia inhalants
Nylon stretcher
First aid book

Leg splint
Full arm splint
Hypothermia thermometer
Lubricating jelly (small tube)
Blanket pins (2)
Syringe (60 cc)
Tongue depressors (2)
Oral airway (3 sizes)
N-P airway
Heat packs (optional for cold
    weather)

3. Expedition Recommendations

This kit would include all the contents of the group kit for day use, with the number of individual items increased according to the length of the expedition and the number of participants. The additional items below require training in their use and should be varied according to the medical background of the members of the expedition.

Blood pressure cuff
Stethoscope
Thermometers (oral and
    hypothermia)
Adult airway

Bulb syringe (for suction)
Intravenous kit
Drug kit
Tooth-fracture kit

Appendix D
Ground-to-Air Signals for Survivors

These signals are intended for communication with a helicopter. They are advisory, and a pilot is under no obligation to obey them. When these signals are used, it is important that the signaler be positioned beyond the path of the main rotor where he may be readily seen.

Clear to start engine. Make a circular motion above your head with your right arm.

Hold on ground. Extend your arms horizontally, thumbs pointing down.

Clear to lift. Extend your arms horizontally, palms up.

Move the helicopter back. Extend your arms forward and "push" the helicopter away.

Move the helicopter forward.
Extend your arms forward and
wave the helicopter toward
you.

Move to signaler's right. Extend
your right arm horizontally
and motion to your right with
the palm of your left hand.

Move to signaler's left. Extend
your left arm horizontally and
motion to your left with the
palm of your right hand.

Release sling load. Touch your
left forearm with your right
hand, palm extended.

Cleared for takeoff. Extend
both arms above your head,
thumbs up.

Wave off: Do not land. Wave
your arms from the side to
over your head.

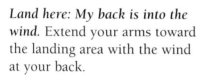

Land here: My back is into the wind. Extend your arms toward the landing area with the wind at your back.

Shut down. Cross your neck with your right hand, palm down.

The following signals are generally used for attracting the attention of the pilots of fixed-wing aircraft, though they may also attract a helicopter. Make the signs by placing rocks on the ground, spreading out clothing, scratching in the dirt, or stamping in the snow. In any case, make the signs large enough to be visible from high above.

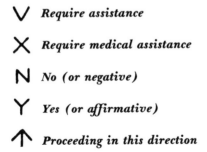

V *Require assistance*

X *Require medical assistance*

N *No (or negative)*

Y *Yes (or affirmative)*

↑ *Proceeding in this direction*

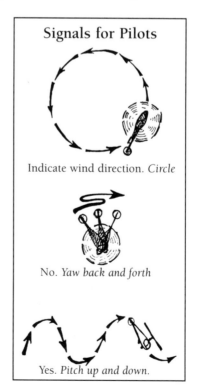

Signals for Pilots

Indicate wind direction. *Circle*

No. *Yaw back and forth*

Yes. *Pitch up and down.*

Appendix E
Cardiopulmonary Resuscitation (CPR)

When a person's heart and lungs stop functioning because of shock, drowning, a heart attack, or other causes, it is possible to save that life by administering cardiopulmonary resuscitation, or CPR.

CPR provides artificial circulation and breathing for the victim. External cardiac compressions administered manually are alternated with mouth-to-mouth resuscitation in order to stimulate the natural functions of the heart and lungs.

1. *Determine whether the victim is unconscious.* Tap or gently shake the victim's shoulder. Shout "Are you OK?" If there is no response, shout "Help!" (Someone nearby may be able to assist.) Do the Airway step next.

2. *Airway step.* Place one hand on the victim's forehead and push firmly back. Hook the fingers of the other hand on the bony part of the lower jaw and lift up and forward on the chin until the teeth are almost closed. Tip the head until the chin points straight up. This should open the airway. Place your ear near the victim's mouth and nose. LOOK at the chest for breathing movements, LISTEN for

breaths, and FEEL for breathing against your cheek. If there is no breathing, do the Quick step next.

3. Quick step. Give two slow, independent breaths. To do this, keep the victim's head tipped and pinch his nose. Open your mouth wide and take a deep breath. Make a good seal on the victim's mouth, then give the breaths, watching for the chest to rise.

4. Check step. CHECK the pulse and breathing for at least five but no more than ten seconds. To do this, keep the victim's head tipped with your hand on his forehead. Place the fingertips of your other hand on his Adam's apple and slide your fingers into the groove at the side of the neck nearest you. If there is a pulse but no breathing, give one breath every five seconds. If there is no pulse or breathing, send someone for emergency assistance while you locate the proper hand position for chest compression. Begin chest compressions.

5. Hand position for chest compressions. (A) With your middle and index fingers find the lower edge of the victim's rib cage on the side nearest you. (B) Trace the edge of the ribs up to the notch where the ribs meet the breastbone. (C) Place your middle finger on the notch, your index finger next to it. Put the heel of your other hand on the breastbone next to the fingers. (D) Put your first hand on top of the hand on the breastbone. Keep the fingers off the chest.

6. Chest compressions. Push straight down, without bending your elbows, always maintaining the proper hand position. Keep your knees a shoulder width apart. Your shoulders should be directly over the victim's breastbone. Keep your hands along the mid-line of his body. Bend from your hips, not your knees. Keep your fingers off the victim's chest. Push down 1 1/2 to 2 inches. Count "1 and, 2 and, 3 and..." and so on.

7. Push 15—Breathe 2. Give 15 compressions at a rate of 80-180 per minute. Tip the victim's head so the chin points up and give two quick full breaths. Continue to repeat 15 compressions followed by two breaths. Check the pulse and breathing after the first minute and every few minutes thereafter. NOTE: Do not practice chest compressions on people—you might cause internal injuries.

This information does not take the place of CPR training. Contact your local Red Cross or American Heart Association chapter to find out how you can learn this lifesaving procedure.

Appendix F

Patient Assessment
System (PAS)

I. Survey Scene
  Danger
  Mechanism

II. Primary Survey
  A—Airway
  B—Breathing
  C—Circulation
  D—Disability

III. Secondary Survey
  Head
  Eyes
  Ears
  Nose
  Mouth/Throat
  Neck
  Chest
  Abdomen
  Pelvis
  Genitalia
  Legs
  Arms
  Back
  Buttocks
  Neuro

IV. Vital Signs
  T—Time
  BP—Blood Pressure
  P—Pulse
  R—Respiration
  C/MS—Consciousness/
    Mental Status
  T—Temperature
  S—Skin Color

V. History
  A—Allergies
  M—Medications
  P—Past History
  L—Last Meal
  E—Events

VI. SOAP
  S—Subjective
  O—Objective
  A—Assessment
  P—Plan for Treatment

VII. Monitor
  S
  O
  A/A = Problems/
    Anticipated Problems
  P

PAS Notes

I. Survey Scene

1. **Danger**—Immediate danger to victim or rescuer (falling rock, explosions, etc.).

2. **Mechanism**—Trauma vs. illness (fall, sudden chest pain, MVA, etc.). Both may be possible. Determine possible mechanism for spine injury.

This survey is done before or during approach to the victim. It is done quickly and generally takes no extra time.

II. Primary Survey

	Green Flags	Red Flags
A—Airway	air in/out	no air in/out
B—Breathing	ventilation adequate	ventilation not adequate
C—Circulation	1. pulse	1. no pulse
	2. no severe bleeding	2. severe bleeding
D—Disability	1. no mechanism for spine injury	1. mechanism for spine injury
	2. consciousness *AVPU*	2. consciousness *AVPU*

1. Primary Survey can be performed with all elements done in sequence or done simultaneously. Stop and treat problems (Red Flags) as they are found. Survey and treatment of problems may be done simultaneously.

2. Basic Life Support (BLS) is treatment of problems in the Primary Survey. Cardiopulmonary Resuscitation (CPR) is a limited form of BLS that is more useful for illness than for trauma.

3. The term Primary Assessment is sometimes used for: I. Survey Scene + II. Primary Survey.

Reproduced courtesy of the Wilderness Medical Society.

Bibliography

Ohio Department of Natural Resources, Division of Watercraft, *River Rescue*, Columbus, Ohio: 1980

Walbridge, Charles and Wayne Sundmacher, *Whitewater Rescue Manual*, Camden, ME: Ragged Mountain Press 1995

Smith, David S. and Sara J., *Water Rescue: Basic Skills for Emergency Responders*, St. Louis, MO: Mosby-Year Book 1994

B. Chris Brewster (ed.) *The United States Lifesaving Association Manual of Open Water Rescue*; Englewood Cliffs, NJ: Prentice-Hall 1995

Ray, Slim, *Swiftwater Rescue: A Handbook for the Rescue Professional*, Asheville, NC: CFS Press 1996

Medical

American Red Cross CPR: Basic Life Support for the Professional Rescuer; American Red Cross, 1988

Emergency Care of the Sick and Injured, 4th ed. Chicago: The American Academy of Orthopedic Surgeons, 1987

Forgey, William W.; *Hypothermia, Death by Exposure*, Merrillville, IN: ICS Books 1985

Issac, Jeff, and Peter Goth, *The Outward Bound Wilderness First Aid Handbook*, New York: Lyons & Burford 1991

Wilkerson, James A., ed. *Hypothermia, Frostbite, and other Cold Injuries*, Seattle, WA: The Mountaineers 1986

Wilkerson, James A., ed. *Medicine for Mountaineering*, 2nd ed. Seattle: The Mountaineers 1985

Dickison, Anne E.; *Drowning and Near-Drowning, Medical Problems Associated with Whitewater Activities*; unpublished manuscript

Paddling and Rafting

Nealey, William, *Kayak,* Birmingham, AL: Menasha Ridge Press
1986

Ray, Slim, *The Canoe Handbook,* Harrisburg, PA: Stackpole Books
1992

Bennett, Jeff, *The Complete Whitewater Rafter,* Camden, ME: Ragged
Mountain Press 1996

Walbridge, Charlie, *Knots for Paddlers*, Springfield, VA: American
Canoe Association 1995

Bennett, Jeff, *The Complete Inflatable Paddler,* Camden, ME: Ragged
Mountain Press 1995

Davidson, James and John Rugge, *The Complete Wilderness Paddler*
New York: Alfred A. Knopf, 1976

McGinnis, William, *Whitewater Rafting,* New York: Quadrangle/The
New York Times Book Company, 1975

McGinnis, William, *The Guide's Guide: Reflections on Guiding Professional River Trips,* El Sobrante, CA: Whitewater Voyages, 1981

Rowe, Ray, *White Water Kayaking.* London: Salamander Books, 1988

Lessels, Bruce, *AMC Whitewater Handbook,* 3rd Ed. Boston:
Appalachian Mountain Club, 1994

Safety

Walbridge, Charlie, Ed. *Best of the River Safety Task Force Newsletter
1976-1982,* Springfield, VA: American Canoe Association, 1983

Walbridge, Charlie, Ed. *River Safety Report 1982-1985,* Springfield,
VA: American Canoe Association, 1986

Walbridge, Charlie, Ed. *River Safety Report 1986-1988,* Springfield,
VA: American Canoe Association, 1989

Walbridge, Charlie, Ed. *River Safety Report 1989-1991,* Springfield,
VA: American Canoe Association, 1992

Walbridge, Charlie, and Jody Tinsley, *River Safety Anthology,*
Springfield, VA: American Canoe Association 1996

Technical Ropes

Adkins, Jan, *Moving Heavy Things,* New York: Houghton Mifflin 1980

Blandford, Percy W., *Knots and Splices,* New York: Arco Publishing 1978

Crocket, Ken, *Climbing Terms & Techniques,* Essex (UK): Fraser Stewart Ltd. 1993

Fleming, Steve, *Low Angle Rope Rescue,* 3rd ed., Ft. Collins, CO: Technical Rescue Systems 1987

Frank, James A. and Jerrold B. Smith., *CMC Rope Rescue Manual,* 2nd ed., Santa Barbara, CA: CMC Rescue 1992

Frank, James A. and Donald E Patterson, *CMC Rappel Manual,* rev. ed., Santa Barbara, CA: CMC Rescue 1993

Hudson, Steve (ed.), *Manual of U.S. Cave Rescue Techniques,* 2nd Ed., Huntsville, AL: National Speleological Society 1988

Long, John, *Climbing Anchors,* Evergreen, CO: Chockstone Press 1993

Luebben, Craig, *Knots for Climbers,* Evergreen, CO: Chockstone Press 1993

March, Bill, *Modern Rope Techniques,* 3rd Ed,, Edison, NJ: Hunter Publishing 1985

May, W.G., *Mountain Search and Rescue Techniques,* Boulder, CO: Rocky Mountain Rescue Group 1973

Owen, Peter, *The Book of Outdoor Knots,* New York: Lyons and Burford 1993

Padgett, Allen and Bruce Smith, *On Rope,* Huntsville, AL: National Speleological Society 1987

Setnicka, Tim, *Wilderness Search and Rescue,* Boston, MA: Appalachian Mountain Club 1980

Thorne, Reed, *Rope Rescue Nomenclature,* 3rd Ed., Lake Elizabeth, CA: Thorne Group 1988

Vines, Tom and Steve Hudson, *High Angle Rescue Techniques,* Dubuque, Iowa: Kendall/Hunt Publishing 1989

Wheelock, Walt, *Ropes, Knots, and Slings for Climbers,* Rev Ed., Glendale, CA: La Siesta Press 1967

Helicopters

Office of Aircraft Services, *Basic Aviation Safety (NFES #2097),* Boise, ID: Department of Interior, Office of Aircraft Services 1990

Rescue 3 International, *Aviation Aquatic Rescue Manual,* Elk Grove, CA: Rescue 3 International 1994

Setnicka, Tim J., *Wilderness Search and Rescue,* Boston, MA: Appalachian Mountain Club 1980

Stoffel, Skip and Patrick LaValla, *Personnel Safety in Helicopter Operations,* Olympia, WA: Emergency Response Institute, 1988

Foreign

Reithmaier, Peter, *Sicherheit im Wildwasser,* Vienna, Austria: Naturfreunde Österreich 1994

Alpiner Kayak-Club, *Kanu-Gefahren,* Munich 1983.

Videos

Heads UP, VHS video, American Canoe Association, 7432 Alban Station Bvd B-226, Springfield, VA 22150

Whitewater Boating: A Safe Beginning, VHS video, KUSA-TV, 1098 Bannock St. Denver, CO 80204

The Awesome Power; VHS video, National Oceanographic and Atmospheric Agency (copies available from Dubs, Inc. 6360 Delongpre Ave, Hollywood, CA 90028)

Flash Floods: A Warning to Beware; VHS video, Arizona Flood Plain Management Association, 2801 W. Durango St. Phoenix, AZ 85009

Water, the Timeless Compound; VHS video, Buzz Fawcett Productions, for the Lutheran Brotherhood, 1983, PR Dept,

Lutheran Brotherhood Insurance Co., 625 Fourth Avenue, Minneapolis, MN 55145; or W.H. Fawcett III, 3305 Highway 101 S., Wayzette, MN 55391

No Way Out, VHS video, Los Angeles County Office of Education (RETAC), 9300 Imperial Highway, Downey, CA 90242

Car in the Water and Swiftwater Survival, VHS video, Public Education Series from KXTV Channel 10, Steve Baxter, 400 Broadway, Sacramento, CA 95818

Organizations

Alpiner Kayak-Club
Stundstrasse 21
D-8000 München 80
Germany

American Canoe Association
7432 Alban Station Boulvard
B-226
Springfield, VA 22150
703-451-0141

American Red Cross
8111 Gatehouse Road
Falls Church, VA 22042
202-737-8300

American Whitewater
Affiliation
P.O. Box 636
16 Bull Run Road
Margaretville, NY 12455
914-586-2355
914-586-3050 (Fax)
74663.2104@compuserve.com

National Association
for Search and Rescue
4500 Southgate Place
Suite 100
Chantilly, VA 22021
703-222-6277

Ohio Department
of Natural Resources
Division of Watercraft
Fountain Square
Columbus, OH 43224

Rescue 3
P.O. Box 519
Elk Grove, CA 95759-0519
800-457-3728

Rigging For Rescue (The
Technical Ropes School)
Box 399
Invermere, British Columbia
V0A 1K0

Canyons, Incorporated
Box 823
McCall, ID 83638
208-634-4303

Canyonland, Field Institute
Box 68
Moab, UT 84532
801-259-7750

Nantahala Outdoor Center
13077 Hwy 19W
Bryson City, NC 28713
704-488-2175

Index

Note: Numbers in **boldface** indicate pages on which illustrations or major discussion of the entry are found.

About the AMC

Since 1876, the Appalachian Mountain Club has promoted the protection, enjoyment, and wise use of the mountains, rivers, and trails of the Northeast. The AMC believes that successful, long-term conservation depends on first-hand experience and enjoyment of the outdoors. A nonprofit organization, AMC's membership of more than 72,000 enjoy hiking, canoeing, skiing, walking, rock climbing, bicycling, camping, kayaking, and backpacking, while—at the same time—help to safeguard the environment. All AMC programs and facilities are open to the public.

AMC Huts & Lodges

AMC offers unique overnight lodgings throughout the Northeast. Spend an overnight at one of eight huts, each a day's hike apart, in the White Mountains of New Hampshire, or drive to Bascom Lodge atop Mt. Greylock in western Massachusetts. Also accessible by car are Pinkham Notch Lodge or Crawford Hostel in New Hampshire, and Mohican Outdoor Center in the Delaware Water Gap of western New Jersey. For reservations, call 603-466-2727.

AMC Outdoor Adventures

Whether you're new to the outdoors or an old hand, the AMC offers workshops and guided trips that will teach you new skills, refine your expertise, or just get you outside in good company. Choose from more than 100 workshops and adventures offered in New Hampshire, Massachusetts, New York, and New Jersey. Whether you're going solo, with your family and kids, or with friends, there is something for everyone.

Each of our 11 chapters—from Maine to Washington, D.C.— offers hundreds of activities close to home. Chapter leaders arrange hiking and bicycling trips and teach the basics of cross-country skiing, whitewater and flatwater canoeing, and other outdoor skills.

Madison Spring Hut, one of the eight trailside huts maintained by the AMC, offers hikers hot meals, warm bunks, and mountain hospitality. (Paul Mozell)

Volunteering

If you like to hike, discover the lasting satisfaction that comes with volunteering to maintain or build trails. No experience is necessary—we'll teach you what you need to know. The AMC leads volunteer trail building and maintenance crews throughout the Northeast. Our professional and volunteer crews take great pride in maintaining 1,400 miles of trails throughout the region.

Paddlers can help clean up a river, monitor water quality, or help negotiate access with private landowners. Volunteering is a great way to give something back to the rivers and trails that have taken you to so many wonderful places.

Conservation Leadership

Much of the northeast's outdoor recreation opportunities would not be possible without a commitment to protecting land and keeping trails, rivers, and mountains accessible. Since its founding, the AMC has been at the forefront of the conservation movement. AMC members fought for the creation of the White Mountain National Forest in 1911. More recently we have been active in protecting the Appalachian Trail corridor, improving access to and the health of rivers and land around hydroelectric dams, and improving water and air quality. Our conservation policies are backed by solid scien-

Discover the outdoors with AMC! Sign up for a workshop to learn outdoor activity skills and enjoy the company of new friends. (Rob Burbank)

tific research, conducted by our own professional researchers in conjunction with organizations such as the Harvard School of Public Health, Dartmouth College, U.S. Forest Service, and the National Park Service. We're working to keep our air clean and healthy, our waterfalls clear, our rivers running free, and recreational activities open.

AMC Books & Maps

The AMC publishes an extensive line of books, including nature guides, New England history, outdoor skills, conservation, and our famous trail guides and maps. AMC guidebooks are essential companions for all kinds of outdoor adventures throughout the eastern U.S. Our publications are available at most bookstores and outdoor retailers as well as our main office in Boston and Pinkham Notch Visitor Center in New Hampshire. To order by phone, call 800-262-4455. Also available through the AMC is *Appalachia*, the country's oldest mountaineering and conservation journal.

AMC Membership

We invite you to join the Appalachian Mountain Club and share the benefits of membership. Your membership includes a one-year subscription to *AMC Outdoors*, the Northeast's premier outdoor magazine—telling you where to go for outdoor recreation and keeping you informed on conservation issues. Members also enjoy discounts on AMC books, maps, workshops, and lodgings, as well as free affiliation to one of AMC's eleven chapters.

For more information on AMC, call 617-523-0636. To join, send a check for $40 for an adult, or $65 for a family to AMC Membership, 5 Joy Street, Boston, MA 02108; or pay by Visa or MasterCard by calling 617-523-0636 .

About the Authors

SLIM RAY is an author, writer, and photographer whose work has appeared in a number of national publications. He has taught river rescue in the U.S. and internationally, and has developed river rescue courses with several organizations, including Rescue 3, Canyonlands Field Institute, and the Nantahala Outdoor Center. An active kayaker who has worked professionally as a canoe and kayak instructor and raft guide, he is the author of two other books on paddling technique and swiftwater rescue.

Slim was involved in a severe kayaking accident on the Green River in North Carolina in 1991 which left him a paraplegic. He continues to write and paddle and he lives in Asheville, NC.

LES BECHDEL, president of Canyons Incorporated, has represented the U.S. in five world championships, and has been national slalom champion four times. Les and his wife, Susan, continue to run wilderness trips for boaters on the Middle and Main Forks of the Salmon River in Idaho.

ISBN 1-878239-55-4